First Steps in Counselling

A students' companion for introductory courses

4th edition

Pete Sanders

PCCS BOOKS
Ross-on-Wye

First edition published 1994
Second edition published 1996
Third edition published 2002
Fourth edition published 2011
Reprinted 2013

PCCS BOOKS
2 Cropper Row
Alton Road
Ross-on-Wye
HR9 5LA
UK
Tel. 01989 763 900
www.pccs-books.co.uk

First Steps in Counselling: A students' companion
for introductory courses
4th edition

ISBN 978 1 906254 41 4

Cover design by Old Dog Graphics
Printed by Ashford Colour Press, Gosport, Hants, UK

Contents

Acknowledgements

The 'Steps' series of books has a complex structure that involves a huge amount of work. The possibilities for errors are manifold and it is mostly due to the skilful and diligent work of copy-editor and proofreader Sandy Green that *First Steps in Counselling* has been published. This simple acknowledgement hardly seems sufficient to honour her part in the work. I would like to thank the following publishers and authors for their kind permission to use the material listed below.

ONCE IN A LIFETIME
Words and music by David Byrne, Chris Frantz, Tina Weymouth, Jerry Harrison and Brian Eno. © 1982 EG Music Ltd/co-publisher notice (provided by Warner Chappell Music Ltd) for the world. All Rights Reserved. © 1992 Index Music Inc/Bleu Disque Music Co Inc, USA. Warner Chappell Music Ltd, London, W1Y 3FA.

HUMAN BEHAVIOUR
Words and Music by Björk Gudmundsdóttir, Nellee Hooper, Antonio Carlos Jobim © 1993 by Famous Music Corporation, Ensign Music Corporation and Warner Chappell Music Ltd. International Copyright Secured. All Rights Reserved.

I AM AFRAID
Words and music by David Couse. Reproduced by kind permission of Chrysalis Music Ltd.

BOYS DON'T CRY
The Cure. Lyrics used with kind permission from Fiction Songs Ltd, London W1P 1LB.

IF
Words and music by Roy Harper. Lyrics reproduced by kind permission of Roy Harper.

TELEVISION, THE DRUG OF THE NATION
Words by Michael Franti. Lyrics reproduced by kind permission of Guerrilla Management.

FIFTEEN YEARS
Words and music by Simon Friend, Charles Heather, Mark Chadwick and Jonathan Sevink. ©1992 Universal/Empire Music Ltd, 77 Fulham Palace Road, London. Used by permission of Music Sales Ltd. All Rights Reserved. International Copyright Secured.

ALL PURPOSE LATE TWENTIETH CENTURY CREED
Simon Rae. First published in *The Guardian* newspaper.

WHITE COMEDY
Benjamin Zephaniah (1995) from the book *Propa Propaganda* published by Bloodaxe Books.

Dedicated to the memories of
John and Joan Sanders

introduction

The 'Steps' series

This book is a revised and enhanced version of the third edition of *First Steps in Counselling*. Others in the series are *Next Steps in Counselling Practice* and *Step in to Study Counselling*. These, this book and *First Steps in Practitioner Research* form a 'family' of related books designed to lead you through what you need to know as you progress through your training and practice in counselling and psychotherapy or the application of counselling as a complement to other activities in a wider context.

You will almost certainly be encountering the *Steps* series for the first time. This series is conceived as comprising interrelated books, and each also stands alone. However, as well as offering a progression into which it is possible to dip in or out at any point, they share a style and approach. The series is characterised by the way in which the usual conventions of academic writing are modified and adapted. They are written in such a way as to directly address you, the readers. This isn't about being different for the sake of it. Each author who contributes to the series, as well as being a practitioner and writer across the broader field of counselling and psychotherapy, is or has been a counselling trainer. So in these books I am using experience to, for the most part, relate to you as I would to a new group of students.

You may also already have noticed another peculiarity of books in the *Steps* series. Each page has an unusually wide margin. On most pages (as this one) you will find something written. Here, I have given references to the other books in the series and you will find other references (and all sorts of things) in the margins as you work with this book. What I have done is to write the main text so that it can be read without interruption or diversion. However, there are many points at which there is more there that at least some of you may like to know, and the margin is where you will find 'extra' information. This includes references, explanations of terms used in the main text and activities that will aid your learning.

Another important feature of this book is that it is not about any particular theoretical approach to counselling and psychotherapy. It is designed to be of use to you and to facilitate your learning irrespective of the theories that underpin your training programme

Sanders, P, Frankland, A & Wilkins, P (2009) *Next Steps in Counselling Practice: A students' companion for degrees, HE diplomas and vocational courses* (2nd ed). Ross-on-Wye: PCCS Books.

Sanders, P (1995) *Step in to Study Counselling: A students' guide to tackling counselling training and course assignments* (3rd ed). Ross-on-Wye: PCCS Books.

Sanders, P & Wilkins, P (2010) *First Steps in Practitioner Research: A guide to understanding and doing research for helping practitioners.* Ross-on-Wye: PCCS Books.

Branch, R & Dryden, W (2008) *The Cognitive Behaviour Counselling Primer.* Ross-on-Wye: PCCS Books.

Sanders, P (2006) *The Person-Centred Counselling Primer.* Ross-on-Wye: PCCS Books.

Worsley, R (2007) *The Integrative Counselling Primer.* Ross-on-Wye: PCCS Books.

Klein, M (2006) *The Psychodynamic Counselling Primer.* Ross-on-Wye: PCCS Books.

Note

Courses will have their own lists of recommended books, e.g. the *Counselling in Action* series, published by Sage.

and your own approach to practice. Although all the authors associated with the *Steps* series have a clear commitment to the person-centred approach, we are not seeking to persuade you of its virtues. You will find brief introductions to the ideas behind the fundamental approaches to counselling in Chapter 2 of this book – as much as I think is appropriate and, for some, bearable, at an introductory level. Some readers may have a real interest in theory or have their curiosity awoken by Chapter 2, in which case I will suggest you try books such as the *Primers in Counselling* series which have been written specifically to support this book and the rest of the *Steps* series.

This book

When I started writing the first edition of this book it seemed a good idea to produce a book for students on introductory courses, since I could find precious few books (actually, none!) written for this group. I soon found out why. A very broad spectrum of people come to introductory counselling courses – or are simply interested in basic helping – for a wide variety of reasons. Trying to write something that would be a useful and rewarding read for the majority proved challenging. I realise that some readers, whether course participants or not, will have no prior knowledge or experience of counselling, whilst others may have come across counselling before, may have been a client, or may even be doing it as a volunteer or as part of their job.

I have tried hard to pitch the book so that it is a 'catch-all' with something for everyone at this basic, entry level, whatever their starting point. In attempting this, I realised that three things would need to be made clear: first, that the book is not trying to teach or train readers standing alone, but is intended as a supplement to a course, a 'course text' if you like. Second, that the course level aimed at is below counselling skills courses; they would need a different type of book. Finally, that the key themes of the book are *information* and *self-awareness*.

I am not the first to suggest that personal development is achieved via many routes and that our ideas in counselling come from many different sources. It is to underline this for the benefit of beginning helpers right from the start, that I decided to include quotes from a wide range of sources. The quotes are ones that have special meaning for me and it would be a bonus if they strike a chord with some readers too.

I think that the participants on introductory courses are a very influential group. Not only are they the seed corn for certificate and diploma courses, but even if they do not proceed any further with their counselling training, they carry away with them a view of counselling. This view of counselling will be passed on to friends, relatives, colleagues, or the person in the pub. These participants, whose introductory course experience is their one and only contact with counselling, will pass judgement on counselling on the basis of this contact. My aim with this book is to help make that judgement as well-informed and positive towards the value of counselling as possible.

None of the chapters in this book is complete. It is in the nature of helping and counselling to be a process moving towards something rather than arriving at a state of completion. I have tried to raise as many issues as possible through the examples in the book, issues which I make no attempt to resolve. It is for the course tutors (and you the reader) to decide how best to work with them.

How I have used the margins

In this introduction to the *Steps* series, I have already said a bit about how, in general, the extra-wide margin is used to convey 'extra' bits of information and to suggest activities that will help you understand the points being made in the main text. In the margins of this book, you will find:

Activities – to make this book more personal and to facilitate your learning, from time to time I use the margin to invite you to try a brief activity. This will inevitably slow down your reading, but just as in your training, a new dimension is added by active engagement, getting directly involved with the ideas, perhaps remembering or noticing aspects of your own life and experience, or taking sides in arguments and debates, or registering your responses to ideas or scenarios I put in front of you. Since some of you will be working with this book alone, the activities are designed to be done by a single person, but for those of you who are using the book while undertaking training, it may often be useful to work with a friend or colleague from the programme because discussion and the attempt to put an idea or feeling to someone else is an excellent way of increasing your grasp of it.

Notes – I include 'notes' in the margin when, to the interest of some of you, there is more to say about a particular point I have raised in the text. This may involve the expansion of some point of theory, a point of detail about a professional organisation, the definition of a term I have used, something interesting about someone I cite or quote or, indeed, anything else I think may be valuable or interesting to know.

References – I have put references in the margins for two main reasons. Firstly, I didn't want to interrupt the text by doing this in the conventional way but also, perhaps more importantly, because I wanted you to be able to see what I am referring to

Note: Learning styles

This book has been written to encourage you to explore, to learn from all of your experience and to adapt material to your own needs. Everyone has their own way of learning – just because the margins in this book suggest certain things, don't think that this is the right or only way.

Activity: Your learning style(s)

Consider the following questions:

1. *Do you prefer to do learning activities:*
   - *on your own?*
   - *with a partner?*
   - *in a group?*
2. *Do you prefer learning by:*
   - *thinking through ideas?*
   - *experience (doing something)?*
   - *sometimes by thinking, sometimes by doing, depending on what you're learning?*
3. *When 'getting your head around' something new do you prefer to:*
   - *draw a diagram of it to make sense of it?*
   - *draw a picture of it to make sense of it?*
   - *talk about/discuss it to make sense of it?*

> IF YOU WANT TO KNOW MORE ABOUT
> FIRST STEPS IN COUNSELLING

Read this book.

SMALL CAPITALS running glossary margin entries in small capitals define words as I go along that I think might be specialist or technical.

at the point at which I make the reference.

If you want to know more about – does what it says on the label – suggestions for further reading or sources of information, e.g. websites.

Running glossary – helping you get to grips with jargon words if you've no background in social sciences – look out for words in SMALL CAPITALS in the text and corresponding words in bold in the margin.

Language

The language I use in the text is carefully chosen to avoid stereotyping and oppressive imagery. There are a lot of snide jokes and unhelpful misconceptions about political correctness. I have no wish to be po-faced or pious, but attempts to diminish the abuse of power in creating images which risk stereotyping or in using language which may demean others are important to me, even if they are sometimes easy targets for parody.

Questions about good practice in relation to the language we use and the way we are with each other are vital if we want to establish a safe learning environment for ourselves. These will probably also relate closely to what you expect of your peers, tutors, and supervisors (and yourself) in a formal training group. This is invaluable preparation for being a helper, since an essential ability is to provide a safe environment for exploration and change, and to that end we must pay attention to our language so that it does not oppress others.

Recording your experiences

Another way of getting a hold on ideas and understandings (both intellectual and personal/emotional) is to *write* about your learning on a regular basis. Many people keep a personal journal quite naturally from the very earliest stages of their contact with counselling training, and would not think of giving it up. If you progress to professional counsellor training you may be surprised to find that your course expects some form of journal as part of assessed work or as a developmental task in order to pass the course.

There are so many forms that such a journal could take, from literally day-to-day comments and observations of self/others, developing thinking and reactions etc., to weekly or occasional reflections, perhaps particularly after course or client days or after supervision. You might also see your responses to the kinds of activities I suggest through the book as potentially part of a journal.

what is counselling?

Introductions – Who are you?

Most introductory courses in counselling begin with an activity where each person in the group has to introduce themselves to the rest of the group. Sometimes the activity is made a little more complicated and you will be asked to choose another person in the group to pair up with and talk to for a minute or two. Then you will be asked to introduce your partner to the rest of the group.

This can be quite a challenge if you're not used to speaking in groups, especially if you feel a little awkward talking about yourself. Counselling training is a challenging business, so most courses start as they mean to continue. Also, it's important for you to get to know each other reasonably well so that you can feel relaxed about talking in the group. Most of the learning in introductory courses happens through the process of sharing your ideas with others and listening to what they have to say. The listening bit here is important, since nearly everyone would agree that it is a skill which lies at the very heart of counselling, so the more we practise the better.

Would you like to introduce yourself now? It's just as true for this book as it is for your counselling course group – if we can form a relationship through the pages of this book, it will be all the easier for me to write and you to read. So, who are you, and how would you introduce yourself to me, what kind of information would you include?

As for me, my name is Pete Sanders. I decided to call myself 'Pete' rather than 'Peter' when I was an impressionable 17-year-old and still at school, after reading a book on numerology. With my friends we worked out, according to the system in the book, versions of our names that had the best 'star potential'.

I am married to Maggie, my second wife (I am her second husband). Between us we have four children, all of whom have grown up and live away from us in different parts of the world, each pursuing their own lives.

I was interested in psychology from my late teens when I worked, first during the school holidays, as a nursing assistant (now called a mental health support worker) in a large mental hospital and later in what was called in those days a 'hospital for the mentally subnormal'. My first day was like a descent into hell and I was sure that there were better ways of treating the patients I met in those hospitals –

Note
Counselling courses do not spend lots of time with the lecturer standing up in front of the students and talking at them for hours. Whilst this will happen some of the time, most time will be spent doing excercises and role plays, and then discussing your experience. This is called 'experiential learning', or learning through experience.

the regimes and methods seemed mediaeval and brutal to me – so I went to study psychology at the University of Newcastle-upon-Tyne.

I got involved in counselling by accident in 1972 when I was an undergraduate by joining a phone-in and drop-in youth counselling agency called 'Off the Record' as a volunteer and decided that I wanted to do counselling as a job. After my psychology degree I went to Aston University and completed the Diploma in Counselling in Educational Settings course in 1975. In those days there were very few courses in counselling in the UK (about six) and most ran alongside careers advice or educational psychology courses. I went from there to work as a counsellor and lecturer in further education colleges until I took voluntary redundancy in 1993 to go freelance.

'Spare' or 'leisure' time for me has become a rather curious concept since I gave up my previous job working in a college. Maggie gave up her job as a teacher at the same time and we both now work from home which means we see a lot of each other. Since writing the third edition of this book I have retired from practising as a counsellor, supervisor and trainer after over 25 years. I now work as a publisher of counselling books and so I have to maintain an active interest in counselling and psychotherapy in order to stay up to date with what's happening in the profession.

Now I've introduced myself and I think back to what I wrote, it makes me wonder why I chose the bits of my life that I did. I deliberately put in the things that I thought you might be interested in (and puffed me up a bit!) and wanted to keep it brief so that you didn't get bored or think that I was showing off too much.

What about you? Did you think of 'who you are' in terms of your family and home life? Your hobbies and the things you enjoy? Values, beliefs or faith? Or, work-related things like the job you do or whether you are in employment? Which are the most important, the most acceptable, and which would you choose to tell me? Which are the most private and which would you choose not to tell me?

How do these questions sound to you at this stage? Perhaps you feel puzzled by them, worried by them or pleased to be asked them. Counselling training tends to emphasise feelings more than other subjects, so you will find more of this as we go along.

This book is intended to be your companion on a journey of discovery. When you see this symbol:

✍ MAKE A NOTE OF YOUR OWN ANSWERS or EXAMPLES

Expectations

Why are you reading this?

There are few courses of study that do *not* start with the tutor asking some or all of the students why they have chosen to study that particular subject. There are not so many books, however, which begin by asking the reader why they've chosen to read it. Something, or someone, has brought counselling and you together.

As you begin learning, it is probable that you will find the answers to some important questions to help you decide whether you really do want to pursue this interest in counselling any further. Questions such as:

- Why am I interested in counselling?
- What got me interested in this course?
- What do I think counselling is?
- What will counselling be like?
- What do I hope will come of it?
- What are my fears about this course?
- What will be expected of me – what are the demands of counselling as a counsellor and as a client?
- Will I be up to it?

It will take some time before you feel satisfied that you can answer these questions fully, but now is a good place to start. The emphasis is on discovering what is right for you. Having learned something about counselling and weighing up all the pros and cons, you might find that counselling is not for you, or that now is not the right time. I'm sure every reader realises that counselling cannot be for everyone, yet it might be difficult to acknowledge this if you have set your heart on it after experiencing the benefits of counselling as a client. It might be that you have invested too much of your own sense of identity or wellbeing into becoming a counsellor. I suggest proceeding with an open mind, curiosity and a pinch of caution.

The answers will be found over the duration of your introductory course by:

- finding out more about *what counselling is*, and
- finding out more about *yourself*

You may be wondering why finding out more about yourself and your motives is so important. Chapter 3 on *The Importance of Self-Development* looks in some detail at this issue. Counselling is challenging. Learning about counselling is almost certain to be challenging too. It would be very strange if the process of learning about helping was a complete breeze, never causing you to break your stride. One of the challenging things is that you probably have to think differently about the world, people and yourself.

Definitions

After the introductions and getting us to ask ourselves why we've chosen to learn about counselling, it's time to move on to looking at what counselling is. This question usually reveals the variety of ideas, attitudes and opinions regarding counselling, what it is, who it's for and who should be doing it. This isn't surprising since counselling has risen from almost total obscurity to become the

Note
Some people's interest in helping stems from their own experience of needing help and being helped. Being a client can be such a restorative, positive experience – life-saving even – that they want in some way to repay a debt they think they owe, especially if the help was received through a voluntary organisation.

Over the years there has been a somewhat uneasy tension between, on the one hand, thinking that people who want to be helpers should not use training as a substitute for therapy, and on the other, realising that counsellor training *must* involve personal development and growth. There is no doubt that we require people to change on courses – some courses even have an assignment asking students to account for their self-development. So where should we draw the line between acceptable growth, and the inappropriate use of training as therapy?

Why are *you* doing this course, or reading this book? Where would you draw the line?

word on nearly everyone's lips in the past 30 years. A counsellor (in the UK) and a psychiatrist (in the USA) have even been the central characters in situation comedies, but I would caution any readers who think that the media representation of counselling bears any resemblance at all to the real thing!

Helping

You may think it goes without saying that whatever else counselling might be, it is primarily a form of *helping*. You may be surprised to find that there is no single definition of helping that holds true for all contexts. By contexts I mean a whole range of possibilities, from individual episodes between two people through families to whole cultures and belief systems. The meaning of an idea changes from place to place and person to person. In part this book will be discovering the shape-shifting properties of 'helping', so be prepared to have your ideas about helping loosened up a little.

Key to our understanding of helping is knowing something about the purpose of the help being offered. To a large extent it is, of course, the person being helped who determines this aspect of the helping. The side panel takes a brief, broad view so that we can better understand the range of what might be defined as helping in different ways, depending upon the purpose.

We will continue to look at how contexts change the way we think about helping throughout this book and you will find that counselling, as a form of helping, has at its core the willingness and ability to see things from other people's points of view. A key facet of this ability is to be able to do this without finding the stability of our own values or viewpoints threatened. This will come to the fore when we try to help people, for example, who are very different from us, or who want to be helped to do something that we wouldn't want to do ourselves. Personal values, political and spiritual beliefs, family and cultural traditions, all shape our ideas about what good helping is and is not, and these will be explored in several chapters in this book.

Counselling

Over the last 40 years there have been various attempts to arrive at a definition for counselling, but the situation is not helped by the fact that people will keep on using the word 'counselling' to describe so many different activities:

- In educational settings, counselling is often used with the term 'guidance', to mean helping people find the right course or job.
- In medical settings and the armed forces some people still use 'counselling' in a rather old-fashioned way to mean 'to discipline'. If you have been 'counselled' it means you have been told off or warned that some misdemeanour will go on your record.

Note

To illustrate the idea that helping can come in many different guises for many differing purposes, lets briefly look at the differences between:

- *Helping to solve problems*
  This is probably the first definition of help that comes to mind, the sort of help that we are all familiar with because we've almost certainly needed it and, on the other hand, offered or provided it. It's a kind of help that clients sometimes want: they have a problem – distressing feelings or thoughts, difficulty controlling their behaviour, or needing to change an aspect of their lives urgently. It is one of the ways of understanding a type of help that counsellors can offer. It is sometimes referred to as problem-centred helping for obvious reasons.

- *Helping for self-improvement*
  This is different from problem-centred helping in that the client does not have a specific problem to 'solve'; they are not necessarily in acute distress. The client might feel they are not getting the best out of life, might want to look at where their life is going, feel happier or want to be a better partner, team member or citizen. None are life-threatening, panic-inducing or especially urgent, but they are clearly important to particular clients. They might even be 'early warnings' of problems around the corner.

- *Overlaps between types of helping*
  These two types of helping are not mutually exclusive. A client coming with a particular problem, e.g. wanting to give up smoking, might find that their smoking is in part a comfort because they are generally unhappy in their relationships.

  Similarly a person seeking help for general self-improvement might find that they smoke less as a 'side effect'.

- The phrase 'debt counselling' is now used to describe the help you can get to arrange your finances by making regular payments and budgeting.
- Some agencies use the term 'counselling' to describe information and advice given on a particular topic, a healthcare issue perhaps such as family planning or safe sex.
- Many people use 'counselling' to mean any kind of helping activity that they do that hasn't got another more commonplace name like 'tutoring' in education, or 'treatment' in medicine.
- In the broadcast and print media we see the term 'counselling' used daily to mean anything from support for contestants on reality TV shows to a makeover in a lifestyle show.

Each of us brings our own definitions of counselling and ideas about what counselling is. Where do these ideas, feelings, sounds and images come from?

- personal experience of being counselled?
- the beliefs of friends and family?
- what you've read in the papers or seen on TV?
- someone you know who is a counsellor?
- books about counselling or psychology?
- other books, e.g. novels, biographies or books about health or spiritual matters?
- the prevailing view of counselling held at your workplace?

As you begin to explore counselling and therapy, it might be useful to write down your answers to these, and other questions. It would be interesting to look at them again at the end of the course to see if, and/or how, your views have changed.

The flip chart in the margin shows some possible responses from a hypothetical training group on an introductory course (the blank spaces leave room for your ideas). How do they compare with the thoughts and feelings you came up with? Each phrase says something about a person's view of counselling, what it is and what it means to them. Let's look at some in a little more detail to find out what people mean by these words.

BEING HEARD

Means being really heard. It feels as though the other person is really interested in me, and is trying to understand.

WARMTH

This is when I feel welcomed by someone. As if they're pleased to see me and really mean it. It seems as though they genuinely like me.

CONFIDENTIALITY

This is very important if I'm to feel safe. I must be sure that

Activity

So, what do you think? Just what is counselling? *What happens to you when you see or hear the word?*
- *What* images *does the word conjure up for you?*
- Who *do you think of?*
- *What* sounds *do you hear?*
- *What* thoughts *come into your mind?*
- *What* feelings *do you have?*

COUNSELLING IS

BEING HEARD   CARED-FOR   TRAGEDY

WARMTH   CONFIDENTIALITY   LOVE

EQUAL   NON-JUDGEMENTAL

NOT TOLD WHAT TO DO   HONESTY

TWO-WAY   FLEXIBLE   SUPPORT

ONLY FOR PEOPLE WITH PROBLEMS

GRIEF   FRIENDSHIP   NO LIMITS

TIME FOR ME   HELP   COOPERATION

EMERGENCY   CRYING   BEREAVEMENT

A GENUINE RELATIONSHIP

....

'People become engaged in counselling when a person, occupying regularly or temporarily the role of counsellor, offers or agrees explicitly to offer time, attention and respect to another person or persons temporarily in the role of client.

The task of counselling is to give the client an opportunity to explore, discover and clarify ways of living more resourcefully and towards greater well-being.'

British Association for Counselling (1991) Counselling: *Definition of Terms in Use with Expansion and Rationale.*

'Counselling is an activity freely entered into by the person seeking help, it offers the opportunity to identify things for the client themselves that are troubling or perplexing. It is clearly and explicitly contracted, and the boundaries of the relationship identified. The activity itself is designed to help self-exploration and understanding. The process should help to identify thoughts, emotions and behaviours that, once accessed, may offer the client a greater sense of personal resources and self-determined change.'

Janice Russell, Graham Dexter & Tim Bond (1992) *Differentiation between Advice, Guidance, Befriending, Counselling Skills and Counselling.* Advice, Guidance and Counselling Lead Body.

'Counselling: is an interactive learning process contracted between counsellor(s) and client(s), be they individuals, families, groups or institutions, which approaches in a holistic way, social, cultural, economic and/or emotional issues.

Counselling may be concerned with addressing and resolving specific problems, making decisions, coping with crisis, improving relationships, developmental issues, promoting and developing personal awareness, working with feelings, thoughts, perceptions and internal or external conflict. The overall aim is to provide clients with opportunities to work in self-defined ways, towards living in more satisfying and resourceful ways as individuals and as members of the broader society.'

European Association for Counselling definition of counselling adopted AGM 1995. Retrieved 10/01/2011 <http://www.eac.eu.com/index.php?/Standards-and-Ethics/definition-of-counselling.html>

the other person *isn't going to tell anyone else* about what I've said, or even that I've been to see them, in case it's embarrassing.

BEING EQUAL

I like to feel I'm on an equal footing with the other person. So that they're not acting in a superior way like an 'expert' or have any power over me.

NON-JUDGEMENTAL

I don't like the feeling of being judged or told off. Some people make me feel as though I've done wrong by the way they speak to me. I prefer to feel accepted as a person, then I feel safe.

IT'S ONLY FOR PEOPLE WITH PROBLEMS

Counselling is for people with problems, e.g. marriage guidance. I don't have problems so I don't need to see a counsellor.

NO LIMITS

If I go to a counsellor I should be able to talk about anything at all that I think is important.

CRYING

It's OK to cry when you're upset, e.g. if someone close to you has died. Counselling should help you express your feelings.

RELATIONSHIP

Counselling is a helping *relationship*, a caring *relationship*. It's about what happens between two people. Most counsellors believe this is a central pillar of counselling. Some counsellors (this is explained in Chapter 2: *Where Do Ideas in Counselling Come From?*) do not see the relationship as important as the techniques the counsellor teaches the client to use.

Having looked in more detail at some of the meanings behind the key words on the flip chart, do you agree or disagree? (Remember that these are the fictitious views of an imaginary group.)

I have found it helpful to look at counselling in comparison to other helping roles and activities to see where the boundaries are between counselling and the rest of everyday life. Most of us are familiar with the roles of parent, friend and doctor. By this I mean that we have experience of being a patient visiting the doctor, of being a son or daughter and of being someone's friend. What do we want from people in

---

PARENT

EVER-OPEN POCKET   SENSITIVE

SENSE OF HUMOUR   TOUGH LOVE

UNSELFISH   ENCOURAGING

DISCIPLINE   TEACHING SELF-CONTROL

PROTECTING   GUIDANCE

UNCONDITIONAL LOVE   FORGIVENESS

GENEROUS WITH TIME   ALWAYS THERE

ASKING FOR, AND VALUING, YOUR CHILD'S OPINION

....

DOCTOR

HAS PROFESSIONAL KNOWLEDGE AND EXPERTISE

RESPECTFUL   NOT INTIMIDATING

SEES ME AS A PERSON   PRIVATE

AVAILABLE WHEN I WANT

USER FRIENDLY   TRUSTWORTHY

COMMUNICATION SKILLS (BEDSIDE MANNER)

SAFE   KIND

WON'T LAUGH AT ME WHEN I TAKE MY CLOTHES OFF

....

FRIEND

ON YOUR SIDE & WILL STAND UP FOR YOU

HONESTY   SPEAKS UP FOR YOU

LOYALTY   BEING A GOOD COMPANION

FALL OUT & MAKE UP AGAIN   RELIABLE

LENDS MONEY   COMMITTED   SHARING

ALWAYS AVAILABLE   SPARES TIME

RESPECTFUL OF YOUR PRIVACY

YOUR BEST FRIEND WILL TELL YOU

....

Note

Naturally your past experiences will affect the kinds of words you use to describe roles like parent, friend and doctor. It could be that you felt rejected by your parents, betrayed by a friend or treated like a bag of symptoms by your doctor. If that is the case and you feel up to it, you could write down some words that describe the experience – this will help define counselling by what it is not. Alternatively, you could use words to describe your ideal parent, friend or doctor or how you are or would like to be as a parent, friend, and so on.

these roles and what do we try to offer when we are in these roles? They are all 'helpers' of one sort or another, so it's clear that helping comes in many different shapes and colours. You could also try other helping roles such as teacher, nurse, priest, etc., if you are wanting to practise counselling skills in conjunction with your work. On the previous page are three more flip charts with ideas from our hypothetical group.

How do your thoughts about these helping roles fit in with the flip charts above? The sidenote acknowledges that not everyone experiences these roles as helping, but these roles do represent the ways of helping and caring that are commonplace in our culture and that we've probably grown up with. Our ideas about good caring tell us a lot about ourselves and it seems as though there might be some common themes about helping which are shared by these roles. This activity also helps us understand where counselling-style helping begins and ends, where it overlaps with other helping activities and where it's different. These limits are called *boundaries*.

Counselling and non-counselling ways of helping

Some ways of helping in our culture are fine as counselling ways of helping. On the other hand, some perfectly good ways of helping as a friend, parent, or doctor would be no good as counselling ways of helping. For example, taking some items from our flip charts on pages 5 and 7:

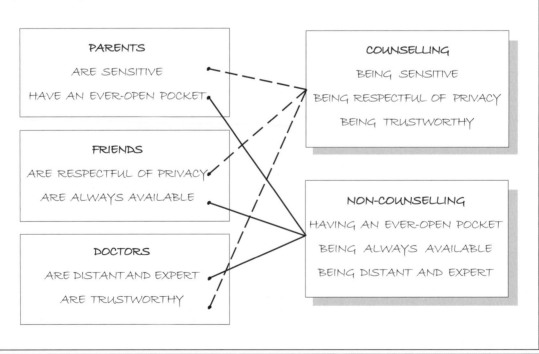

Boundaries between counselling and other ways of helping

Boundaries help define an activity by creating a space within which the activity can take place. 'Space' brings to mind *my* space, *safe* space, *sufficient* space, *open* space, *private* space, *sacred* space – these are all ways clients and counsellors might understand the helping or therapeutic space. One of the ways we make the counselling space safe for the client, for their exclusive use, is to protect it with boundaries. These boundaries will keep certain non-counselling things or ways of being out and certain counselling-style helping things or ways of being in.

As can be seen in the panel in the margin, some ways of helping are role- or context-specific. In most circumstances, it would not be considered appropriate for a counsellor to lend clients money or be constantly available for them. Things are likely to be more complicated if you work as an employee or volunteer in a helping agency or institution – you will have to get to grips with the policies of the agency when it comes to boundaries. For example, you might not be allowed to tell a client your surname, yet you might be allowed to lend them money to get home on the bus. These different boundaries are always context-specific, in other words the context in which the helping takes place will bring its own sensible rules regarding how helpers conduct themselves with clients. Some of these agency or institution rules will be informed by the type of helping that is being offered – whether 'counselling' is taking place, or 'counselling skills', or whether the staff or volunteers are offering 'coaching', 'mentoring' or what I call in this book 'basic helping' (others might call this 'listening' or 'support').

I hope you can now appreciate why making distinctions between types of helping is important. The boundary between what counselling is and what it is not has been, and is currently, the subject of serious debate. The debate is held by just about everyone involved in counselling, including organisations and professional associations. The debate is important for both clients and counsellors so that safe effective practice can be asked for and offered, and it is obviously also a core element of initial training. To that end some groups in the helping professions are involved in developing and agreeing a set of competencies for counselling so that qualifications in counselling can be standardised. One of their first tasks will be to identify what counselling is and how it is different from other forms of helping such as befriending, guidance, advice, coaching, mentoring, etc.

Professional organisations, networks and other groupings of helpers have contributions to make regarding appropriate boundaries of helping in that they define good, safe, *ethical* practice.

Note

To say that it would not be appropriate for a counsellor to lend money is correct. However, when counselling was in its infancy in the late 1960s and early 1970s, many further and higher education counselling services were 'generic'. That is to say that the counselling service offered help with a wide range of student problems from changing course through accommodation to personal problems. If a student at a further education college turned up at the counselling service having had an argument with their parents and needed the bus fare home, the counsellor might well have given them the money.

Similarly, helpers in some residential settings are clearly supposed to be available to residents – their clients – 24 hours a day, seven days a week. Clearly boundaries, like so many issues of theory and practice in counselling, have their appropriateness dictated by the context. There are few rules that can be mechanically applied. Most – but not all – are matters of judgement, and this judgement comes with experience as well as good training and personal development.

Activity

Don't take it as read that giving money to clients is not allowed without thinking about it. Are there any circumstances when you might think it would be OK for an individual counsellor to give a client money? There might be agency policies that allow money to be given to clients in special circumstances such as in the above note.

Note

I look at ethics and helping in some detail in Chapter 7, and we describe some of the work of groups and professional associations in various places in the book, starting on the next page.

What are counselling and psychotherapy?
A set of useful summaries can be found on
the BACP website including:

 • BACP Definition of counselling and
 psycho-therapy: Counselling and psychotherapy are umbrella terms that cover a range
 of talking therapies. They are delivered by
 trained practitioners who work with people
 over a short or long term to help them bring
 about effective change or enhance their
 wellbeing.
   • What is therapy?
   • Types of therapy
   • Therapeutic models in brief
   • What therapy is not

Retrieved 10/01/2011 <http://
www.bacp.co.uk/information/education/
whatiscounselling.php>

Other links to BACP information take us
to alternative definitions:

 Counselling and psychotherapy are often
 described as "talking therapies" and involve
 a contractual arrangement between the
 therapist and the client where they meet,
 in privacy and confidence, to explore a
 difficulty or distress the client may be
 experiencing. Therapy should always be
 at the request of the client and no-one
 should be sent.

From Information Sheet T1, retrieved 10/
01/2011 <http://www.bacp.co.uk/admin/
structure/files/pdf/811_t1.pdf>

And an older, more detailed *BACP
definition of counselling* can still be found
on some agency and department websites:

 Counselling takes place when a counsellor
 sees a client in a private and confidential
 setting to explore a difficulty the client is
 having, distress they may be experiencing
 or perhaps their dissatisfaction with life, or
 loss of a sense of direction and purpose. It
 is always at the request of the client as no
 one can properly be 'sent' for counselling.

Retrieved 10/01/2011<http://www.nott
inghamcounsellingcentre.org.uk/
index.php/frequently_asked_questions/>

British Association for Counselling and Psychotherapy

The professional organisation representing the largest number of
counsellors and therapists in the UK is the British Association for
Counselling and Psychotherapy. It was established in 1977 as the
British Association for Counselling (BAC) with just a few hundred
members, steadily growing until in 2000 it changed its name to the
British Association for Counselling and Psychotherapy (BACP) and
its members now number over 30,000. Clearly the definition of
counselling held by BACP would be important and useful for people
in the UK. The side panel details some of the information provided
by BACP on the subject of what counselling is and is not.

Readers might be interested to realise that BACP carries slightly
different definitions in different parts of its website. Don't be
confused by this. In part it is simply a confirmation that a single
definition is probably impossible and not particularly useful when
the contexts in which this type of helping have so much influence
on the aims and methods of 'counselling'. It also provides us all
with the altogether more educational task of distilling the common
components across the definitions.

For many years BACP was interested in the distinction between
using counselling skills and *being a counsellor* for a number of
reasons. Primarily, BACP would like to assure prospective clients
that someone claiming to be a counsellor and/or psychotherapist has
a minimum level of qualifications and experience. At the same time,
BACP acknowledges that many people offer helping relationships in a
variety of settings and contexts. The type of helping is counselling-
like, but the person doing the helping would not call themselves a
counsellor. The BACP developed a framework over many years to
help clients, other non-counselling professionals and the public at
large understand the different types of helping that are available.
This framework evolves to reflect changes in the helping professions
and we will refer to this framework and its development throughout
the book.

Also, in Chapter 9: *Counselling Contexts and Connections*,
we will look at the emerging 'profession' of counselling and there
will be more on the role of the BACP there.

Basic helping

In some previous editions of this book I used the phrase 'helping
in a counselling way' to describe the type of *informed helping* we
might aspire to on completion of a 20–30 hour Introduction to
Counselling course. Because this is a cumbersome phrase to fit
into sentences, from the third edition onwards I have preferred to
use the term 'basic helping'.

> The wise ruler says:
> I take no action and the people are transformed of themselves;
> I prefer stillness and the people are rectified of themselves;
> I do not interfere and the people prosper of themselves;
> I am free from desire and the people of themselves become simple like
> the uncarved block.
>
> Lao Tzu: *Tao Te Ching*, LXXIII,179
>
> 'Look here,' Furii said. 'I never promised you a rose-garden. I never promised you perfect justice … and I never promised you peace or happiness. My help is so that you can be free to fight for all these things. The only reality I offer is challenge, and being well is being free to accept it or not at whatever level you are capable. I never promise lies, and the rose-garden world of perfection is a lie – and a bore too!'
>
> Hannah Green: *I Never Promised You a Rose Garden*, p. 101

This basic helping will incorporate an awareness of what theories of helping there might be without necessarily *knowing* them in any detail. Allied to this will be an awareness of helping and counselling skills, but not necessarily the ability to consistently offer a good range of them. In addition, this basic helping includes an awareness of the goals of counselling and the ethical framework within which professional counsellors work. And of course, we will be aware of the central role of self-development in the effective and responsible training and development of helpers, together with the requirement for adequate support and supervision.

Finally, basic helping can also be understood as a stage in the development of an individual helper's skills – a springboard from which the person can pursue the full-time use of counselling skills in their job, or progress to become a qualified counsellor and/or psychotherapist.

As a result of this new and developing awareness our ability as a helper at the most basic level will be improved. We will also be able to confidently assure ourselves, our relatives, friends, colleagues and others that we may try to help, that counselling is a responsible, skilled and useful helping activity whenever they might be in distress. This is basic helping. In Chapter 13 we will briefly review the learning on basic introductory courses and see where you might want to go next in the development of your helping skills.

Being a better parent, friend, neighbour and citizen

There are many reasons why people embark upon basic helping training. Whatever the reasons for starting, there may well be some side benefits that you might not have signed up for. Since the skills

Note
The definitions in the margin on p. 10 and the box on p. 13 emphasise the quality of the relationship. Helping another human being is built on the ability to establish a good relationship, so all training starts there, rather than the level of psychological theory. There are thousands of good theoreticians who are poor helpers, and thousands of people, for example, hairdressers, who are good natural helpers but know nothing about psychological theory. To be a well-rounded helper, you need to have a grounding in both.

and attitudes central to basic helping are also central to good human relationships, you will find that an introductory course is quite likely to enhance your qualities as a parent, friend, neighbour or even citizen. You may find that you feel more able and prepared to help a friend or neighbour in their grief when someone dies, or in making a difficult life decision. Also, as we work through the values, qualities and skills of good helping, you might see how these can develop in you a sense of being a more fulfilled person and responsible citizen. In short, being able to help someone frequently leaves us feeling better about ourselves.

Basic helping in a voluntary agency

One of the most popular ways to share your basic helping is through voluntary work. You will see more about this and who might benefit in Chapter 10. Some people on your course group will already be volunteers in a helping agency. Some will have already participated in some agency-specific helping training. What you will find in this book is intended to back up and add to the training you will receive from your agency. In the unlikely event that some of the things you read in this book appear to conflict with agency policy, that is not bad news. There are lots of different views in counselling and basic helping, and by exploring these different views through discussion you will learn much more. Discuss any differences you find in your course group and with your agency trainers, managers and supervisors. They should be pleased to explain the agency policy.

Using counselling skills

Counselling skills can be used by anyone, either as a separate set of techniques or, more usually, as a set of skills either integrated with, or alongside, an already well-established set of professional or 'people' skills. In such a case we might find:

- a nurse using counselling skills when he listens to a patient or comforts grieving relatives
- a teacher using counselling skills when she is told by a school pupil that he is being bullied
- a manager using counselling skills when an employee tells her that he is thinking of quitting work to look after an ageing parent
- a person working at home to bring up children might use counselling skills to comfort a neighbour when their spouse is made redundant
- a colleague listening really well in order to resolve a disagreement in a meeting
- a priest helping members of her congregation to deal with witnessing a tragic accident in the parish

You might have chosen to attend a basic counselling course to help you in a similar setting at your place of work or in the community. We will look at *who counselling is for* in more detail in Chapter 10.

Some years ago (Sanders, 2007) I offered the following definition of counselling skills:

Sanders, P (2007) *Using Counselling Skills on the Telephone and In Computer-Mediated Communication* (3rd ed). Ross-on-Wye: PCCS Books.

Counselling skills are interpersonal communication skills derived from the study of therapeutic change in human beings, used in a manner consistent with the goals and values of the established ethics of the profession of the practitioner in question. In addition, the user of counselling skills will find that their own professional skills are enhanced by the process. (p.19)

Definitions of non-counselling helping

Guidance
To offer a confidential, accountable service which helps the client to develop self-awareness. To enable the client to be aware of and have access to accurate, appropriate information on available opportunities in order to make informed choices. The client is offered opportunities to explore relevant concerns and to develop decision-making skills. The activity is designed to help the management of transition appropriate to the client's needs and wishes.

Befriending
To provide on-going quality support to distressed individuals for an indeterminate period of time. The activity should enable appropriate, realistic and healthy coping skills to be developed in a warm and trusting relationship. Befriending is intended to lessen the person's sense of social or personal isolation.

Advice
Advising enables the client to solve problems and make decisions by offering accurate, current and appropriate information. It seeks to widen the client's choice by informing them of their rights, options and possible action programmes.

Janice Russell, Graham Dexter & Tim Bond (1992) *Differentiation between Advice, Guidance, Befriending, Counselling Skills and Counselling.* Advice, Guidance and Counselling Lead Body.

Personal/Life Coaching
A collaborative solution-focused, results-orientated and systematic process in which the coach facilitates the enhancement of work performance, life experience, self-directed learning and personal growth of the coachee.

Anthony Grant, University of Sydney, 2000. Retrieved on 10/01/2011 <www.associationforcoaching.com/about/about03.htm>

Mentoring
… is a process for the informal transmission of knowledge, social capital, and the psychosocial support perceived by the recipient as relevant to work, career, or professional development; mentoring entails informal communication, usually face to face and during a sustained period of time, between a person who is perceived to have greater relevant knowledge, wisdom, or experience (the mentor) and a person who is perceived to have less (the protégé).

B Bozeman, & MK Feeney (2007) Toward a useful theory of mentoring: A conceptual analysis and critique. *Administration and Society, 39*(6),719-39.

Counselling

There are many different ways of understanding the nature of counselling. It can be seen as:

- a counselling *approach* to people – a way of understanding or caring for and helping our fellow humans
- a set of counselling *skills* – therapeutic ways of behaving
- a set of counselling *goals* – caring and helping aims which we are hoping to achieve
- counselling *boundaries* – a set of limits, inclusions and exclusions appropriate for counselling
- counselling *roles* – one person identified as the client and one person identified as the counsellor
- counselling *ethics* – caring values and behaviours, primarily doing no harm and protecting the client

Some other ways of helping may share some of these features, but not all. When you have all of the above, then you have counselling.

Basic helping may share a counselling approach to helping and some of the skills, goals and ethics, for example. When using counselling skills, we may share the counselling skills but have a different approach, goals, boundaries and ethics, e.g., using counselling skills in a nursing setting to achieve nursing goals with nursing boundaries and ethical code.

We can see that the issue of definition of counselling is dependent upon the boundaries of the activity, the qualities of the relationship, and the aims or functions of the activity.

The essential boundaries of counselling are:

- that it is practised by someone designated as a counsellor
- that the counsellor be appropriately trained to be able to practise to an acceptable standard
- that the counsellor abides by a code or framework of counselling ethics and practice (see Chapter 7)
- that the client knows that the service being offered by the counsellor is counselling (not coaching, advocacy or mentoring, for example)
- that the counsellor is honest about what counselling can reasonably achieve and refers the client on to different, specialised help where appropriate

The essential qualities of the relationship are:

- that the counsellor shows deep respect for the client
- the counsellor and client will agree on what the relationship will set out to achieve and how it will seek to achieve it
- that the client will feel safe enough to be challenged

Note

One of the key differences between counselling and using counselling skills is that the counsellor is bound by a framework of ethics and practice, carrying a set of professional responsibilities. When using counselling skills, you are primarily governed by another set of ethical principles and professional responsibilities, which spring from the work setting, role or professional title, e.g. nursing, teaching, management or youth work.

Note

Another of the key differences between counselling and the use of counselling skills is that the counsellor and client will make an agreement regarding what the client wants from the counsellor and what the counsellor is prepared to offer.

- that the client will feel valued as a person
- the counsellor does not judge the client

The aims or functions of counselling are:
- that the client will feel empowered, i.e. have a greater sense of personal autonomy
- the client has a greater sense of self-understanding
- to enable the client to live in a more 'satisfying and resourceful way' (see Russell et al., 1992)
- that the client has a greater sense of wellbeing
- that any specific problems identified by the client are actively addressed and resolved where possible
- that the above 'gains' should be enduring

The elements of the definitions above should find agreement amongst a wide range of counsellors. Hopefully it is now clear that there is a general convergence of views on what counselling actually is, albeit expressed in slightly different ways.

What counselling is not
Like so many things, counselling is defined as much by what it isn't as by what it is. It can also be instructive to look at the ideas and activities that lie just outside counselling, since counselling, whilst similar to so many helping activities, has distinct differences.

Counselling is not:
- being a friend
- caring in a parental way
- 'treating' or 'healing' someone like a doctor
- instructing or teaching
- advising
- giving guidance
- using the skills of counselling disconnected from the elements described in the previous section

These helping styles and activities are so well known they are practically second nature to most of us. They are also easily confused with counselling – so much so that if we find counselling difficult we often tend to revert back to a way of helping which is more familiar to us. Some take the view that counselling is potentially a very natural helping style for us as long as we can *stop* trying to do something else, like taking control of the situation, thinking we know best, or judging the person we are trying to help.

Throughout your basic introductory course you will get feedback from your fellow students and tutors. Some of this feedback might

Russell, J, Dexter, G & Bond, T (1992) *Differentiation between Advice, Guidance, Befriending, Counselling Skills and Counselling.* Advice, Guidance and Counselling Lead Body.

Activity
How do the various definitions and elements of definitions we have looked at compare with your own ideas?

Activity
The chances are that you will prefer to help in a particular way or style. Perhaps because of your job or because of your personality, you tend to help in a 'teaching' style or a 'parental' style or a 'friendly' style, etc.
- *What tendencies do you have to rescue, judge or take control when you are trying to help in a counselling way?*

Activity

If you are in a situation where things feel difficult and you find yourself considering another style of helping, how should this choice be exercised? Here are two examples to get you thinking:

- *Your children might generally prefer you to help them in a parent-like way rather than be a counsellor.*
  - *Would it be appropriate to offer them counselling-style helping under some circumstances?*
- *People in a client role might expect you to help them in a counselling way.*
  - *Would it be appropriate to offer them help in a parental style, teaching style, friendly style or healing style under some circumstances?*

Note

The BAC Code of Ethics and Practice, May 1996 reads:

It is not possible to make a generally accepted distinction between counselling and psychotherapy. There are well-founded traditions which use the terms interchangeably and others which distinguish them. (para 3.3.)

There is much more on ethics in Chapter 7.

Thorne, B (1999) Psychotherapy and counselling are indistinguishable. In C Feltham (ed) *Controversies in Counselling and Psychotherapy* (pp. 225-32). London: Sage.

concern how they experience your natural style of helping. It will be useful to take note of this so that you can identify those occasions when you feel most tempted to stop a counselling style and revert to your natural style. When this happens you have a choice between two styles of helping. It is good to remember that both are useful under different circumstances. One of the themes of this opening chapter is that each helping style has its time and place. Helping is context-specific.

Each way of helping is fine under the right circumstances. Counselling, using counselling skills and basic helping, is no better or worse than other ways of helping, just different and suited to certain circumstances. People seeking help have the right to ask for a helping style that suits them – however, we are under no obligation to provide a helping style that we don't feel comfortable with.

There are few of us for whom a counselling way of helping is easy the first time we try to do it, even though we think it is 'right' for us because it is in harmony with our values. We need to practise and work at it on a number of levels – our self-awareness, our knowledge and our skills. The remaining chapters in the book look in more detail at each of these at a level appropriate to basic helping and an introductory course in counselling or counselling skills.

Counselling or psychotherapy?

I have made some effort to come to some helpful definitions in this first chapter, but the truth is that the whole area of professional counselling and psychotherapy is still rather ill-defined in this country. One of the most frequently asked questions is 'What is the difference between counselling and psychotherapy?' Worse still from a public relations point of view, I cannot say that there is an answer on which most professionals can agree. This lack of agreement about the labels we use is an indication of the genuine uncertainty regarding precise definitions of these activities.

At the 1992 Annual Conference of the then British Association for Counselling (BAC, now BACP) Brian Thorne delivered a keynote speech with the title 'Psychotherapy and Counselling: The Quest for Differences' – see *Counselling, 3*(4), December 1992 – and he wrote again on this topic in 1999 (Thorne, 1999).

At the 1993 Annual General Meeting, the BAC debated whether it should embrace the word 'psychotherapy' in its title and changed its name in 2000 to the British Association for Counselling and Psychotherapy. So in professional circles it is a matter for debate, but some would say that the debate is really about professional status or even control of the psychological side of the helping professions.

In his 1992 paper Brian Thorne looked at possible grounds for distinction including:

- the type of problem: psychotherapy is for deeper-seated problems
- the type of treatment: psychotherapy uses the dynamics of the relationship between therapist and client
- duration of treatment: psychotherapy lasts for a longer time than counselling
- the setting: psychotherapy takes place in medical settings, counselling in educational settings

He concluded that there are no grounds for maintaining any difference in usage of the terms 'counselling' and 'psychotherapy'. He emphasised the need to clear up any confusion for the sake of clients and reiterated these conclusions in 1999 in a debate in print with Jan Harvie-Clarke (Thorne, 1999, Harvie-Clarke, 1999). Harvie-Clarke took the position that 'There are real differences between psychotherapy and counselling' and started by saying that she was only speaking from the view of a PSYCHODYNAMIC practitioner. Her chapter is based upon her understanding of how her own practice changed over the years, rather than points of general difference which can apply to all practitioners. And this could be the key to resolving the puzzle – perhaps differences are only really evident at the level of individual therapists and their practice, not at the level of more general principles. How deep a particular practitioner works with a particular client, for how long, how frequently, and in what setting, are all factors which will define what the therapist believes they are offering. They may call it what they choose.

An Internet search in 2011 – twelve years after the Thorne/ Harvie-Clarke debate – for differences between counselling and psychotherapy yields much less certainty. Perhaps the change in title of BAC to BACP has had an effect on the public and professionals alike.

Counselling, psychotherapy, call it what you like, has a valuable contribution to make to our quality of life in the 21st century and confusion over names and titles is likely only to serve to keep valuable skills and services away from the people whom they are most likely to benefit.

Activity

A definitive answer is no nearer if some groups of professionals have been saying for years that counselling and psychotherapy are the same whilst other groups of professionals have been saying they're different.

- *Do you think there are any differences between counselling and psychotherapy?*
- *What general impression do you get from media, publicity, friends, family and personal experience?*
- *Maybe you think you are not qualified to answer? If not, who do you think ought to be supplying an answer?*
- *Is a definitive answer necessary?*

Thorne, B (1999) Psychotherapy and counselling are indistinguishable. In C Feltham (ed) *Controversies in Psychotherapy and Counselling* (pp. 225-32). London: Sage.

Harvie-Clarke, J (1999) There are real differences between psychotherapy and counselling. In C Feltham (ed) *Controversies in Psychotherapy and Counselling* (pp. 233-40). London: Sage.

PSYCHODYNAMIC Derived from psychoanalysis and the work of Sigmund Freud and later psychoanalytic theorists, with unconscious processes at the heart of the work.

If I am
Helping in a Counselling Way

I am **informed** by:
counselling aims,
counselling skills,
counselling boundaries,
counselling and
counselling skills ethics.

I will:
have *my own* aims,
use *my own* helping skills,
use *my own* boundaries,
be guided by *my own* ethics.

If I am
**Helping in a Counselling Way in a
Voluntary Agency**

I will also:
• know and work
according to *agency*
policies and protocols.

I am also **informed** by:
the aims *of the agency.*

If I am
Using Counselling Skills

I will **practise**:
• *counselling skills*
– within *counselling
skills* ethics,
• other *professional skills*
(e.g. nursing, teaching)
– within other *professional
ethics* (e.g. nursing).

I am **informed** by:
counselling aims,
counselling boundaries.

If I am
a Counsellor

• I will **practise** *counselling* skills.
• I will **keep** *counselling* boundaries.
• I will **have** *counselling* aims and goals.
• I am **governed by** *counselling* ethics.

There has been much debate amongst counsellor trainers regarding the preferred blend of ingredients in training. Just how much skills, theory, personal development and so on, make the perfect training course? On a short 20 or 30 hour introduction to counselling course for basic helping, the debate was whether to have any theory at all. My view then is expressed in this chapter, the title of which should give the game away; it's a thinly disguised 'Counselling theory' chapter. I think that now, in the new millennium, it is almost universally accepted that an awareness of the theories of helping is essential. Otherwise basic helping would simply be a collection of the best ideas the helper can come up with at the time.

When I first started helping as a volunteer at 'Off the Record' in Newcastle-upon-Tyne the training consisted of around three months of weekly meetings in which we discussed ourselves and did some role plays of 'problem' situations. At no time did anyone mention 'theory' or *where ideas in counselling come from*. Of course, it may have been assumed that, as a psychology undergraduate, I knew it all anyway. (This was not true, since my psychology degree didn't even have any lectures on 'personality'.) When I asked one of the trainers for more information, it was suggested that I read *On Becoming a Person* by Carl Rogers. (I misheard the title and approached puzzled bookshop assistants asking if they knew 'I Am Becoming a Person'!)

When I finally got hold of a copy I was thrilled to discover that someone had been thinking about helping skills in such a systematic yet approachable way. I then discovered that Carl Rogers wasn't the only person to have thought deeply about human psychological distress – there were several approaches, theories and systems. Each one made claims to be successful and a new one seemed to be added to the list every week! That was in 1972, and the situation seems much the same today, with new approaches coming along with familiar regularity.

At any one time, readers would be forgiven for thinking that the latest theory had all the answers or was the method guaranteed to be successful for certain problems. Whatever you read in magazines or on the web, or see on TV, most approaches to helping are about as effective as each other, give or take some very small

Rogers, CR (1961) *On Becoming a Person*. London: Constable.

'All theory is autobiographical ... no theory is universal ... in the history of ideas, every choice has personal motives ...'

John Shlien (2003) *To Live an Honorable Life*. Ross-on-Wye: PCCS Books, pp. 217-18.

Sigmund Freud (1856–1939), originally trained as a medical doctor, was the originator of PSYCHO-ANALYSIS in the early 1900s.

PSYCHOANALYSIS Extensive theory of the mind developed and modified by Sigmund Freud throughout his professional life. It kicked off interest in the possibility of 'talking cures' and, via Freud's students and followers, stimulated the further development of many variations and countertheories. We look in more detail at Freud's contribution and psychoanalysis on pp. 27-33.

- *Behaviour*
- *Defences*
- *Using your own resources*
- *Emotions*
- *Active listening*
- *Positive thinking*
- *Coping*
- *Goals*
- *Non-interfering*
- *Self-discipline*
- *Problem-solving*
- *At your own pace*
- *Acceptance*
- *Dreams*
- *Logical thinking*
- *Irrational beliefs*
- *Step-by-step*
- *Avoidance*
- *Homework*

differences. Knowing this could cut two ways, you could be confused and not know which approach to choose either as a counsellor/helper or as a client. Or you could be relieved, knowing that you can choose from a number of approaches if you want to be an effective helper, or choose a particular approach as a client.

When I decided to try to unravel this tangle of ideas, claims and counterclaims, I discovered that the roots of the ideas can be traced as far back as you have the resources and energy to go. From centuries-old philosophies and ancient cultures, through to current ideas in our own white European culture. A summary of the more recent landmarks in the Western world would go back over 100 years to the work of Sigmund Freud.

Freudian ideas are important because they have slowly but surely slipped into our understanding of the world over the past 100 years. When we use Freudian ideas, we don't announce it, we just do it – most of us do not know the ideas come from Freud. These ideas occur in many forms in literature, films, and plays, as well as everyday conversations, e.g. we talk about 'Freudian slips', 'the unconscious', interpreting the meaning of dreams, and so on. These ideas are with us constantly and we use them in our understanding of the world without thinking.

When starting to think about becoming a helper or counsellor, we need to have a go at exploring where our own ideas and assumptions about helping come from. So first I want to look at some of the popular ideas we share about helping today, starting with the language we use. Look at the list of words and phrases in the margin. They all may be associated with counselling, listening and helping. Which ones are most likely to come to mind when *you* think about helping?

These words and phrases can be traced to five fundamental and very influential approaches to the psychology of human mental distress which are covered in this chapter. When we explore

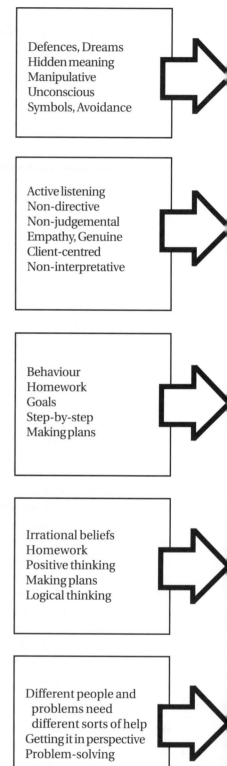

Defences, Dreams
Hidden meaning
Manipulative
Unconscious
Symbols, Avoidance

Active listening
Non-directive
Non-judgemental
Empathy, Genuine
Client-centred
Non-interpretative

Behaviour
Homework
Goals
Step-by-step
Making plans

Irrational beliefs
Homework
Positive thinking
Making plans
Logical thinking

Different people and
problems need
different sorts of help
Getting it in perspective
Problem-solving

Psychodynamic Approaches
Several contemporary approaches can all be traced back to the original work of Sigmund Freud (1856–1939), founder of *Psychoanalysis*.

No contemporary psychologist or psychotherapist could claim not to be influenced by the work of Freud. Many schools of therapy grew more directly out of his work, sometimes founded by Freud's ex-students or associates, including CG Jung, Wilhelm Reich, Melanie Klein and DW Winnicott. Modern counselling approaches influenced by Freud include *Transactional Analysis*.

Humanistic Approaches
Developed by a group of American psychologists in the 1950s. In counselling terms, the most influential was Carl Rogers (1902–1987), founder of the *Person-Centred Approach*.

Other influential humanistic psychologists, contemporaries of Rogers, include Abraham Maslow and Rollo May. Rogers' ideas have had a very wide influence in counselling and psychology. Many modern approaches to helping and education now incorporate his ideas or claim to be person- or student- 'centred'. Also, confusingly, the term 'person-centred' is used in the UK in the field of social care, but is not based on Rogerian theory.

Behavioural Approaches
Modern psychological approaches based on scientific learning theories of Russian psychologist IP Pavlov (1849–1936) and American psychologists JB Watson (1878–1958) and BF Skinner, founders of *Behaviourism*.

Skinner (more so than Watson or Pavlov) is another highly influential psychologist whose work has touched many modern ideas. 'Behaviour Therapy' became popular in the 1970s after Joseph Wolpé refined the work of the early Behaviourists. Elements of learning theories can be found in most modern counselling approaches since all psychologists would acknowledge the role of learning processes of some sort in human development.

Cognitive Approaches
Emphasising the central role of thoughts in mental processes, cognitive approaches were developed by Aaron Beck and Albert Ellis, founder of *Rational Emotive Behaviour Therapy*.

Beck and Ellis separately developed cognitive approaches to mental distress and change. Cognitive approaches have influenced the development of time-limited helping work which enjoys some support in healthcare settings. Other cognitive approaches have had an impact upon the treatment of severely disturbed people with enduring mental health problems.

Integrative Approaches
The quest to blend components of different therapeutic approaches has enjoyed varying success since the mid-1970s, popularised by Gerard Egan, founder of *Developmental Eclecticism*.

At the forefront of the development and popularisation of integrative approaches in the UK were Egan and Arnold Lazarus with his 'Multimodal Therapy'. In recent years models (some without names) have been developed by Anthony Ryles, and many others. Few are widely practised in the UK apart from Egan's model and Ryles' Cognitive Analytic Therapy.

Three forces in modern psychology

Many references can be found in the literature to three major forces in psychology. Freudian psychoanalysis and its various offshoots are considered to be the 'first force' in psychology, having been developed in the late 19th century and become dominant in the earlier part of the 20th century. The rise of behaviourism in the United States in the early 20th century led to it being called the second force in psychology.

As a reaction to the huge edifice of psychoanalytic theory and the instrumental nature of behaviourism, more holistic, natural ways developed in psychology in the 1950s. This is the third force in psychology – humanistic psychology. It was thought at the time that humanistic psychology would become the dominant major force, but since then cognitive psychology gained ground and now looks as though, combined with behaviourism, it is sweeping all before it. Readers should also be aware of 'positive psychology', a recent movement in Western psychology seeking to concentrate on what 'goes right' in human functioning rather than what 'goes wrong'.

No one has continued naming these waves of psychological theory as forces in psychology since Maslow. This idea was rather culturally arrogant – similar to the way the United States refers to its national baseball championship as the 'World Series'. If we change our field of view to 'world psychology', we can see that many of the ideas proposed by psychoanalysts, behaviourists, etc. are probably not new. It is certain that there have been very sophisticated ideas about healing mental distress in many great, and lesser, civilisations throughout the ages, from China to Africa. Many of these ideas do keep cropping up in modern thinking. Psychology in the 21st century appears to be more open to wider cultural influences.

these approaches later in the chapter you may find that you are familiar with many of the ideas reflected in these approaches. People tend to make certain assumptions about effective helping that are culturally based and again we might find some reflected in these approaches to human psychology. We will learn that each approach has its founders and many more recent approaches to helping have been directly or indirectly influenced by these schools of thought.

The founders of the approaches didn't invent these ideas out of thin air. Each theory is a product of the summation of a person's experiences in a particular social context at a certain moment in history. Each had their own influences from which they borrowed, sometimes acknowledged, sometimes not. The real picture of where ideas come from is, of course, extremely complicated. Indeed it is impossible to understand the origin of ideas fully, but fun and interesting to try.

This short introduction to the history of the ideas behind modern counselling will look first at the three foundation stones of counselling theory: psychoanalysis, behavioural psychology and humanistic psychology. These are sometimes referred to as the first, second and third force in psychology respectively.

In addition to looking at these 'three forces' in psychology, we will look at a couple of slightly more recently developed ideas in counselling, namely the notion that our *thoughts* are important in shaping our feelings (called the *cognitive* approach) and the idea that the best way of helping is to blend together or *integrate* the best of each approach (called *integrative* counselling).

Although psychological theories are important and form the basis of helping practice, do not be completely overawed by them. I will be asking you to discover your *own* ideas about helping and to look at how these fit in with the approaches covered in the book. At this stage in your learning as a helper it is useful to know how your own ideas fit in with classical theories. If you decide to progress to developing and using counselling skills, or to counselling proper, such an appreciation of your own and other people's ideas is essential.

You may be reading this and thinking that you don't have any ideas about helping other than 'common sense'. Do not be too hasty to dismiss common sense, since it is the helping approach used by the vast majority of the human race. Of course what is 'common' sense will depend upon your cultural setting (family, community, class, religion etc.). In other words, your own version of common sense will be a blend of personal experience of being helped, things you've learned from your parents, guardians, priests and teachers, the impact of literature, films, etc. on your thinking and … well, perhaps you could complete the rest in the activity in the margin at the top of the page opposite.

The problem with most counselling theories

It will not take you long to work out, as you read through the next few pages, that each of the 'theories' or approaches I am going to cover was developed and presented by a white man from Northern Europe or North America. This is a serious problem since, as I have repeated several times already, the ideas that people have spring from the culture in which they live. The ideas that white men can think up are limited by their whiteness and their maleness, and in the case of the theorists covered here, by their privileged, educated status in First-World countries.

We have to ask ourselves whether it is reasonable to believe that such privileged, white, middle-class, educated men are the only people with anything useful to say about helping and counselling, and the answer is, of course, no. We should realise that the ideas that have guided our thinking about counselling for the last 100 or so years are, for the most part, androcentric (centred around male ways of thinking and doing things) and ethnocentric (centred around the culture and race of the theorist, i.e. white culture).

So, I have talked about how the men whose ideas have shaped contemporary helping and counselling were and are products of their time and how we can reasonably expect the ideas to reflect and be shaped by the cultural biases and mores that prevailed. In my view it would be unfair to criticise Freud, for example, for coming up with a helping system based on the expert knowledge of the therapist, since society in Northern Europe in the late 1800s revolved around the experts who held knowledge (and therefore power), such as priests, judges and physicians.

It would be less forgivable for someone to base a 21st century theory of helping on the powerful 'expert' knowledge of the helper, since Northern European/American culture is now much more 'customer-centred'. Doctors are now much more likely to ask patients if they have any idea why they are ill and few priests still claim to have direct links with gods. Most professional expert helpers try to 'give away' their expertise by being more collaborative. Anyone who resists this tendency in the 21st century is likely to be tripped up by the increasing number of 'smart', or 'informed' clients/patients who have thoroughly researched their symptoms and available services online before approaching a doctor or helper.

In terms of individual persons, the effect of basing a helping approach on theory that is so culturally narrow, that only supports the status quo, is that it simply passes on any culturally endorsed practices in, for example, child rearing, that are likely to lead to mental health problems in adulthood. In terms of groups of people, a narrow monocultural theory both absorbs and reproduces any institutionalised stigmatisation, discrimination and oppression that

Note

The same can be said, of course, for me. I try to acknowledge the undoubted privilege and advantage conferred on me by various accidents of birth and the effect they might have on the things I write about and how authoritative I might sound. It is just as well, however, that readers do their best to scrutinise my writing for the inevitable biases that will remain.

Note

Many people suffering from physical ailments turn to the Internet to make sure they get the best diagnosis and services. The same is happening with those suffering psychological distress or mental health problems. An Internet search for symptoms or diagnostic labels will turn up a number of helpful sites.

Note

In addition to Chapter 4 on *Prejudice, Oppression and Counselling* you will find more material related to the current topic elsewhere in the book, including Chapter 9: *Counselling Contexts and Connections.*

Note

This isn't an activity as such, it is a suggestion that, as you read about psychology theories later in this chapter *you might find it useful to make notes as you go along.* Don't be afraid of having your own ideas – remember the activity on page 16 – let your own experience and your common sense be your guides.

are features of that culture. So to different extents, all of the theories are presenting very narrow views of people – namely psychologies based on being white, being a man, being able-bodied, being educated, being heterosexual, etc. Black people, women, gay men, lesbians, disabled people and non-Westerners all ask *'Where do I fit in to this theory?'* and *'Where is my psychology in this?'* You will find more material on prejudice and oppression in Chapter 4.

For the moment I am suggesting that you read about the ideas which have shaped helping in our culture on the following pages with some questions in your head:

- How do these ideas measure up to *your* views on:
    - the nature of human beings?
    - the causes of human distress?
    - the nature of helping?
- Can you find yourself, your family, your community in the ideas? In other words, if you are gay, black, a woman, disabled or non-European, do the ideas at least describe or account for your experience?
- To what extent are these ideas still relevant to helping today in our 21st century culture?

Why is theory important at this stage?

Helping is a skilled and responsible activity. Anyone wanting to improve their helping capacity needs to look at three aspects which contribute to their final performance as a helper:

- Theories
- Skills
- The personality of the helper

A quick look at the contents page will reveal that each of these three aspects is represented in this book.

You may have thought that you knew nothing about the theoretical origins of counselling before you started reading this chapter. I hope that I have shown how theory is not always something we get from books. Theories about how and why humans behave as we do are all around us, from the small, micro-culture of our family and its myths to the large, macro-culture of white Northern Europe and Anglo-America, we get ideas about the way humans are. And ideas don't come out of thin air – Freud, Rogers, Skinner, Beck and others were all influenced by their respective micro- and macro-cultures.

If I were to answer the question in the chapter title as concisely as possible, I would say 'Ideas in counselling come firstly from our own personal theories and secondly from books on counselling.' The aim of this section is twofold. Firstly, to help you think about your personal ideas about human behaviour. Secondly, to help you identify the possible origins of these ideas. You can then find and understand your starting point on theory in terms of ideas in contemporary psychology.

I am fascinated by theories, who thought them up and the circumstances under which they came to think them up. Add to that my belief that helpers should always be ready to explain what they are doing in terms a little more elegant than 'just listening', 'being caring' or 'allowing the client to let off steam', and you will understand why I've included this chapter in an introductory book. I like to know a little about the main players in the theoretical field, so I've included some short biographical sketches of Freud, Rogers, Skinner, Beck and Egan in this chapter.

I will start by introducing a framework with which we will evaluate ideas. At first glance it might look complicated, but I hope you will not be put off, that you will find it valuable and even entertaining. I'll also include some definitions of terms for those of you who have not encountered any psychology before. It's worth noting that it's easy to think you know what a word means because it occurs in everyday conversation. However, the meaning in psychology texts might differ crucially from the meaning in everyday use, so I'll include some basic terms to clear up any confusion.

On the next page, after the definitions, you will find a series of scales on which we might have opinions about human personality and behaviour. Do you think, for example, that we learn to be 'who we are' or that our personality is largely inborn, the result of hereditary factors? Do you think that we have conscious free will and can make emancipated decisions about how we act, or is our behaviour determined by unconscious motives beyond our knowledge and control?

If you go through the scales noting your position on each, we will move on to looking at how each of the major approaches fares on the scales. Then we will be able to find out where we fundamentally agree and disagree with each approach. It is common for people to find that their personal views are reflected by a mixture of ideas from each approach.

Motivation is the term used by psychologists to describe the study of why people do things, so after a moment's thought it is clear why it is central to our understanding of distress, change and fulfilment. It may come as no surprise to discover that there are many competing theories as to what 'makes' us do things and there is hardly any actual 'evidence' that any of these theories are correct. Traditionally, in an effort to understand why animals exhibit any behaviour at all, psychologists start with the obvious behaviours that seem connected to survival of the individual and the species

'Life is, and we are, far bigger and more vital than the ultimately flimsy, hero-worshipping thought systems and prized ingots of intellectual property with which we weigh ourselves down. Institutions institutionalise us. Core theoretical models infantilize and zoologize us and our clients – that is, deny us our autonomy, cage, shrink and dehumanize us. At least, that's my theory – for now!'

Colin Feltham (1999) 'Against and beyond core theoretical models'. In *Controversies in Psychotherapy and Counselling*. London: Sage, p. 191.

'Thus psychotherapists ignore the fact that we do not really know what goes on in anyone else's mind, that people are very suggestible and that we do not understand how some of them manage to get better. These facts are disguised by a variety of elaborate conjectures about mental processes which are presented as hard data.'

Katharine Mair (2011) 'The myth of therapist expertise'. In R House & N Totton, *Implausible Professions* (2nd ed). Ross-on-Wye: PCCS Books, p. 88.

The idea for these scales comes from:
Hjelle, LA & Ziegler, DJ, (1981)
Personality Theories: Basic assumptions, research and applications. New York: McGraw-Hill.

regarding eating, drinking, pain avoidance and reproducing. More apparently complicated behaviour is very much more difficult to understand.

Personality is the relatively stable organisation of qualities, attitudes, dispositions, motivations and tendencies that mediate behavioural responses to the social and physical environment. Personality is what makes a person psychologically different from other people, so different that in all probability each personality is unique. The study of personality concerns both the differences between people and what binds us together as human beings.

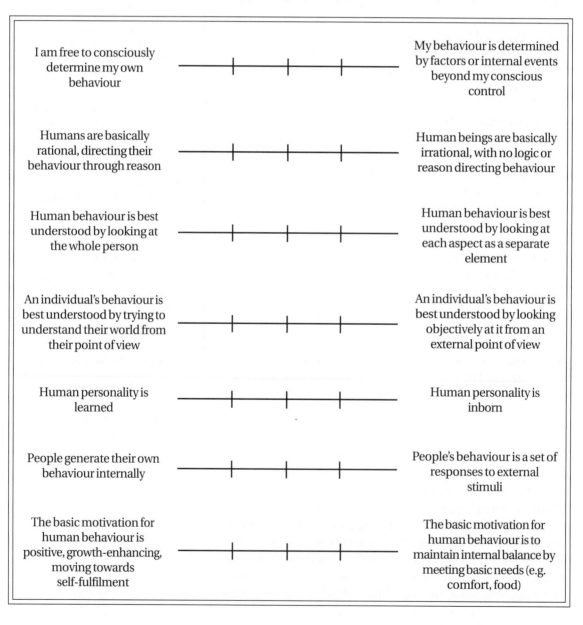

Psychoanalysis

Freud based his ideas on case studies and his own self-analysis. Both of these methods are open to us all to gain insight into common human problems, which is why we encourage evaluation of new ideas through our own experience.

The nature of mental activity

Freud hypothesised that mental activity existed in three domains:

- *Unconscious* or beyond our awareness and inaccessible. The mental processes in the unconscious domain are primitive, oriented towards survival and almost certainly too antisocial, and chaotic for comfort – that is why they are contained, restrained away from awareness. They do not obey social constraints or laws of logic. An individual cannot gain access to her unconscious because it always remains hidden from her conscious mind. Hidden and inaccessible though it is, unconscious mental activity motivates or directs much of our daily actions. The unconscious makes itself known through symbols, for example in dreams, which our conscious mind needs help in interpreting. Only through the process of psychoanalysis can this be revealed.
- *Pre-conscious* activities are those which although unconscious can be drawn into awareness through memory. Anything out of our immediate awareness which can be recalled, such as telephone numbers, postcodes, names, and certain events, etc. are pre-conscious.
- *Conscious* mental activity, fairly obviously, is the domain of full awareness. All thoughts and feelings of which I am aware are conscious. The conscious domain is governed by logical processes obeying the laws of reason.

Freud believed that everything we do and think has a 'goal'. There is no such thing as an accident or chance event. This is where the phrase 'Freudian slip' comes from, indicating that our slips of the tongue are by no means accidental – each 'slip' points to something unsayable in our unconscious.

Structure of personality

Freud divided human personality into three distinct areas or structures (sometimes called 'objects'):

- *Id* This is the part of the personality that we are born with. Freud described the id as a seething cauldron of instincts and desires which seek gratification at all costs. Id processes are unconscious, therefore chaotic and are ultimately pleasure- and comfort-seeking. The id has no values, morals or concept of

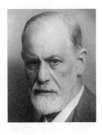

Sigmund Freud 1856–1939
Freud was born in Moravia, then part of the Austro-Hungarian Empire. When he was four years old, his family moved to Vienna where he lived until the last year of his life, 1939, which he spent in London having fled from the Nazis.

In 1873 Freud began his studies at the University of Vienna where his original interest was medicine and he conducted some important research on the anatomy and physiology of the nervous system. In 1885 Freud went to Paris to study under Charcot who was experimenting with hypnosis in the treatment of hysteria. (Hysteria is when a person shows apparent physical symptoms such as blindness or paralysis without any physical cause. The condition also has the apparent purpose of gaining attention, e.g. hysterical paralysis of my writing arm before my exams!)

On returning to Vienna, Freud continued to use hypnosis in his treatment of patients during which time he learned that, under hypnosis, people were able to 'reach down' below their ordinary consciousness and recall old, painful memories. Freud identified links between these memories with the present mental troubles his patients were experiencing.

From the case studies of his patients, from dedicated self-analysis over a period of 50 years (he set apart half an hour at the end of each day for this), and from discussions with his teachers and contemporaries, Freud developed his theories of psychoanalysis. His early theories place a strong emphasis on the role of sexual energy or drive in the development and structure of the personality. It would seem, for example, that during the informal discussion of a case, Charcot suggested that the only thing that would surely benefit the patient was an active sex life, of which she was deprived. Freud was deeply impressed by this and returned to Vienna with a deepening conviction regarding the role of sex in human psychology.

His work has attracted criticism since the late 1960s from many quarters, including feminists, who contend that his basic ideas are anti-women. He believed that anything other than heterosexual penetrative sex was a 'deviation' from the natural, biological function of adult sex. It was a symptom of the sexual energy stuck in an infantile stage of development and therefore a suitable subject for treatment. Such views have been used for years to make the oppression of gays and women legitimate, by appearing to give academic or scientific credibility to prejudices.

Whatever our views might be regarding the role of sex in our lives, it is clear that Freud's contribution to psychology has been incorporated into our culture even though we may not now realise it. Many people accept that the unconscious mind exists and that it directs our behaviour, hidden from view. We talk of Freudian slips, interpret each other's dreams and speculate about the 'real meaning' of a colleague's absence from work on the day his appraisal is due. Although it might be argued that people had similar notions before Freud, the way we incorporate such ideas into our everyday lives today must be credited to Sigmund Freud.

right and wrong. Its workings are most clearly seen in the behaviour of a newborn baby. Freud called the inborn energy of the id the life energy or *libido* and he believed that it was largely sexual in nature.

- **Super-ego** This is the conscience, the internalised parent part of the personality. Freud believed that the super-ego forms when the child identifies with the same-sex parent, changing 'You mustn't do this' to 'I mustn't do this' so internalising (taking them inside themselves and believing the rules are their own) rules, morals, notions of right and wrong, sex roles, etc. The development of the super-ego is basically a learning process. The strength of the super-ego is accounted for by the fact that it develops at a very early age (around five years old) when young children are very vulnerable and impressionable.
- **Ego** The ego develops through childhood, first as a mediator between the chaotic id and the outside world. The ego works out the consequences of behaviour aimed at satisfying the id and checks the id impulses based on reality. Later the ego has to appease the demands of the super-ego, so its task becomes a delicate balancing act. The ego is only fully developed at maturity. A properly adjusted adult is governed by the ego, balancing the 'I want it now!' demands of the id against the 'You mustn't do this, you naughty boy!' admonishments of the super-ego.

Defence mechanisms

The ego maintains control by using defence mechanisms which are unconscious. They help protect us from the demands of the id, often by simply avoiding the issue. Our awareness of this method of avoiding uncomfortable things crops up increasingly in everyday speech in phrases such as 'he's in denial'.

The ego defends the conscious mind against raw id impulses by creating a barrier through which they can only gain admission by various circuitous routes, becoming acceptable in the process. This re-routing creates the aforementioned defence mechanisms, sometimes called *ego defences* for obvious reasons. Since id energy must gain expression somehow (the id *demands* it!) we are all using defence mechanisms all of the time.

Ego defences can be successful: allowing expression of the forbidden impulse in a way that gives the id satisfaction; or unsuccessful: simply preventing expression and causing the impulse to re-present itself over and over again, each time demanding satisfaction. Unsuccessful ego defence leaves undischarged energy in the system which must go somewhere and so is eventually expressed as anxiety.

Successful ego defence is called *sublimation* and is achieved by deflecting the impulse into an acceptable activity, so:

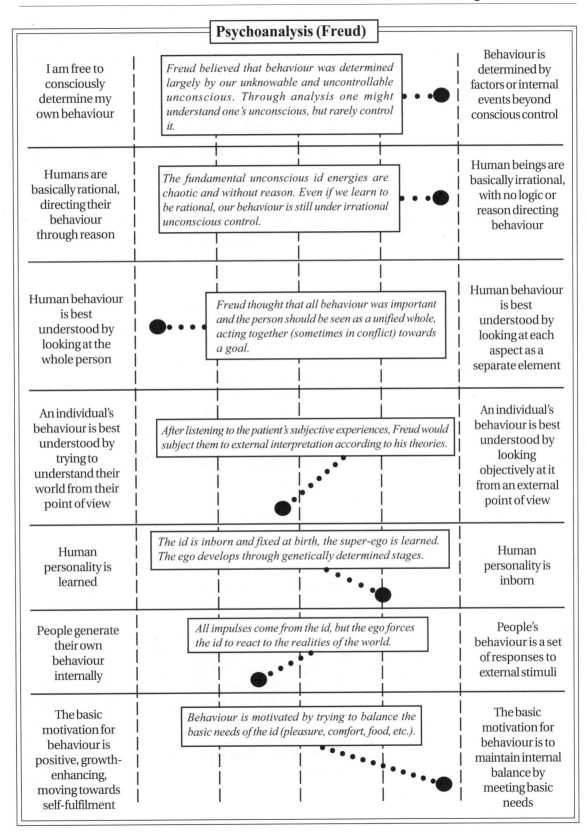

Psychoanalysis (Freud)

I am free to consciously determine my own behaviour

Freud believed that behaviour was determined largely by our unknowable and uncontrollable unconscious. Through analysis one might understand one's unconscious, but rarely control it.

Behaviour is determined by factors or internal events beyond conscious control

Humans are basically rational, directing their behaviour through reason

The fundamental unconscious id energies are chaotic and without reason. Even if we learn to be rational, our behaviour is still under irrational unconscious control.

Human beings are basically irrational, with no logic or reason directing behaviour

Human behaviour is best understood by looking at the whole person

Freud thought that all behaviour was important and the person should be seen as a unified whole, acting together (sometimes in conflict) towards a goal.

Human behaviour is best understood by looking at each aspect as a separate element

An individual's behaviour is best understood by trying to understand their world from their point of view

After listening to the patient's subjective experiences, Freud would subject them to external interpretation according to his theories.

An individual's behaviour is best understood by looking objectively at it from an external point of view

Human personality is learned

The id is inborn and fixed at birth, the super-ego is learned. The ego develops through genetically determined stages.

Human personality is inborn

People generate their own behaviour internally

All impulses come from the id, but the ego forces the id to react to the realities of the world.

People's behaviour is a set of responses to external stimuli

The basic motivation for behaviour is positive, growth-enhancing, moving towards self-fulfilment

Behaviour is motivated by trying to balance the basic needs of the id (pleasure, comfort, food, etc.).

The basic motivation for behaviour is to maintain internal balance by meeting basic needs

- the desire to handle faeces becomes an interest in pottery,
- the impulse to be aggressive is satisfied by playing competitive sport.

Unsuccessful ego defences are manifold, we will look at a few:

- *Repression* is the process of keeping taboo impulses and any related ideas out of consciousness – so that we are completely unaware of them. For example, my repression of attraction to other men means that I have no hint of its existence. I cannot be made conscious of it by suggestion or logical argument. Repression is a natural involuntary process according to Freud, not a learning process, so I would not repress my homosexuality because my parents told me it was bad; repression is an unconscious automatic process.

- *Reaction formation* is the formation of feelings in the conscious that are the opposite of the unconscious id impulses. Examples are love becoming hate, whilst overmoralising and disgust are reactions against sexuality. Once again, the defence process is unconscious and cannot be appealed to by reason.

- *Projection* is the attribution of our own taboo impulses to others. So 'I hate him' becomes 'he hates me'. Combined with reaction formation a chain of events is revealed; 'I love him' becomes 'I hate him' (via reaction formation) which in turn becomes 'He hates me' (via projection). Since the original taboo impulses are unconscious and therefore not known to us, the process of projection is also unconscious. A common form of projection is when self-hatred (which is unacceptable) is projected onto the other person as *'You don't like me',* or, *'You hate me!'*

- *Turning against self* might seem to be an idea in conflict with projection, yet it is still another way of denying an unacceptable impulse. This time if I have aggressive feelings towards someone I love (an unacceptable impulse) I can turn them back upon myself. This leads to self-doubt, self-loathing and in extreme cases, self-harm and suicide.

Psychodynamic approaches

The modern generic name for approaches based on Freud's theory is 'psychodynamic'. Different approaches have developed different themes or emphases over the years and some now make claims to be completely separate approaches. Nowadays, only the traditional psychoanalysts hold the more rigid ideas strictly, such as the *unknowable* unconscious. Many psychodynamic therapists will, for example, incorporate in to their practice the *instrumental* (see Chapter 5) use of, for example, empathy and positive regard for their clients.

Attachment theory

British psychiatrist John Bowlby was originally a psychoanalyst, but became interested in research into how young chicks, and other animals, become 'imprinted' on or attached to – and follow around – the first available adult or even an inanimate object if it is in the right place at the right time.

Attachment theory argues that a baby's first relationship with an adult (in most cultures, the mother, but this is not essential) is hugely important in how we relate to others as adults – the quality of that first relationship largely determines how we relate to other people when we are grown-ups. At a very young age we develop 'internal models' of what we expect relationships to be like. Unsurprisingly, those of us who experienced secure attachments as children tend to find it fairly easy to make friends and to trust them. In contrast those of us with problematic attachments might find it difficult to depend on, and trust others, often trying to keep a safe distance, whilst others of us may want to have a very close (almost merged) relationship with someone but spend a lot of time worrying about whether they love us as much as we love them.

More recent attachment theory is considered by some to apply to all approaches, in the sense that it is taken to be presenting 'universal truths' about the effects of impaired attachment. In particular, the work of psychodynamic psychologist Peter Fonagy goes into great detail about types of attachment, saying that stable adult mental health requires the attachment figure (again, usually the mother) to provide a relationship with is both contained (safe) and regulated. If the parent is themself beset by problems, ranging from drug dependency through to poverty, their ability to provide the right sort of attachment relationship is compromised.

A way of looking at common human problems?

It is a fairly common first reaction to psychodynamic ideas that they have no relevance to common human problems. Yet as we have seen, psychodynamic theory concerns itself with explaining the origin of such everyday experiences as anxiety, guilt, aggression, self-doubt and unsatisfactory relationships. The question remains, however, as to whether these feelings and issues are the result of human problems or the cause of them. There are many more layers of psychodynamic theory which seek to explain more and more about human mental life (for those interested, I suggest some further reading on page 33). The approach attempts to do justice to the complexity of human experience whilst providing a core of explanations that have an elegant simplicity.

Some critics argue, however, that the emphasis on sexual, violent energy in the core of human personality (the id) is not in accord with their experience. This is, of course, not news to

Note

Bowlby's seminal work *Attachment and Loss* – in which he presented the findings from his research for the World Health Organization on homeless and orphaned children in post-war Europe – is still available and should be your starting point for reading about attachment theory. His book *Child Care and the Growth of Love* influenced the provision of care for orphaned children throughout the developed world. His work is still instructive reading for anyone interested in the causes of mental health problems. Early separation from parents was a major problem in Britain during Word War II because of the deaths of so many men in active service, and the deaths of whole families due to bombing, and also the prolonged separation due to evacuation of children from the cities.

Bowlby, J (1997/1998) *Attachment (Vols 1-3)*. London: Pimlico.

Bowlby, J (1990) *Child Care and the Growth of Love*. London: Penguin.

Bowlby, J & Holmes, J (2005) *A Secure Base*. Hove: Routledge.

Fonagy, P, Gyorgy, G, Jurist, E & Target, M (2004) *Affect Regulation, Mentalization and the Regulation of Self*. London: Karnac.

Activity

Take some time to debate these points with a friend, fellow student or yourself.

- *What does your experience of yourself and others tell you?*
- *Do you notice some of these processes going on in other people's lives?*
- *Do you think they might be going on in yours?*
- *Do you think you could bring these into awareness and accept them, or do you believe that they really originate in unacceptable impulses forever beyond your own conscious awareness?*

psychodynamic practitioners and theorists, since the energies of the id are confined to the unconscious and we should not expect our experience to do the impossible, i.e. bring the unacceptable unconscious impulses to our conscious attention for the purposes of theoretical debate!

A view of the helper and helping process

Each set of distinct ideas about human distress bring a different 'flavour' to the helping process. It could be argued that the whole question of *'What is helping?'* was opened by Freud and has been vigorously conducted by psychodynamic practitioners the world over ever since. How have psychodynamic approaches contributed to our understanding of the way in which helping relationships are constructed? We have already looked at some aspects of theory and now I will briefly consider some of the general philosophy of helping that has been informed by psychodynamic theory.

The helper is:
- a knowledgeable expert
- fully conversant with the psychodynamic theoretical framework

The relationship is:
- structured upon the theoretical framework of the helper
- focused equally around the experience of the person being helped and knowledge of the helper
- is hierarchical with the helper as expert

The main active skills are:
- information collection from the person being helped and subsequent assessment/diagnosis
- interpretation of thoughts, feelings and behaviour of the person being helped according to the theoretical framework

The helping process is:
- led, directed and driven by the helper according to their expert opinion
- is out of the hands and beyond the reach or understanding of the person being helped
- trying to reveal the previously unconscious motives that drive an individual's thoughts, feelings and behaviour
- aiming to restore executive control of our lives to the conscious part of our personality

The model assumes:
- that people cannot help themselves, but need their experiences interpreted by others
- core self is destructive and antisocial, so people must be protected during helping
- helping can be dangerous
- helping can only be done by experts

Psychodynamic Approaches

Inborn instincts are the foundations upon which childhood experiences build our personality

Our true motives are unconscious and hidden from us because the instincts and urges are taboo

Our unconscious only lets itself be known to us indirectly through symbolic events like dreams or behaviour

Using their knowledge and skill, the therapist interprets our experiences and behaviour (e.g. dreams) to unveil our unconscious motives, giving us an opportunity to be free of these unconscious controls

For the majority of psychodynamic practitioners, helping is a skilled professional activity with few skills which transfer easily to less formal helping settings. The level of knowledge and personal preparation required to make helpful interpretations will ordinarily rule out the use of psychodynamic methods as a subset of counselling skills.

There are psychodynamic practitioners who have actively challenged the role of the expert in psychodynamic helping, see for example the work of John Southgate and Rosemary Randall (1978) and the recent popularisation of psychodynamic counselling (as opposed to psychoanalytic psychotherapy) by the publication of books emphasising skills rather than knowledge, e.g. Michael Jacobs (2010).

Psychodynamic ideas have been in continuous development for 100 years. Of the many offshoots, some have attempted to make the ideas accessible to everyone and to enable everyone to be their own expert. One such approach that has enjoyed considerable popularity is Transactional Analysis developed by Eric Berne. The radical contribution made by Berne was the demystification of the core psychodynamic ideas by the use of accessible everyday terms like 'parent', 'adult', 'child' and 'games'.

The helping process, according to most psychodynamic approaches, is represented as a diagram in the margin, opposite.

Southgate, J & Randall, R (1978) *The Barefoot Psychoanalyst.* London: AKHPC.

Jacobs, M (2010) *Psychodynamic Counselling in Action* (4th ed). London: Sage.

Berne, E (1964) *Games People Play.* New York: Grove Press.

Activity
• *Take a few moments to consider these psychodynamic propositions regarding the nature of the helping process. (It might help to think of times you have needed help yourself or times you have helped someone.)*
• *Can you apply these psychodynamic ideas to those situations?*

IF YOU WANT TO KNOW MORE ABOUT PSYCHODYNAMIC THERAPY

As well as the books mentioned above, try:

Klein, M (2006) *The Psychodynamic Counselling Primer.* Ross-on-Wye: PCCS Books.

Jacobs, M (2010) *The Presenting Past: The core of psychodynamic counselling and therapy* (3rd ed). Maidenhead: OU Press.

Humanistic approaches

The views developed by several American psychologists (Abraham Maslow, Carl Rogers, Rollo May) in the 1950s constitute what has become known as *humanistic psychology*. Whilst there are some differences between their ideas, there is an overwhelming agreement about key themes. Carl Rogers is best known for his theories as they relate to the practice of counselling and psychotherapy, and it is his ideas I will use as the basis for evaluation on the framework on page 37. However, in order to build a well-rounded picture, I will begin with some of Maslow's ideas.

Humanistic theories of personality maintain that humans are motivated by the uniquely human need to expand their frontiers and to realise as much of their potential as possible. These theories emphasise 'growth motives' and so contrast with both psychoanalytical and behavioural (of which, more later) approaches which highlight the reduction of biological needs.

According to Maslow, the motive to develop and fulfil one's basic potential can take precedence over other motives including, occasionally, those related to biological needs. Maslow called this striving to achieve personal potential 'self-actualisation'. He saw it as a pyramid of needs with the needs at each level having to be met before the next level can be approached meaningfully. We are always striving for self-improvement according to Maslow, and this goes beyond the simple meeting of our basic needs.

Maslow's ideas did not translate into a therapeutic approach, but American psychologist Carl Rogers (1902–1987) developed a theory of distress and a therapeutic method which influenced psychology worldwide. Some of Rogers' ideas are, like Freud's, influential enough to have been incorporated into psychological therapies so successfully that they are practically taken as read and have become a sort of therapeutic common sense.

Note

Maslow's motivation theory explains why a person cannot find true fulfilment if their needs for food, shelter and safety are unmet, which include not only physical deprivation and abuse, but also psychological threat, such as emotional abuse.

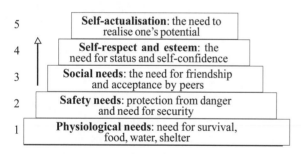

5 — **Self-actualisation**: the need to realise one's potential

4 — **Self-respect and esteem**: the need for status and self-confidence

3 — **Social needs**: the need for friendship and acceptance by peers

2 — **Safety needs**: protection from danger and need for security

1 — **Physiological needs**: need for survival, food, water, shelter

Person-Centred Therapy
Human personality

Rogers' theory is easy to oversimplify and make sound ridiculous. It has a very 'common sense' feel to it and at the same time has several components which set it against almost all other theories and many accepted practices in helping. In a nutshell, he stated that human infants (and adults for that matter) need unconditional acceptance in order to grow (and maintain) a healthy self-structure (Rogers' term for personality). There are no complicated stages or processes, just the basic need for love and approval, and freedom from threat. These qualities, Rogers called 'unconditional positive regard', meaning being loved for simply 'being', regardless of what you did. By these interactions with significant others (parents, relatives, peers, teachers, etc.) the person develops as a unique being – at least as unique as society and family will allow.

A way of looking at common human problems?

Societies and families are not too good at providing unconditional love. Every time we are offered *conditional* love (on the basis that we behave in a certain way) we build up a set of ideas about ourselves based not on our own experiences, but on the values and judgements of others. Rogers is talking about a very wide range of things from, for example, sexuality (only loved and accepted if I am straight) through to expression of thoughts and feelings (only loved if I keep quiet about abuse). This withholding of love can be unspoken and very subtle, or quite brutal.

This results in an 'imported' self-structure which starts to operate separately from the person's natural ability to experience the world for themselves. When these two elements are in conflict he called this 'incongruence'. If a person has a lot of imported material (rather than that based on self-evaluated experience) they experience more and more unpleasant conflict between these two parts of themselves as they go about their everyday life experiencing the world.

Some experiences will be congruent in that they 'fit' the person's view of themselves (I am gay and being attracted to men feels good) but many will not fit and are experienced as a threat to the whole of the self-structure (I have these feelings which are wrong – I am bad and unlovable). Since incongruent experiences suggest that either the experience or the self-structure is 'wrong', something has to give. Either the person denies or distorts the experience (to make it fit), or they suffer from anxiety (anything from a relentless niggling discomfort to a panic attack), which in turn is an experience which may not fit with their image of themselves (I'm a positive person, not someone who feels afraid all the time).

The more discrepancy there is, the more threatened my self-structure will be and I fortify my wobbly self-structure by making it more solid and rigid (ironically, trying to support the elements within it that are causing the problem in the first place). A healthy self-structure needs to be flexible, since life unfolds in unexpected ways and we must respond creatively, not with the same old rigid patterns.

A view of the helper and helping process

Carl Rogers' work concerning the process of change in therapy and education is based on the following fundamental propositions:

- The underpinning or 'core' of human personality is constructive and forward-moving – best understood as maturation,

Carl Rogers 1902–1987

Rogers was born in rural Illinois in 1902. A shy and quiet child, he went to the University of Wisconsin to study agriculture. Rather than pursue agriculture he decided to join the Christian ministry and went to Union Theological Seminary in New York City shortly after marrying his childhood friend Helen Elliot.

He studied psychology at Teachers' College, Columbia University after becoming disillusioned with the more rigid doctrines of the church. He worked with children and their families for 12 years in Rochester, New York and during this time began to develop his ideas about the individual's capacity for self-healing and the role of the counsellor as co-worker rather than expert in the helping process.

He continued to develop his theory in 1950s and was particularly concerned to validate his ideas through research, making a huge contribution to research in psychotherapy throughout his life, inspiring thousands of projects in the 1960s, 70s and 80s to evaluate the effectiveness of counselling and psychotherapy. Rogers himself undertook one of the largest studies into the use of psychotherapy with schizophrenic patients whilst at Wisconsin in the 1960s.

He then settled in California and founded the *Center for Studies of the Person* with like-minded colleagues. He continued to broaden his vision beyond counselling and psychotherapy to relationships, education, politics and world peace until his death in 1987. His particular contribution to contemporary culture was to put the individual, their experience and self-healing potential at the heart of the change process. This was a serious challenge to mainstream psychology at the time, which was busy trying to convince the world that psychologists were the 'experts' on human behaviour.

Honoured by the American Psychological Association with their first Distinguished Scientific Contribution Award and twice voted 'The Most Influential American Psychologist', Rogers never stopped being controversial in his views, which have now been incorporated into our culture in many ways. Not only do psychologists talk about being person- or client-centred, but educationalists now talk about being 'student-centred'. Many in the 21st century are attracted to the basic humanity of this approach.

Rogers, CR (1957) The necessary and sufficient conditions of therapeutic personality change. *Journal of Consulting Psychology, 21,* 95-103. Reprinted in H Kirschenbaum & VL Henderson (eds) (1990) *The Carl Rogers Reader.* London: Constable, pp. 219-35.

> '... if I am willing to take that one hour in and for itself ... I myself am the remedy at this moment, if there is any, and I can no longer escape my responsibility ...
>
> Here is just one hour to be lived through as it goes, one hour of present immediate relationship, however limited, with another human being who has brought himself to the point of asking for help. If somehow this single contact proves to have value for the applicant, how does this happen?'
>
> Jesse Taft (1937) *The Dynamics of Therapy in a Controlled Relationship.* New York: Macmillan, p. 11.

IF YOU WANT TO KNOW MORE ABOUT
PERSON-CENTRED THERAPY

Try:

Sanders, P (2006) *The Person-Centred Counselling Primer.* Ross-on-Wye: PCCS Books.

Mearns, D & Thorne, B (2000) *Person-Centred Therapy Today.* London: Sage.

development or in biological terms, growth.

- Humans have this instinctive movement towards achieving their full potential in a constructive way, which he calls being 'fully functioning'.
- This movement towards fulfilling one's potential (actualisation) includes the organism's capacity for self-healing, or 'self-righting' (including psychological healing).
- If the counsellor can provide the right conditions, then this self-fulfilling, self-righting process can emerge and develop.
- The right conditions are primarily when there is a complete absence of threat to the individual (see below).
- The best vantage point from which to understand another person's behaviour is from their internal world – trying to understand it as if it were your own.
- People respond better if they experience the helper as a genuine ('real') person, rather than someone in the role of 'expert'.

It is easy to see why Carl Rogers called his approach *Person-Centred*: the client is the centre of the helping process in the sense that helping is seen as activating the self-healing process located in the client themselves by providing basic or *'core'* helping *conditions*. It is a respectful, non-threatening method, letting the client direct the process themselves through the wisdom of their self-healing tendencies.

In 1957 Rogers detailed the six conditions that are necessary for therapeutic change. These are:
- that the helper makes psychological contact with the person to be helped
- that the client is vulnerable or anxious
- that the helper is congruent or genuine
- that the helper experiences non-judgemental warmth, acceptance or unconditional positive regard (UPR) towards the client
- that the helper experiences empathy
- that the client receives the empathy, UPR and genuineness of the helper

The helper is
  - a cooperative companion rather than expert
  - skilled in the provision of a safe environment in which the person being helped can contact and activate their own self-healing energy

The relationship is:
  - either seen as unstructured or structured upon the needs of the person being helped
  - focused around the experience of the person being helped
  - is non-hierarchical; the helper is not in the role of expert

The main active skills are:
  - providing certain 'core conditions' for effective helping,

Person-Centred (Rogers)

I am free to consciously determine my own behaviour	*Rogers believed that behaviour is determined by conscious processes that are controllable and in awareness. There are no unknowable causes of behaviour.*	Behaviour is determined by factors or internal events beyond conscious control
Humans are basically rational, directing their behaviour through reason	*The fundamental self is neither rational nor irrational in a superficial sense, but has a deep wisdom based on an underlying rationality.*	Human beings are basically irrational, with no logic or reason directing behaviour
Human behaviour is best understood by looking at the whole person	*Rogers believed that humans act as organised, integrated whole organisms.*	Human behaviour is best understood by looking at each aspect as a separate element
An individual's behaviour is best understood by trying to understand their world from their point of view	*One of Rogers' fundamental propositions is that the best vantage point from which to understand someone's behaviour is from their point of view.*	An individual's behaviour is best understood by looking objectively at it from an external point of view
Human personality is learned	*The fundamental self, with the positive, growing (actualisation) tendency of the human organism is inborn. Almost everything else is learned.*	Human personality is inborn
People generate their own behaviour internally	*Impulses come from the self, and are acted upon. The organism reacts to a limited extent to the external world.*	People's behaviour is a set of responses to external stimuli
The basic motivation for behaviour is positive, growth-enhancing, moving towards self-fulfilment	*A fundamental humanistic proposition is that behaviour is motivated by the tendency to seek self-fulfilment (self-actualisation). Even if human needs are arranged in an ascending order, the energy moves us to ascend to the highest level.*	The basic motivation for behaviour is to maintain internal balance by meeting basic needs

Person-Centred Approach

Human beings have an inborn capacity to grow and achieve their full potential. This is called the actualising tendency

The actualising tendency can be harnessed, given the right conditions, and people can then solve their own problems and heal their own psychological hurts

The 'right conditions' are the 'core' conditions of empathy, congruence and non-judgemental warmth

The helper provides these core conditions, enabling exploration of experiences, strengthening the self-concept and the tendency towards actualisation

This restores control of our lives to our 'organismic' self, facilitating a more fulfilling life

Activity

• *Take a few moments to consider these propositions regarding the nature of the helping process. It might help to think of times you have needed help yourself or times you have helped someone.*

• *Can you apply these ideas to those situations?*

namely: empathy, congruence or authenticity and non-judgemental warmth, which of course means no interpretation of the other person's experience

The helping process is:
- directed and driven by the person being helped:
  - however mysterious this may seem to the helper
  - however long it may take (healing wisdom is located in the person being helped)
- out of the hands and beyond the reach of the helper, they simply facilitate the emergence of the process
- an attempt to empower the individual's capacity for self-help
- aiming to restore executive control of our lives to the organismic core of our personality

The model assumes:
- that only people can help themselves
- there is no need for their experiences to be interpreted by others, indeed interpretation is philosophically invalid and practically damaging to the helping process
- core self is intrinsically positive, social and healing so people can be encouraged to connect with their core self without fear
- the person-centred helping process, based on the core conditions, is affirmative and empowering, not dangerous
- helping can be done by anyone who provides the core conditions, regardless of age, status, or professional qualification

The process of helping following a person-centred model can be summarised in the diagram in the margin. It seems to be well suited to helping in a wide range of situations with its emphasis upon developing generic helping skills rather than particular expert knowledge. The real ramifications of this approach can be felt in the way it gives the helping process back to ordinary people. Indeed, what could be more ordinary than the human qualities of empathy, genuineness and non-judgemental warmth? If the change process really is located in each one of us, just waiting to be activated by the core conditions within a relationship, then the challenge is a serious one to all who seek to keep helping expert-based.

One criticism of his approach made by behaviourists is that person-centred counselling only works because when the counsellor is understanding, genuine and warm towards her clients she is doing nothing more than teaching them to do the same and so they become understanding, genuine and warm themselves. If this is a criticism of the approach, I for one can't think of a better way to get things wrong!

Behavioural approaches

Academic psychology has made a patchy contribution to theories of helping and counselling. What often happens is that psychotherapists and counsellors call upon the findings of academic psychology to support their ideas, usually integrating several diverse findings to try to form a coherent therapeutic approach. As they do this they often leave out any academic findings that do not support their approach. This way of doing things is not limited to one of the counselling approaches – they all do it to a greater or lesser extent.

The behavioural approaches used academic psychology as their starting point. Much of modern psychology owes a great deal, at least in part, to the work of early behaviourists. Behaviourism grew in the early 1900s to all but dominate American psychology by the middle of the century. J.B. Watson and B.F. Skinner, working separately and on different learning processes, founded the movement which Skinner hoped would set humans free from the shackles of their existence by developing a technology of change and making it available to everyone – science to set the common man free. Armed with an understanding of learning processes, humankind would take control of their destiny.

The basic principles of behaviourism are:

- Apparently complex behaviour is a collection of more simple elements which can be understood in terms of basic learning principles.
- Learning, or the acquisition of new responses, requires reward. Ignoring unwanted behaviours leads to their 'extinction' or disappearance. (Punishment suppresses the expression of responses but doesn't eliminate them.)
- Whatever has been learned can be unlearned and modified through the application of learning principles.

There are two ways in which a new pattern of behaviour can be acquired – two types of learning. They are called classical conditioning and operant or instrumental conditioning. These ideas are often called learning theories and 'learning theory' is a popular shorthand title for the discoveries of behaviourism. Later, psychologists added 'social learning theory' to explain learning in social settings rather than the laboratory settings which studies individual animals.

Classical conditioning

Classical conditioning is where a stimulus becomes associated with a REFLEX RESPONSE (see margin overleaf). Ivan Pavlov, a Russian physiologist, stumbled on the procedure in the early 1900s. He noticed that if a dog was fed from the same bowl by the same lab

Burrhus F Skinner 1904–1990

Skinner was born in 1904 in Susquehenna, Pennsylvania into what has been described as a warm, stable family environment in which learning was esteemed, discipline prevailed (never physical punishment), and rewards were given when deserved.

During his childhood, Skinner devoted time and energy to building a variety of contraptions from sledges and trolleys through to a device that would not allow him to leave his bedroom without hanging up his pyjamas! This early fascination with mechanics foreshadowed his later interest in modifying observable behaviour – also done in a somewhat mechanical way.

Although he majored in English at college, he became progressively more interested in psychology through the works of early behaviourists such as John Watson. He went to Harvard University in 1928 to study psychology.

In order to update himself on the emerging field of behavioural psychology he set himself a rigorous schedule of study involving an early rise, study before breakfast, his usual working day, then study until bedtime with breaks of no more than 15 minutes – a routine he maintained for two years.

Like other innovators Skinner 'lived' his belief in behavioural principles, even using a controlled environment (referred to as a 'baby box') in the raising of his daughter. Similarities have been drawn between this device and the eponymous 'Skinner Box' he developed to train rats and pigeons to press levers for food.

Watson is known as the 'father of behaviourism', but Skinner took the initial ideas and moulded them into a comprehensive scientific perspective. He produced a large amount of published work and made a massive contribution to contemporary culture. Through his rudimentary attempts to help people with their problems using learning processes, he inspired a rejuvenation of interest in *behaviour therapy* and, indirectly, the new popular cognitive approaches.

His ideas have been very influential in education, an area which he felt passionately about. His assertion that punishment does not help us get rid of unwanted behaviour, and the idea that learning should be a process of small steps to ensure almost continuous reward for inevitable success, have given rise to changes in classrooms all over the world. He developed the first (what now seem very rudimentary) programmed learning devices in which students progressed through set steps, revisiting the same problem until they had successfully conquered it. These were the forerunners of present-day computerised, interactive learning programmes.

REFLEX RESPONSE is effectively hard-wired to a stimulus, e.g. pulling your hand back from a hot surface or blinking when you get a puff of air in your eye. Reflex responses cannot, in everyday circumstances, be controlled by conscious thought or force of will.

Note

Operant conditioning is so-called because the animal/person has to 'operate' on the environment (do something) in order to get a reward.

VOLUNTARY BEHAVIOUR is consciously, deliberately controlled behaviour.

Note

In psychological terminology, reward is called 'reinforcement' and getting rid of a behaviour is called 'extinction'.

Note

An aversive stimulus is anything unpleasant. In the early animal experiments electric shocks (mostly through the metal floors of the Skinner Box to the animals' feet) were typically used. They were easy to control and keep to a constant level.

technician repeatedly, the dog would start to salivate at the sight of the bowl alone and even at the sight of the lab technician. Note that salivation is a natural reflex that happens in anticipation of food to prepare for the digestion of food. The principle of classical conditioning is that a previously 'neutral' stimulus (the sight of the lab technician) can produce a 'conditioned response' (salivation) through its association with a stimulus (food) that automatically produces the same response.

John B. Watson and Rosalie Rayner conducted a study with an infant called Albert (the study became known as the 'Little Albert' experiment) in which they simultaneously presented Albert with a white rat (to which Albert had previously been attracted) and the loud noise of metal bar being struck by a hammer behind the child's head. Albert was frightened by the noise and began to associate the noise with the presence of the white rat. After a few pairings, Albert cried every time the rat was brought near him. This demonstrated that a fear reflex could be learned and associated with a neutral object – one way we become fearful of 'neutral' objects, animals or situations.

Operant conditioning

Operant conditioning is essentially different because it is the way VOLUNTARY BEHAVIOURS (as opposed to reflexes) become associated with stimuli. It describes the process by which behaviours are 'shaped' by whether they are reinforced (rewarded) or not. The basic idea is that we are more likely to repeat a behaviour if something good happens immediately after every time (or most times) we do it. B.F. Skinner conducted the pioneering experiments where he automated the whole process of training rats and pigeons to do a range of things, in his 'Skinner Box', by giving them food pellets as rewards immediately afterwards.

Behavioural approaches attempt to understand problems in terms of the person's history of what had and had not been reinforced. If a person's history is understood in terms of stimuli and responses, their problem behaviour will be better understood.

Parents use 'operant conditioning' every time they praise their children for being helpful or polite without realising there is a scientific name for it. Most of us instinctively recognise the value of rewarding certain behaviours and ignoring the behaviours we don't want. It's worth noting that Skinner and others clearly demonstrated that the way to get rid of unwanted behaviour is to not reward or reinforce the behaviour you want to get rid of. The application of aversive stimuli – popularly known as punishment – does not extinguish unwanted behaviour. It only suppresses it until the punishment stops. People who advocate the 'carrot and stick' have only got it half right. The carrot works but the stick doesn't.

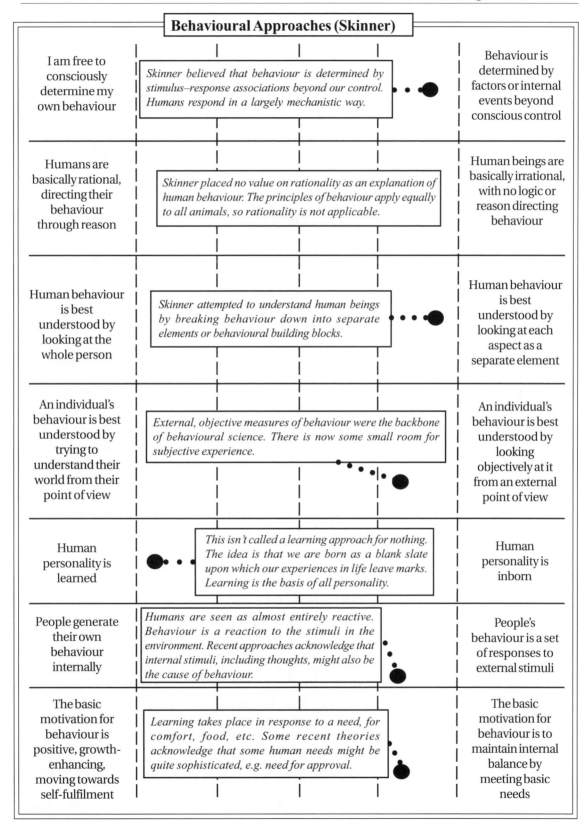

Behavioural Approaches (Skinner)

I am free to consciously determine my own behaviour	Behaviour is determined by factors or internal events beyond conscious control

Skinner believed that behaviour is determined by stimulus–response associations beyond our control. Humans respond in a largely mechanistic way.

Humans are basically rational, directing their behaviour through reason	Human beings are basically irrational, with no logic or reason directing behaviour

Skinner placed no value on rationality as an explanation of human behaviour. The principles of behaviour apply equally to all animals, so rationality is not applicable.

Human behaviour is best understood by looking at the whole person	Human behaviour is best understood by looking at each aspect as a separate element

Skinner attempted to understand human beings by breaking behaviour down into separate elements or behavioural building blocks.

An individual's behaviour is best understood by trying to understand their world from their point of view	An individual's behaviour is best understood by looking objectively at it from an external point of view

External, objective measures of behaviour were the backbone of behavioural science. There is now some small room for subjective experience.

Human personality is learned	Human personality is inborn

This isn't called a learning approach for nothing. The idea is that we are born as a blank slate upon which our experiences in life leave marks. Learning is the basis of all personality.

People generate their own behaviour internally	People's behaviour is a set of responses to external stimuli

Humans are seen as almost entirely reactive. Behaviour is a reaction to the stimuli in the environment. Recent approaches acknowledge that internal stimuli, including thoughts, might also be the cause of behaviour.

The basic motivation for behaviour is positive, growth-enhancing, moving towards self-fulfilment	The basic motivation for behaviour is to maintain internal balance by meeting basic needs

Learning takes place in response to a need, for comfort, food, etc. Some recent theories acknowledge that some human needs might be quite sophisticated, e.g. need for approval.

PHOBIA Persistent, irrational 'morbid fear' of a situation or object, e.g. spiders, knives, or flying, etc.

AUTONOMIC NERVOUS SYSTEM is self-regulating and controls involuntary actions such as heart rate and digestion. It is divided into two branches, the Sympathetic, which actively responds to stimuli (e.g. the fight/flight response) and the Parasympathetic, which rebalances our bodily responses.

Note
This is called 'systematic desensitisation' and is a successful treatment for managing anxiety when caused by relatively simple, single stimuli, like moths, snakes, flying, etc.

A way of looking at common human problems?

Learning theories have been used to explain a whole range of complicated human abilities. They do this by putting the basic building blocks of classical and operant conditioning together in various ways. There is a huge amount of literature covering this work since the early decades of the 20th century. Here I'll just start off with a couple of examples to get you thinking about the possibilities with regards to understanding human problems.

Classical conditioning

This basic conditioning of reflex responses has provided a potentially useful model to help us understand, for example, PHOBIAS, because fear is a response of the AUTONOMIC NERVOUS SYSTEM. Several classical conditioning experiments demonstrated the important idea of 'generalisation' whereby we can become fearful of things because they are similar to the initial stimulus we became frightened of. Watson and Rayner discovered that Albert became frightened of anything that resembled the white rat – anything white and furry. Albert demonstrated what is known as a 'generalisation gradient' – the more the stimulus resembled a white rat, the more fear he showed.

This idea is nothing new – soldiers returning from active duty often find that they are panicked by any loud noise that is similar to their frightening battlefield experiences. People who have been abused as children often feel fearful in the presence of someone who resembles the abuser. Behavioural psychology brought measurement and predictability to both the stimuli and responses.

Some of these basic classical conditioning principles were marshalled into therapeutic methods by therapists such as Joseph Wolpé who refined a step-by-step method of overcoming irrational fears (PHOBIAS) by presenting people with more and more fear-provoking stimuli whilst they were relaxed.

Operant conditioning

Since operant conditioning is a process involving voluntary behaviour, it is only useful in helping us understand behaviours in which we (at least initially) have a choice. Gambling addiction is an example of a problem to which operant conditioning might be applied. The key bit of theory here involves 'schedules of reinforcement' – the relationship between the operant responses and the reward.

When the association between, e.g. a bar-press and a food pellet is learned by a rat in a Skinner Box, there are various options (or 'schedules') for reinforcement:

- the rat could receive one pellet of food every time it presses the bar
- the rat could receive one pellet of food every, e.g. five times it

presses the bar – or ten times, or twenty times, etc. – (called a *fixed ratio* reinforcement schedule)
- the rat could receive one pellet of food *on average* every ten times it presses the bar (called a *variable ratio* reinforcement schedule)

The different reinforcement schedules have a significant effect on how easy it is to extinguish the behaviour that has been learned – in this case bar-pressing. Skinner showed that after a behaviour has become established through repeated reinforcement it can be extinguished by removing the reward. After a few repetitions of pressing the bar the rat learns that the food pellet no longer arrives and stops pressing. However if the original learning had involved a schedule of reinforcement (the relationship between how many times the bar is pressed by the rat in order to get one pellet of food) where it's impossible to predict when the food will arrive (typically a *variable ratio* schedule, i.e. every so often with no pattern to it) then the bar-pressing behaviour becomes extremely difficult to extinguish.

This is the type of reinforcement schedule programmed into slot and gaming machines and the responses (putting the money in and pulling the handle) are very difficult to stop – just one more press, the next one might be the one!

In terms of therapeutic applications, two basic behaviourist principals apply to operant conditioning:
- what can be learned can be unlearned – responses, behaviours which distress a person can be extinguished
- new more adaptive (useful, more fulfilling) responses or behaviours can be learned in place of the previously distressing ones

Application of these principles led to step-by-step interventions, some of which are now almost taken for granted as ways to discipline ourselves or control our behaviour, such as:
- individuals might reward themselves with a treat after not smoking for one week
- in institutions, systems of reward have been used where tokens are given to, e.g. patients in psychiatric hospitals for 'good' behaviour (perhaps related to their individual treatment plan) which they could exchange for privileges such as tobacco (called token economy systems)

Social learning theory
The rather uncompromising views of the early behaviourists did not gain widespread support. They quickly became tempered by the incorporation of more 'human' factors (ruled out initially because they couldn't be observed or measured) such as thought

Behavioural Approaches

We are born as 'blank slates'. Human personality, in fact everything we are, is learned

Behaviour is the objectively observable manifestation of our personality, although thoughts and feelings are important

Learning is a *relatively* permanent change, so what can be learned can be unlearned

We can unlearn behaviour, thoughts and feelings which cause us distress and replace them by learning 'good' ways of thinking, feeling and behaving

The therapist helps us identify our aims and goals, then designs learning programmes that will achieve our goals if followed

Activity
- *Take a few moments to consider these propositions regarding the nature of the helping process. It might help to think of times you have needed help yourself or times you have helped someone.*
- *Can you apply these ideas to those situations?*

processes, attitudes and emotions, etc. Models of the learning processes themselves were broadened to include more 'soft' processes such as learning by observation and learning without obvious physiological reinforcement (i.e. getting food or drink as a 'reward').

Parents of teenagers understand just how powerful an influence peer pressure can be. In fact, peer pressure actually starts much earlier than that. As children we all copy mum and dad, or older brothers and sisters, then school friends and even teachers and so on. Learning by copying what we have seen appears to happen without the person doing the learning actually being reinforced. We seem to just do it because we have seen it. Other experiments have found the perhaps equally obvious fact that we are particularly likely to copy certain types of people, especially powerful people, those we like or respect, or those we want to be like – we are all familiar with the term 'role model'.

Albert Bandura conducted a famous experiment in which children observed an adult behaving violently towards a large child-sized skittle-like doll which bounced back upright when hit or kicked. When the children were allowed back in the playroom, they imitated the adult's violent behaviour. This became known as 'vicarious learning', 'observational learning' or 'modelling', the interesting feature being that the young children were not actively rewarded to copy the adult's behaviour. They just seemed to do it naturally. This finding leads to the social learning theory idea that rather than just being passive victims of reinforcements in our early childhoods, we continually set ourselves goals and can reinforce, or punish, *ourselves* for our progress, or lack thereof, towards those goals.

A view of the helper and helping process

I have looked already at some examples of behavioural therapeutic processes, so I'll summarise the main features of behavioural approaches:
The helper is:
- a knowledgeable expert and companion-in-learning
- fully conversant with behaviourism as a theoretical framework

The relationship is:
- structured upon the theoretical framework of the helper
- focused on both the positive and negative experiences of the person being helped
- is hierarchical with the helper as expert/companion

The main active skills are:
- information collection from the person being helped and subsequent assessment/diagnosis
- analysis of poor past learning and suggesting new behaviours

to be learned, and processes by which this may happen

The helping process is:

- led and directed by the helper according to their expert opinion
- is dependent upon the motivation of the person being helped
- trying to reveal previously unhelpful associations between stimuli and behaviour
- aiming to unlearn unhelpful associations and replace with new, helpful ones

The model assumes:

- that people are active learners, positively motivated
- distressing behaviours can be unlearned
- behaviour change is often best achieved in collaboration with skilled helpers/experts

Cognitive behavioural approaches

As the 20th century progressed, fewer people held the belief that *feelings* had little or nothing to do with human problems. So much of psychology had concerned itself with the links between emotion and behaviour that behaviourism was having difficulty in limiting psychology to observable measurable *behaviour*. 'Cognitive' behavioural approaches grew out of the notion that thoughts and thinking had received little or no attention in the field of helping and human problems or counselling and psychotherapy. This remained the case until the pioneering work of Albert Ellis in the late 1950s and early 1960s. Later, the widespread emphasis on feelings in counselling and the absence of models of how thinking processes could be involved was also challenged by Aaron T. Beck.

Albert Ellis developed Rational Emotive Therapy, or RET, later changing the name of his therapeutic approach to Rational Emotive *Behaviour* Therapy or REBT. It is one of the approaches now known as cognitive behavioural approaches – *cognition* is the psychological term for thinking. The literature suggests that Ellis and Beck (both originally trained in psychoanalysis) developed their ideas more or less in parallel, and I have chosen to look in more detail at Ellis because his ideas are easily put in everyday language.

Ellis described the fundamental process within which irrational thoughts take hold as the ABC of RE(B)T:

A stands for *activating event*. This is usually some noxious or unpleasant experience, e.g. being unsuccessful in an application for a job.

B stands for *beliefs*. This is the person's belief system, which is usually irrational, e.g. saying to yourself 'I'm a failure and a useless person because I've not been selected for the job.'

Albert Ellis 1913–2007
Born in Pittsburgh, Pennsylvania in 1913, Albert Ellis did not believe that his background and upbringing affected his life as a psychotherapist. He said, *'That notion belongs to the "psychoanalytic bag", and fortunately I am no longer suffocating in that particular bag.'* One of three children, he moved at the age of four with his family to New York where he lived for the rest of his life. His childhood was beset with challenges described by Yankura and Dryden (1994) as:

'Benign' parental neglect: He hardly ever saw his father and his mother showed no interest in her children. Ellis looked after his brother and sister.

Poor health in childhood: Ellis suffered a series of health problems, being hospitalised eight times around the ages 5–7.

Shyness and social avoidance: He was very shy and introverted, avoiding any kind of public exposure at school or with girls where he lived.

Yankura, J & Dryden, W (1994) *Albert Ellis.* London: Sage.

He met these challenges in various ways, from learning to manipulate his mother to get what he wanted through to trying to chat up girls he didn't know to prove to himself that getting rejected wasn't the end of the world.

He dreamt of becoming a famous author, but after repeated failures to get any of his writings published he began graduate psychology training at age 28.

His areas of special interest were sex, family, and marital therapy, though he had to abandon his sex research due to pressure from faculty. He initially worked in private practice and then as a clinical psychologist. Unusually for someone with no medical training, he received psychoanalytic

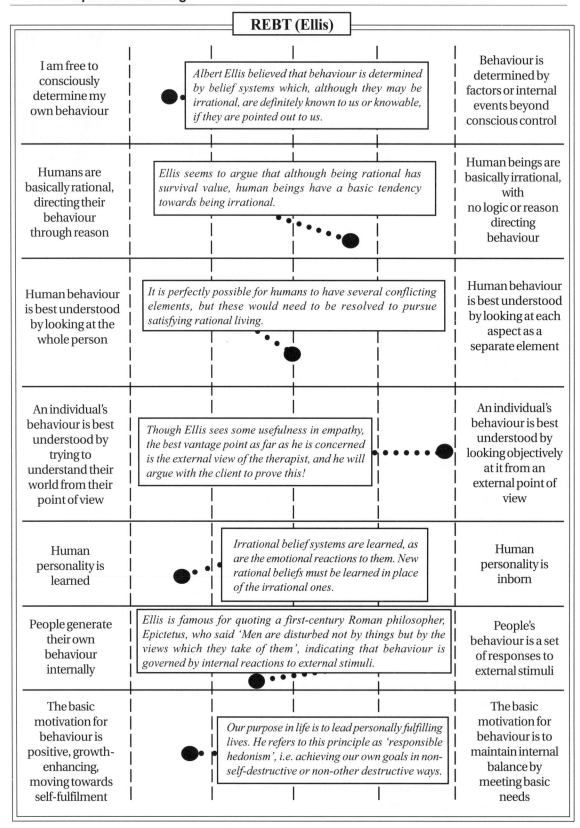

REBT (Ellis)

I am free to consciously determine my own behaviour	Behaviour is determined by factors or internal events beyond conscious control

Albert Ellis believed that behaviour is determined by belief systems which, although they may be irrational, are definitely known to us or knowable, if they are pointed out to us.

Humans are basically rational, directing their behaviour through reason	Human beings are basically irrational, with no logic or reason directing behaviour

Ellis seems to argue that although being rational has survival value, human beings have a basic tendency towards being irrational.

Human behaviour is best understood by looking at the whole person	Human behaviour is best understood by looking at each aspect as a separate element

It is perfectly possible for humans to have several conflicting elements, but these would need to be resolved to pursue satisfying rational living.

An individual's behaviour is best understood by trying to understand their world from their point of view	An individual's behaviour is best understood by looking objectively at it from an external point of view

Though Ellis sees some usefulness in empathy, the best vantage point as far as he is concerned is the external view of the therapist, and he will argue with the client to prove this!

Human personality is learned	Human personality is inborn

Irrational belief systems are learned, as are the emotional reactions to them. New rational beliefs must be learned in place of the irrational ones.

People generate their own behaviour internally	People's behaviour is a set of responses to external stimuli

Ellis is famous for quoting a first-century Roman philosopher, Epictetus, who said 'Men are disturbed not by things but by the views which they take of them', indicating that behaviour is governed by internal reactions to external stimuli.

The basic motivation for behaviour is positive, growth-enhancing, moving towards self-fulfilment	The basic motivation for behaviour is to maintain internal balance by meeting basic needs

Our purpose in life is to lead personally fulfilling lives. He refers to this principle as 'responsible hedonism', i.e. achieving our own goals in non-self-destructive or non-other destructive ways.

C stands for *consequences*. The consequence of the A–B chain is usually an uncomfortable emotional reaction and behaviour.

A way of looking at common human problems?

Ellis proposed that thoughts are key factors in determining feelings and that in fact it is our thoughts that are at the centre of human disturbance. In particular Ellis suggested that it is the beliefs we have about ourselves and the world that shape our emotional and behavioural reactions.

This isn't so different from any other set of ideas about human functioning, since most approaches put beliefs about ourselves and the world pretty much at the heart of things. Ellis went on to suggest that there were two basic types of belief we could have, *rational* and *irrational*. In Ellis' terms, 'rational' beliefs were those which promoted personal fulfilment and 'irrational' ones were self-defeating, or ideas that frustrated our natural efforts to lead personally fulfilling lives.

He then went on to sketch out types of irrational thinking and the consequences of holding irrational beliefs. For example, he suggested that human beings have a tendency to:

- make mountains out of molehills, or in Ellis' terms, *awfulize*. This means, e.g. taking an event or experience which may be mildly distressing and believing that it is a catastrophe or the end of the world. 'If I don't get this job, my life will be ruined.'
- *personalise* events in the world – thinking that things are done specifically to get at us, e.g. believing that the interview panel singled me out for awkward questions rather than thinking that they were just doing their job, or conversely blaming myself when things outside of my control go wrong.
- *overgeneralise* by, for example, thinking that something bad will always happen when it has just happened once or twice, i.e. saying 'I'm no good at job interviews' on the basis of one or two failed applications.

This type of rumination is called *self-talk* and from this selection of irrational thought strategies many readers will, I am sure, recognise them as unhelpful ways of thinking, and may be able to identify such thought patterns in their own lives. Perhaps one of the reasons behind the popularity of REBT and other cognitive approaches is that such beliefs *are* widely held. It is easy to see how an activating event can lead to an irrational emotional reaction. We then construct behaviours based on this irrational, unpleasant, emotional reaction, e.g. in the example of failing a job interview, I might decide that I'm never going to succeed, so I stop applying for jobs. The behaviour now becomes part of a self-fulfilling prophecy – I really am unemployable!

training and then proceeded to try to reform the psychoanalytic movement which he shortly abandoned.

Throughout the 1950s Ellis had been developing his ideas which grew into RET in the latter part of that decade. He founded the Institute for Rational Living in 1959 (now called the Albert Ellis Institute) and changed the title of his approach to Rational Emotive Behaviour Therapy to acknowledge the role of behaviour both in the theoretical constructs and practical applications of the approach.

Albert Ellis has had an enduring impact upon contemporary helping and continued to drive REBT theory and practice with undiminished energy until his death.

Note

It is interesting that in contemporary Western popular culture, people present almost any negative event (sometimes objectively quite trivial) in their lives as 'devastating'. Television reporters ask witnesses or victims 'How did it *feel* to have x, y or z happen to you?' and the interviewee dutifully confirms the devastating nature of the event. The possible consequence of this is that we are positively encouraged to 'awfulize' rather than develop a realistic (maybe I mean 'rational') engagement with our emotional range.

Note

REBT does not provide an absolute definition of rationality; it is pragmatic, based in reality and therefore flexible and adaptable. Cognitive therapies in general do not make value judgements or have theoretical definitions of what constitutes a 'problem' other than anything which obstructs, blocks or prevents us meeting our personally meaningful goals. The definitions are person-specific.

Note

Ellis and Beck disagreed on the importance of the *relationship* between the client and the therapist. Ellis thought that it was *not* helpful to be warm towards the client, since this might help reinforce the client's irrational behaviour.

Beck, on the other hand, believed that the importance of the therapeutic relationship was obvious.

 Aaron T Beck was born on July 18, 1921 in Providence, Rhode Island to Russian-Jewish immigrant parents. He was the youngest of five children. One of his brothers died in childhood and his sister died in 1919 from the influenza epidemic, after which, Beck's mother became severely depressed. His mother's depression, and his own fears and problems caused by a near-fatal illness in childhood sparked the development of his theory and therapies in later years.

IF YOU WANT TO KNOW MORE ABOUT
COGNITIVE BEHAVIOUR THERAPY

Try:

Branch, R & Dryden, W (2008) *The Cognitive Behaviour Counselling Primer.* Ross-on-Wye: PCCS Books.

After successful REBT, Ellis believed that the client will have a 'therapist in their head' who can carry on the battle against irrational beliefs. The question is, how can an awareness of these unhelpful beliefs be turned into an active and effective helping method?

A view of the helper and helping process

There can be little doubt as to the influence of cognitive-behavioural approaches to helping on our understanding of human change processes in the past 40 or so years. Any answer to the question '*What is helping*' now routinely involves a consideration of the cognitive domain, or thoughts and thinking, where previously, some of us may have been tempted to think of counselling as being involved exclusively with feelings. Albert Ellis in particular was concerned with illuminating the possible connection between thoughts and feelings, and so his view of the helping process is one in which the thought processes of the person being helped are seen as primary.

In common with some other approaches, the theory of REBT leads to a clear formulation of the helping process from which springs a set of congruent helping skills. As might be expected, the skills put a high premium on thinking, logic, reasoning and the helper's ability to communicate clearly with the person being helped.

Ellis maintained that because these thoughts or *cognitions* were essentially intellectual events, they should be tackled at that level. He proposed that the best way to defeat these ideas was for the helper to argue with the person being helped, or *refute* the irrational ideas until the person being helped sees the error of their ways. This may seem a little brusque for a *helping* method and indeed, these ideas about helping – and the method developed from these ideas – are very different from the other ideas we have looked at so far. Many people reject the notion that lasting change can be achieved by argument and refutation, however irrational one's position is. It seems to many that if defeating the self-defeating beliefs was so easy they might have been argued out of their troubles much earlier.

According to Ellis, helping is not about *pleasing* the person being helped, or being *nice* to them. The best form of helping is to be brutally honest without any gentle let-downs, frills or apologies. To argue with the person you are trying to help, so that they see how irrational their ideas are, is the kindest thing to do.

The helper is:
• a knowledgeable expert who understands the relationship between thinking and emotion
• skilled in the application of the principles of rational-emotive therapy

The relationship is:
• structured upon the theoretical framework of the helper

- focused equally around the experience of the person being helped and knowledge of the helper
- a vehicle through which the person being helped can learn a more rational way of living, but this learning is not relationship-bound, it can take place through other channels
- is hierarchical – the helper is in the role of expert
- based on the REBT basic conditions of empathic understanding, argument and challenge

The main active skills are:

- information collection from person being helped and subsequent teaching of rational ways of thinking through:
  - understanding and diagnosis of the client's irrational ABC structure
  - explaining the experience – belief – emotion – behaviour chain to the client to improve self-understanding
  - argument and disputation of irrational thoughts
  - teaching the client that neither events nor other people cause feelings
  - planning homework through which the person being helped can experience the benefits of the rationality of their new strategies for thinking and feeling

The helping process is:

- actively led, directed and driven by the helper according to their expert opinion
- one that uses many modes, techniques or methods of communication according to their perceived utility
- a shared responsibility between helper and person being helped – the person being helped must show commitment through, e.g. doing homework between sessions
- trying to unveil the irrational thought processes that govern our emotional lives, dominate decisions and invisibly make much of our everyday behaviour self-defeating
- aiming to assign executive control of our lives to rational, self-affirming, reality-based thought processes

The model assumes:

- that people usually cannot help themselves, although there is some room for self-generated, self-awareness development
- experiences, beliefs and behaviour are interpreted by the helper
- core psychological processes have a biological tendency to be irrational
- the helping process, whilst robust, is safe, adversarial, yet affirmative and empowering, not dangerous
- helping can be done most effectively by experts, but that people come to see their irrational beliefs and change them through a variety of experiences

Note

The idea of adopting an argumentative, adversarial helping style does not sit well with many helpers. For those helpers who see helping and non-judgemental warmth as inseparable, the expression of caring through supportive challenge advocated by REBT practitioners is dubious.

Cognitive Behavioural Approaches

We are happiest when the things we do help us achieve personally meaningful goals

We have a tendency to think in 'irrational' ways that prevent us from leading fulfilling lives

These irrational beliefs cause unpleasant feelings about things that happen to us because our feelings are controlled by our thoughts. We then adjust our behaviour to fit this pattern

We can unlearn these irrational ways of thinking and learn rational beliefs which will lead to pleasant feelings and help us achieve our goal of fulfilment

The therapist helps us identify our irrational beliefs by arguing and suggesting logical reasons showing us how to change

Note

Each year sees the foundation of yet more schools, approaches or methods of counselling and psychotherapy. It would be silly to estimate the total number – it runs into many hundreds. Even limited study reveals that some of these approaches claiming to be new are very similar to other approaches. It is difficult to see some of these as anything other than attempts to make money out of vulnerable people's distress.

Note: The *correct* theory?

I ask this question with an agenda. What does the word 'correct' mean? Effective? Or maybe, cost effective? And what do we mean when we say 'effective'? Is therapy supposed to make us happy, get us back to work or help us become more emotionally self-sufficient, or …? What do you think therapy is *for*?

Norcross, JC & Goldfried, MR (2005) *Handbook of Psychotherapy Integration* (2nd ed). Oxford: Oxford University Press.

PLACEBO A treatment that is intended to have no therapeutic effect or power, e.g. sugar-pill with no active ingredients. Used in research as a dummy-treatment.

> 'To insure the adoration of a theorem for any length of time, faith is not enough, a police force is needed as well.'
>
> Albert Camus (1951, trans. 1953) *The Regicides, pt. 3, The Rebel*

Integrative and eclectic approaches

With several approaches to helping being developed in the 1950s and 60s some helpers began asking the question 'Which, if any, has the *correct* theory and practice for helping people in distress?' With each approach making claims to be the 'right' one, or the most effective, a vigorous debate developed amongst devotees of each approach. In the midst of the claims and counterclaims the current trend towards integration was forged.

It may be that after looking at what the major theorists have to say, you feel that none really covers all of the ground. It may be that you like some of the ideas put forward by Freud, some of Carl Rogers' ideas and some of the proposals of Albert Ellis. Perhaps you would like to draw together and blend ideas from many sources.

This is not a new notion; putting together an approach derived from the 'best' that other approaches have to offer has been tried several times – and different people have different ideas about what is 'best' in each approach. Such approaches that draw from many sources have been called, until very recently, *eclectic*, but are now more likely to be called *integrative*. Recent writing has made important distinctions between the two terms, and within each term, there are nuances of meaning.

Norcross and Goldfried (2005) group methods of integration in psychotherapy into four types: Common Factors, Technical Eclecticism, Theoretical Integration, and Assimilative Integration. Their groupings take into account new ways of thinking about how helping methods can be organised as follows:

Common factors

This method of arriving at an integrative model is based on recent findings regarding the factors which are thought to be responsible for change in psychotherapy. Briefly, these factors include:

- things that happen outside therapy (extra-therapeutic factors)
- the therapeutic relationship
- PLACEBO effect, hope and/or expectancy
- the structure, model or technique of the therapy offered

An integrative model is forged by looking at the last factor above (the type of therapy practised with all its techniques and interventions) as a way of enhancing the other factors, rather than contributing an essential extra ingredient. This way, the elements of many approaches which enhance the strength of the relationship, hope, a positive expectation of change etc., can be brought together with the client's own model of change. This last point is important since one common-factors approach also incorporates the idea that the most important common factors are those contributed by the client – the client's own 'self-righting' ability. This version of common factors integrative therapy is supported by the work of Art Bohart, who, with Karen Tallman, highlighted the client's role in the process of change.

Technical eclecticism

This method involves selecting techniques (hence 'technical' eclecticism – integration of techniques) from various approaches and then arranging them to make a different 'new' approach.

A model well known in the UK was that developed by Gerard Egan – the first edition of his popular book *The Skilled Helper* was published in 1975. He turned away from constructing grand theories of the person and concentrated on looking at the process of helping itself. He described what he thought were the key skills of helping someone with a problem by selecting what he believed to be the most effective elements of different approaches, thus he assembled a number of techniques to be practised in a series of stages, i.e. that you followed a set of steps in a particular order. In this way it is 'systematic' and is sometimes known as systematic eclecticism.

Whilst Egan did not propose a personality theory, he did suggest that human problems were acquired and perpetuated by a number of internal and external factors. The internal factors, he suggested, were deficits in 'skills' (e.g. of problem-solving, having self-defeating attitudes, etc.) and the external factors were mainly destructive social or interpersonal 'systems' (e.g. families, social conditions, etc.). It made sense, then, to help people 'manage' their problems in a skills-centred way.

Egan has revised and refined his model many times since *The Skilled Helper* was first published. Some practitioners think that the model is now overcomplicated and too cumbersome for easy use. Many prefer to use a version of the model published in 1986. In this version, Egan divided the helping process up into three stages. The division of the helping process into stages remains the subject of vigorous debate (revolving around the appropriateness of such a framework) that lies outside any debate about its complexity. There are advantages and disadvantages to this type of integration, and as you will see, the fact that this type of integration has no theoretical underpinnings can be used both ways.

That such approaches have no theoretical integrity, no underlying philosophy or theoretical framework on which to base therapeutic or helping decisions can be seen as a disadvantage. There is no basis on which to really judge the needs of the person being helped other than the hunch or predelictions of the helper – there is no theory to back up the helper's hunch.

This very same aspect of technical eclectisim is claimed by

Bohart, AC & Tallman K (1999) *How Clients Make Therapy Work.: The process of active self-healing.* Washington DC: American Psychological Association.

Egan, G (1975) *The Skilled Helper.* Pacific Grove, CA: Brooks Cole.

Note

There have been nine editions of *The Skilled Helper* since 1975. It has been a hugely popular book but is not cheap in the UK. It is best to seek out an 'International Edition', since these are more reasonably priced, or try the following excellent introduction:

Wosket, V (2006) *Egan's Skilled Helper Model: Developments and applications in counselling.* London: Routledge.

Note

Another well-documented systematic model, better known in the United States, was proposed by Arnold Lazarus. He called his model 'multimodal therapy' and it comprised seven 'modalities' or domains in which therapeutic intervention is coordinated: behaviour, emotions, sensation, imagery, cognition, interpersonal, and drugs and biology.

IF YOU WANT TO KNOW MORE ABOUT
MULTIMODAL THERAPY

You could visit the website Cognitive Behaviour Self-Help Resources <http://www.get.gg/mmt.htm> or take a look at:

Nelson-Jones, R (2010) *Theory and Practice of Counselling and Therapy* (5th ed, pp. 368-97). London: Sage.

It introduces 15 approaches to therapy, not all of which are readily available in the UK. It's intended for diploma-level students and might be worth getting from a library.

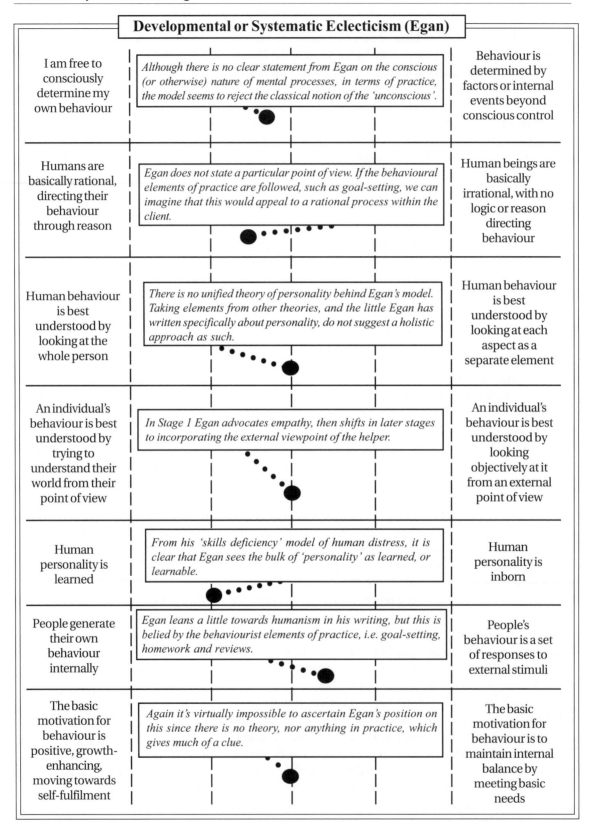

Developmental or Systematic Eclecticism (Egan)

I am free to consciously determine my own behaviour	*Although there is no clear statement from Egan on the conscious (or otherwise) nature of mental processes, in terms of practice, the model seems to reject the classical notion of the 'unconscious'.*	Behaviour is determined by factors or internal events beyond conscious control
Humans are basically rational, directing their behaviour through reason	*Egan does not state a particular point of view. If the behavioural elements of practice are followed, such as goal-setting, we can imagine that this would appeal to a rational process within the client.*	Human beings are basically irrational, with no logic or reason directing behaviour
Human behaviour is best understood by looking at the whole person	*There is no unified theory of personality behind Egan's model. Taking elements from other theories, and the little Egan has written specifically about personality, do not suggest a holistic approach as such.*	Human behaviour is best understood by looking at each aspect as a separate element
An individual's behaviour is best understood by trying to understand their world from their point of view	*In Stage 1 Egan advocates empathy, then shifts in later stages to incorporating the external viewpoint of the helper.*	An individual's behaviour is best understood by looking objectively at it from an external point of view
Human personality is learned	*From his 'skills deficiency' model of human distress, it is clear that Egan sees the bulk of 'personality' as learned, or learnable.*	Human personality is inborn
People generate their own behaviour internally	*Egan leans a little towards humanism in his writing, but this is belied by the behaviourist elements of practice, i.e. goal-setting, homework and reviews.*	People's behaviour is a set of responses to external stimuli
The basic motivation for behaviour is positive, growth-enhancing, moving towards self-fulfilment	*Again it's virtually impossible to ascertain Egan's position on this since there is no theory, nor anything in practice, which gives much of a clue.*	The basic motivation for behaviour is to maintain internal balance by meeting basic needs

some to be an advantage since it encourages wide exploration of possible helpful interventions unfettered by allegiance to any one theoretical model.

A weak version of technical eclecticism involves assembling a collection of techniques on an ad hoc basis according to the requirements of the situation as seen by the helper. So if a person seeking help seems to require a bit of active listening, then having a defence mechanism or two explained to them, followed by instructions on how to defeat negative self-talk, you would have a sort of individually designed client-'centred' approach for each person you were trying to help. However, in the UK, what is most likely to drive this sort of ad hoc eclecticism is what the therapist covered in their training – and there is no real way of predicting that. Sometimes such integrative trainings are 'assembled' according to the qualifications and interests of the staff.

Theoretical integration

This method consists of combining: "two or more therapies are integrated in the hope that the result will be better than the constituent therapies alone" (Norcross & Goldfried, 2005, p. 8). This can happen at a 'deep' level of theory (and usually only two or three approaches can be combined) or identifying the theoretical elements which bring together several approaches. This way of integrating models is sometimes called 'theoretical synthesis'.

An example of this type of synthesis is Cognitive Analytic Therapy (CAT), unsurprisingly integrating ideas from psychoanalytic theory and cognitive psychotherapy. It was developed in the UK by Anthony Ryles in the mid-1980s. It is a highly structured time-limited therapy of around 16 sessions and the therapeutic process has three phases, Reformulation, Recognition and Revision.

Assimilative integration

Throughout this book I've suggested that most counsellors train in a school or approach to counselling that they feel comfortable with and fits their values and understanding of life. Indeed I've encouraged you, the reader to consider carefully your choice of helping style based on who you are as a person – your strengths and weaknesses. Assimilative integration as a model assumes that you have a personal core model which you prefer to practice. As you gain experience, you then incorporate elements of other approaches which also suit your personal style. This way of working rests on gaining experience and feeling secure in your practice of one approach before assimilating other techniques and strategies into it.

Naturally, there is no formula for assimilative integration, since

Gerard Egan

It is telling that the psychologist about whom little biographical information is published should be Gerard Egan. His writing is functional and instructive rather than inspirational or transcendent – rather like the approach he has developed – and he seems to have little time for gurus. I draw heavily on an interview by Adrian Coles in the August 1996 edition of *Counselling*.

The third of four boys, Gerard Egan spent most of his life in Chicago; his parents were born in Ireland and emigrated to the USA on their honeymoon. He describes his mother as having a pragmatic approach to life. School and church were tough and demanding, yet family and community social life was easy-going. He spent nine years in a Jesuit seminary, then obtained an MA in philosophy. He changed his views about religion and education in graduate school, and later, when teaching philosophy, he became interested in psychology. He gained a PhD in clinical psychology which he then taught for 12 years, when the germ of his skills-centred, problem management approach to helping started to grow.

> **Coles, A (1996)** From priesthood to management consultancy. *Counselling* 7(3), 194-7.

> **Norcross, JC & Goldfried, MR (2005)** *Handbook of Psychotherapy Integration* (2nd ed). Oxford: OUP.

IF YOU WANT TO KNOW MORE ABOUT
COGNITIVE ANALYTIC THERAPY

You could look at The Association for Cognitive Analytic Therapy website: <http://www.acat.me.uk/> or read:

> **McCormic, EW (2008)** *Change for the Better: Self-help through practical psychotherapy*. London: Sage.

IF YOU WANT TO KNOW MORE ABOUT
ASSIMILATIVE INTEGRATION

A book using person-centred counselling as the core theoretical model is:

> **Worsley, R (2007)** *The Integrative Counselling Primer*. Ross-on-Wye: PCCS Books.

it is a method of creating a personal practice unique to each counsellor. This is its strength and weakness. Those in favour point to the evidence that effective therapists are 'congruent', i.e. they 'inhabit' the theory and believe in what they practice.

If you feel attracted to this style of helping, it is something to aim for in the future, since it relies upon becoming a fully trained and experienced practitioner in one approach as a first step.

A way of looking at common human problems?

The contribution made by integrative pioneers has forced helpers to think hard about what they are doing and why. Key questions are:

- Is it possible to know what the 'best' bits of the various approaches are?
- Can they be put together to form a seamless and effective helping style?
- Is it necessary to have a theory of personality to help understand why a person is asking for help and to give some idea of what must be done in order to get some relief from their suffering?
- Why have the techniques been assembled in this particular way? (Is there a theory?)
- Is a sequence of techniques sufficient for anything other than the most basic levels of helping, or as Egan termed it later '*problem management*' (Egan, 1982)?

For many people the idea of combining the 'best bits' of several approaches is a very commonsense idea. It is pragmatic – why wouldn't you want to simply put together the effective bits of any skilled activity in life? However a point of difficulty remains – in the previous sections on other approaches to helping, it is clear that the theorists have had a view of human personality which clearly underpins the approach and from which the various helping methods, techniques and skills spring. Beyond the structure of personality, each approach makes some assumptions about human nature.

As we assemble an approach from many sources, can we bring with the various elements the appropriate bit of personality theory to accompany it? Does it matter if we do or we don't? Does our helping model *have* to have a coherent notion of how humans are supposed to function, how they go wrong and how our efforts to help might work?

Sue Culley, a renowned writer on integrative counselling (Culley, 1991), *does* give a very clear indication about the basic assumptions about human nature implicit in integrative counselling. She outlines the following values which underpin her integrative model:

- individuals are deserving of acceptance and understanding because they are human

---

'The wise man regulates his conduct by the theories both of religion and science. But he regards these theories not as statements of ultimate fact but as art-forms.'

JBS Haldane (1927) *Science and Theology as Art-Forms, Possible Worlds and Other Essays.* New York: Harper and Brothers.

Egan, G (1982) *The Skilled Helper: A systematic approach to effective helping.* Belmont CA: Wadsworth.

Culley, S (1991) *Integrative Counselling Skills in Action.* London: Sage.
The latest edition of this book was published in 2011.

- individuals are capable of change
- individuals create their own meaning
- individuals are expert on themselves
- individuals want to realise their potential
- the behaviour of individuals is purposeful
- individuals will work harder to achieve goals which they have set for themselves

A view of the helper and helping process

The idea that psychological helping (to this day regarded by some as the exclusive domain of medically qualified psychiatrists) can be reduced to a series of skills or techniques was inspirational to some and contentious nonsense to others. On the one hand it continued the trend, started by Carl Rogers, to see helping as an activity that is not 'expert-based'. On the other hand, it offended some helpers who saw Egan's approach as stripping away the human *qualities* of helping and replacing them with handy, de-humanised *techniques*. Helpers, then, were to become skilled technicians in Egan's model. Egan took this idea from behavioural psychology, where the whole process could be broken down into steps.

This was the beginning of the equally contentious idea that psychological change (counselling and therapy) could be *manualised*. In other words the steps could be written down cookbook style in a manual and the technician-helper would simply carry them out in the right order. Central to this approach is the ability to assess or diagnose what the problem is, in order to apply the right 'treatment'.

When describing the other approaches to helping in this chapter, in this subsection I looked at the helper, the relationship, the active skills and so on. When looking at integrative approaches, you might have realised by now that these sections have, in effect, already been covered in the pages on other therapeutic approaches. Since all integrative approaches are combinations of other theories and techniques, they are simply a (possibly new) combination of elements that we have already looked at. There is nothing new to be said here.

Integrative Approaches

People suffer from a wide range of psychological distress caused by a lack of personal skills and being caught in destructive social systems

No one approach could possibly be flexible enough to be helpful to all, or even the majority of, people

The best idea is to take the 'most effective' bits of a number of approaches so that the widest range of problems can be tackled

The helper learns techniques from many approaches with a view to applying these elements to help people learn better problem-solving skills

The helper might either apply skills and techniques in a set sequence or select from a range of skills according to the problem and the person

Psychodynamic approaches

Defences   Dreams
Hidden meaning   Symbols
Manipulative   Unconscious
Avoidance

Humanistic approaches

Active listening   Non-directive
Non-judgemental   Empathy
Genuine   Client-centred
Non-interpretative

Behavioural approaches

Behaviour   Goals
Making plans   Step-by-step
Homework

Cognitive approaches

Irrational beliefs   Homework
Positive thinking   Logical thinking
Making plans

Integrative approaches

Different people and problems need
    different sorts of help
Getting it in perspective
Problem-solving

Putting it all into perspective: Take a step back, breathe and …

I hope you didn't try to tackle this whole chapter in one reading! It's time to review what we've covered with a view to putting it in perspective. A good place to start is by re-examining the five panels on pages 20 and 21 to see how the words listed there are linked to the five approaches to human behaviour and helping we have looked at. I hope it is clearer how the words in the margin are attributable to psychodynamic approaches and the work of Freud; humanistic approaches and the work of Rogers; behavioural and cognitive approaches, integrative approaches, and so on.

I hope you can now see how the language of helping has roots in the theories of helping. The words we use are clues to the ideas we hold about helping, helpers and those we are hoping to help, and now you may be able (to some small extent) to trace backwards from the words you use to the theories and the underlying philosophy.

I want to be clear, however, that I am not suggesting that you decide what approach suits you best at this stage. It is too early to 'nail your colours to the mast' in the theories-of-helping sense. It is simply a moment to learn about where the ideas in counselling come from and how, even without being trained in psychology, or even knowing about it, our own ideas have been affected by these theories.

If you decide to continue training in counselling, you will soon have to decide what approach to follow. You have to decide whether you want to practise counselling as a 'pure' approach or as an integration of ideas, ways and methods. This is an inescapable decision, and you can't do both. If you will be continuing in your studies to intermediate level or on to degree level, you will find that some courses offer 'pure' or mono-theoretical training and others offer 'integrative' training. There will be some input from other theories on both kinds of course, but the core of the training will be person-centred, psychodynamic, cognitive behavioural or whatever on the 'pure' style of course.

There are three points to this chapter

One is to help identify the origin of ideas, not to give a comprehensive introduction to these theories. At this level of learning about helping and basic counselling skills, it would not be appropriate to go into any more detail than I do here, but there should be enough to get your teeth into.

The second is to give you an opportunity to discover which of the approaches is most in harmony with your own views. Over the years I have heard many trainees describe the joy of learning about a counselling approach which really resonates with their own life-path as like 'coming home'. If you are on a basic introductory course, or beginning your introduction to counselling through independent study, I hope that you will be able to find your 'home' by working through this chapter.

Finally, I wanted to explain that ideas about helping do not, as I have said elsewhere in this chapter, come out of thin air. You will see that these ideas are all around us in our culture. The ideas and language in our 21st century culture owe much to psychoanalysis, humanistic, behavioural and cognitive psychology, so, more particularly, does the vocabulary of helping.

As you proceed in training, your helping style will be a mixture of your own deeply held views and new theories that you learn along the way. In this chapter I have given you very brief summaries of each approach. I remember when I graduated from O-level chemistry to A-level chemistry the teacher disconcerted me somewhat by saying that most of what we had learned so far in chemistry was wrong! The point he was making was that in order to make the ideas understandable to us, they had been simplified to the point of being inaccurate. Having tried to write about quite 'big' theories of personality and helping along with their philosophical roots, I know just what he meant! I had to both simplify the ideas and try to squeeze it all into a few pages. I am sure that I have not done justice to the complexities of each theory or approach, but I do hope I have been able to give a flavour of each without too much prejudice or inaccuracy.

This chapter includes a very brief look at the lives of the founders of each approach to give us a personal dimension to their ideas. In my view it is clear that, in each case, they were or are passionate about their beliefs, they 'lived their ideas' and also that their personalities are to a greater or lesser extent reflected in the approaches which they developed. This section reminds us that, in addition to the social conditions and cultural background from which these men have come, their personal lives and personalities have an effect too.

Finally, I would return to my previous point that all of these theories are the products of men, developed largely at the expense of women and black and gay psychologies. You could still ask 'Why have you not included any of the feminist counselling literature or the work of Anna Freud, Melanie Klein or Karen Horney?' My answer is that I have chosen the theories here that I believe represent the foundation stones of contemporary helping theory, but you can follow up these other important strands yourself.

I'm sure you will not be surprised to learn that history isn't quite as simple as I have portrayed it in these simple sketches. For example, a little digging around reveals that Carl Rogers credits the

---

WHERE DO YOU AND YOUR IDEAS FIT IN? YOU MIGHT LIKE TO MAKE A NOTE OF YOUR VIEWS ✍

IF YOU WANT TO KNOW MORE ABOUT LGBT COUNSELLING

Lesbian, gay, bisexual and transgender people have developed therapy with minoritised sexualities as the focus. For more information visit: <http://www.pinktherapy.com/>

IF YOU WANT TO KNOW MORE ABOUT MULTICULTURAL COUNSELLING

People from minoritised ethnic groups have developed approaches to helping which take into account psychologies other than Western/European/Anglo-American psychology. These tend to be local culturally sensitive projects and it's difficult to point readers to specific examples. An accessible book introducing multicultural helping that is now out of print, but still available online is:

Lago, C & Thompson, JM (1996) *Race, Culture and Counselling.* Buckingham: Open University Press.

IF YOU WANT TO KNOW MORE ABOUT FEMINIST THERAPY

Feminists argue that feminism implies a particular psychology, not just a psychology of women. An accessible book is:

McLellan, B (2003) *Beyond Psychoppression: A feminist alternative therapy.* Melbourne: Spinifex Press.

work of a social worker (a woman) called Jesse Taft, and his ideas were clearly influenced by the psychoanalyst Karen Horney. These 'schools' of counselling and psychotherapy have complicated histories which you would do well to look at in detail should you continue your studies to diploma level and beyond.

For the moment I will just say that we cannot change the past, but we can learn from it and make a different future.

'Reshaping life! People who can say that have never understood a thing about life – they have never felt its breath, its heart – however much they have seen or done. They look on it as a lump of raw material which needs to be processed by them, to be ennobled by their touch. But life is never a material, a substance to be moulded. If you want to know, life is the principle of self-renewal, it is constantly renewing and remaking and changing and transfiguring itself, it is infinitely beyond your or my theories about it.'

Boris Pasternak: *Doctor Zhivago*

When planning this chapter, I considered calling it 'The importance of self-awareness'. After all, self-awareness is at the centre of developing as a counsellor. But, for those wanting to be a counsellor, essential though self-awareness is, it's just not enough. It wouldn't be sufficient to sit back after a while with a satisfied smile and say, 'That's it, I'm self-aware now.' The emphasis for counsellors is on a continuing *process of improvement,* not arriving at a given *state* of awareness. Ongoing self-development is so important to being a good counsellor that it is built into the ethical frameworks of all of the major professional bodies. Counsellors are *required* to continually pursue self-development, however experienced they are or however highly qualified.

You will most likely find on your introductory course, at the very beginning of learning about a counselling style of helping, that knowing and understanding yourself better is the first step in this process.

In his book *Practical Counselling and Helping Skills* (1993), Richard Nelson-Jones suggests that we could benefit from considering several areas of ourselves as a starting point for self-awareness before we begin counselling, including our:

- motives for helping
- capacity to feel
- sense of worth
- fears
- sexuality
- values and ethics
- culture and awareness of other cultures
- race and attitudes to race
- social class and attitudes to class

The prospect of beginning a journey of self-exploration may seem daunting; many of us feel a strong urge to run a mile in the opposite direction whenever anyone mentions self-awareness. How do you feel about the prospect of looking at yourself, your motives, your fears, your sexuality, etc.?

Looking at the list of self-awareness topics above, how do you feel about exploring any or all of them?

'All they had in them was themselves but they would keep going until they found what was in them to find.'

Russell Hoban: *Turtle Diary*

'What may appear as coincidences are not coincidences at all but simply the working out of the pattern which you started with your own weaving.'

Claude Bristol: *The Magic of Believing*

Note

Training that puts off, or separates personal development from the rest of the course at the beginning, in my view, creates the impression that self-development is an optional extra or takes second place to theory.

Nelson-Jones, R (1993) *Practical Counselling and Helping Skills: Text and Activities for the Lifeskills Counselling Model* (3rd ed). London: Sage.

Note

The fifth edition of this book was published in 2005.

Activity

- *How would you go about the task of exploring or becoming more aware of, for example, your capacity to feel or your sexuality?*
- *Would you like to do this self-exploration alone, in a pair with one other person, or in a small group? Or with friends, family or strangers?*

Whenever we think about developing greater self-awareness, we might have several feelings such as:

Excitement 'Great I can't wait to get started!'

Fear 'Oh no, what dreadful things will I uncover?'

Relief 'At last, I've been meaning to do this for ages!'

What about you? Do you have any hopes or fears about self-development such as 'Leave well alone, all this thinking isn't good for you'?

These feelings often come in conflicting bundles. It's difficult to shake off the notion that self-exploration is *risky*. We think we might get hurt or that, in some vague way, it might not be good for us. 'Better leave well alone, you never know what you might discover, and above all else don't do it with people around because it will make you vulnerable.' I can clearly remember being told as an adolescent that I was too introspective and that I thought too much and too deeply for my own good!

The idea of opening up, sharing our thoughts and fears, may well seem odd or dangerous to many people. Many jobs are very distressing – nursing, social work, emergency services and so on. People working in such jobs have traditionally built up defences to the distress. They have to 'toughen up' and become hardened to the terrible sights and sounds and haunting thoughts they endure

The Johari Window

Self-awareness can be 'mapped out' using a Johari Window:

• **Open** area is your open, conscious, public behaviour, known to you and others.

• **Blind** area is where others can see things about you that you cannot see yourself.

• **Hidden** area represents things we know about ourselves which we do not reveal to others.

• **Unknown** area includes feelings, thoughts and motives within you that are known to neither yourself nor others.

The 'open' area is expanded by, for example, talking honestly about ourselves (*self-disclosure*) and listening to *feedback from others*. Can you think of any other ways of making the open area bigger?

on a daily basis. It is often part of the workplace ethos in such jobs that you just get on with the job and don't talk about it.

Although we feel most at risk when we contemplate baring our soul to others, it is, paradoxically, from the genuine responses of others that we stand to learn something about ourselves. By talking about ourselves as honestly as we can in a *safe* environment and listening to the feedback from others, we can check whether the view we have of ourselves is the one received by others. In addition we may discover some of the hidden motives that may have been influencing our attitudes and behaviour all along. This new self-awareness may make it possible for us to change, if we choose. This prospect of change may also bring new challenges.

Note
Counselling/basic helping is different. Even working as a volunteer you may see and hear many distressing things, but you are not expected to clam up and deal with it yourself. We will look at how counsellors deal with these issues in Chapter 8, *Support and Supervision in Basic Helping and Counselling.*

'It costs so much to be a full human being that there are very few who have the love and courage to pay the price. One has to abandon altogether the search for security and reach out to the risk of living with both arms. One has to embrace life like a lover.'
Morris West: *The Shoes of the Fisherman*

'And you may find yourself living in a shotgun shack
And you may find yourself in another part of the world
And you may find yourself behind the wheel of a large automobile
And you may find yourself in a beautiful house, with a beautiful wife
And you may ask yourself, "Well ... how did I get here?"'
Once In A Lifetime: Talking Heads, words and music by David Byrne, Chris Franz, Tina Weymouth, Jerry Harrison and Brian Eno

It would seem, then, that the right environment is required before self-exploration feels safe. This process that we go through in training is similar to the process that a client might go through in counselling. We can now appreciate how vulnerable and frightened anyone seeking help might feel because we have experienced our own fears and joys on our own road to self-discovery. The conditions which lead us to feel safe enough to disclose some previously private feelings are also similar to the conditions talked about by Carl Rogers (see Chapter 5), namely, empathy, non-judgemental warmth and genuineness, and congruence.

In training, even on an introductory course, we need to be aware of an extra ingredient which will help us move towards greater self-awareness. That ingredient is the balance between feeling supported and feeling challenged. This balance point is different for everyone, and in a group we all share the responsibility for trying to get the balance right. If

High Challenge

Too scary, we get too frightened, defensive or hostile.	*The right balance for active participation in self-exploration. Exciting stuff!*
Low Support	**High Support**
Too dull, we become bored, disinterested and lose heart.	*Too comfortable and cosy, we don't get much work done.*

Low Challenge

some of the issues in this book seem too low or too high in challenge, what can you do to increase the challenge for yourself, or increase the support you need to help you meet the challenge?

It is important to understand challenge. Too much challenge and we close down to learning, too little and we get bored.

Giving and receiving constructive and effective feedback

MAKE A NOTE OF YOUR IDEAS

Giving and receiving feedback are two of the most important activities or processes in training in counselling and counselling skills. Feedback is both verbal communication (the words we say) and non-verbal communication (our actions, facial expressions and posture). It is through receiving feedback that we get an opportunity to see ourselves as others see us. It helps us become more aware of our behaviour – what we do and how we do it.

Giving feedback
- we can tell people how we see them
- we can tell people our feelings about the way they are

Both giving and receiving feedback can feel quite scary. What others think of us may not be in accord with our image of ourselves. This can be hurtful, flattering or simply puzzling. Whichever it is, I find feedback either exciting or uncomfortable to give or receive – a little like playing the children's game of *'truth, dare, kiss or promise'*.

Receiving feedback
- others can tell us how they see us
- other people can tell us their feelings about the way we are

When others receive your feedback, they may also be feeling uncertain, uncomfortable or scared. Your impressions may well not fit in with *their* views of *themselves*. For these reasons, feedback needs to be thoughtful and given sensitively, not hastily, without thinking or like a 'bull in a china shop'.

You might be asked to give feedback to others on some personal issues on your course, such as whether you found the other person helpful, caring, sensitive and why. You may find the prospect of this daunting, but it requires no more than developing a sensitivity to other people's needs, which is at the heart of good counselling. Here are some ground rules for giving feedback:

- All of your observations of another person will include both positive and negative elements. Try to include both positive and negative observations in your feedback. Avoid saying just negative things – or all positive things – to the other person.
- What you are picking up is the behaviour of the other person. Comment on the other person's behaviour rather than give your impression of the person, i.e. 'Your voice had a very harsh quality', rather than 'You are very harsh.'
- Stick to describing *what* you see, think or feel rather than either *making a judgement* about it or saying *why* it's happening, i.e. 'Your shouting frightened me', rather than 'Shouting is a terrible thing to do, you do it because you are inadequate.'
- Try to give feedback on something that the other person can do something about, rather than something beyond their control.

- Speak for yourself not others, say 'I think …' or 'I feel …', rather than 'Everybody thinks …' or 'It's clear to everyone …' or 'I'm sure nobody knows …'.
- Give feedback about specific instances or behaviours rather than generalising, i.e. 'When you did this … I felt threatened.' rather than 'You threaten me' or 'You are threatening'.

The things you say about other people when giving feedback will nearly always say as much about you as they do about the other person. Be prepared to receive feedback on your feedback! It might be, for example, that you always give positive feedback – maybe you can't bear to hurt other people's feelings. Or perhaps you tend to give predominantly negative feedback – maybe you think that people will only learn if you point out their mistakes.

Carl Rogers (see Chapter 2) thought that people learn best when they feel safe. Most counselling courses are organised on this principle. It is important that you feel safe enough to give honest feedback and that you feel safe enough to listen to feedback without feeling got at. The processes of giving and receiving feedback require a feeling of safety if they are to be of any real use.

Personal motives

Examining motives is a good thing to do whatever the activity in question. When considering involvement in counselling it is, at some stage, essential to look at *why* you want to be a helper. It is crucial for us to be as sure as we can be that our motives for offering to help someone will not distort the helping we can give so that it ends up being unhelpful or even damaging. Although we cannot hope to examine *all* motives here, we can look at a couple.

As an extreme example, there have been cases in the news recently where people working in children's homes have been found guilty of sexual abuse of the children in their care. It would seem that their motives for wanting to work with children were more than questionable.

Of course it would be stupid of me to suggest that we do not serve our own needs at some levels when we choose to volunteer or work as a helper. The question is, do our motives get in the way of our ability to offer constructive help, or do they facilitate our offering constructive help? Do these motives add to or take away from our helpfulness?

It is interesting to discover that there are certain safeguards that professional counsellors can make to guard against questionable motives and these are looked at in Chapters 7 and 8 on Ethics and Supervision respectively. Although a professional code of ethics and

'… it is his own hurt that gives the measure of his power to heal.'
CG Jung (1954), *The Practice of Psychotherapy, Vol 16 of The Collected Works*. London: Routledge & Keegan Paul, (par 239).

'The therapist is ultimately not there to treat the patient but, via a circuitous and well-concealed route, to treat or protect or comfort himself.'
T Maeder (1989) *Children of Psychiatrists and Other Psychotherapists*. New York: Harper & Row, p. 77.

'One would rather have a really suitable person for doing this kind of work than an ill person made less ill by the analysis that is part of the psychoanalytic training.'
DW Winnicott (1971) *Therapeutic Consultations in Child Psychiatry*. London: Hogarth Press, p. 1.

Note: Personal motives can be helpful or harmful

- The central issue of *emotional pain* in my life can be the focus of helpful or harmful motives:

Helpful: If I have worked through a past traumatic event, I may have gained personal strength from the experience and also may be more sensitive to others suffering trauma.

Harmful: I may be over-sensitive to certain issues because my emotional pain is unresolved from a recent trauma. I might also be trying to resolve my own trauma through contact with clients, rather than trying to help the client.

- The central issue of *wanting to help others* can be the focus of helpful or harmful motives:

Helpful: Expressing an unselfish concern for others as helping behaviour can be seen as similar to the core condition of warmth or valuing others.

Harmful: If I require others to be dependent upon my help so that I can be seen as a 'good guy', I am distorting helping relationships to meet my own needs.

supervision of counselling practice are not strictly applicable to those interested in learning about a counselling way of helping on an Introduction to Counselling course, the principles of getting support for yourself and helping in an ethical way should be at the heart of everyone's helping activities. We will look at the British Association for Counselling and Psychotherapy (BACP) Ethical Framework in Chapter 7 and how it might relate to basic helping.

> 'From his cradle to his grave a man never does a single thing which has any first and foremost object but one – to secure peace of mind, spiritual comfort, for himself.'
> Mark Twain
>
> 'We are all selfish and I no more trust myself than others with a good motive.'
> Lord Byron
>
> 'Everyone thinks of changing the world, but no one thinks of changing himself.'
> Leo Tolstoy
>
> 'How wonderful it is that nobody need wait a single moment before starting to improve the world.'
> Anne Frank

Personal values

Another of the many possible foci for personal development during a basic counselling course is the area of conflicting values. This might come up in four ways:

- conflicts between different sets of values within myself
- conflicts between my values and my behaviour
- conflicts between my values and the values of the person I am in a helping relationship with
- conflicts between my values and the values of counselling (whatever I understand them to be)

As someone interested in helping others it is necessary for me to become aware of the values that I bring to the helping relationship, since my own strongly held values may distort the help I am hoping to give. It is another tricky balancing act to try and offer genuine help in some areas of life without influencing a person's values by subtle means or maybe by disclosing my own values. You may not intend to influence the other person's values, but it is possible that the other person might see you as a role model or copy you in an effort to get relief from their distress.

In terms of the core conditions discussed in Chapter 5, it is a matter of being simultaneously non-judgementally warm *and* genuine towards a person with whom you feel there is a conflict of values. (You will discover that this in not an easy thing to do.)

Similarly, if I have a conflict between two values or a conflict between my values and my behaviour, this incongruence will almost surely be picked up by the person I am trying to help, possibly making me seem inauthentic or false. For example, I might find myself saying one thing and doing another – imagine what message that would send to the person whom I am trying to help. Examination of my personal values is therefore essential before I can be an effective helper.

Personal values, however, change as a result of life, new experiences, the passage of time or even doing an Introduction to Counselling course. Although we might examine our personal values now, there's every chance that they might have changed by the time this book is finished. If I'm serious about being a helper, I must monitor my personal values to see how I change and develop.

It is likely that there will be no formal time on your course where the named task is to examine your personal values. This does not mean that you will not be aware of your personal values and the personal values of others practically every time you attend a course meeting. It is inevitable that you will have checked out other people's values during class discussions and exercises and also during coffee-breaks. This is a natural part of 'sizing people up', figuring out who our friends are going to be, who might support us, and who will be for us or against us. It is a perpetual social process.

Since you have decided to participate in this course and get a better understanding of human behaviour, you might take some time to reflect on the class discussions and coffee-breaks to see what you think they reveal about you. How have your values shone through the things you have said and done?

Later in this chapter, I will look at the value of the popular practice of keeping a personal journal whilst you are doing your training. It will be the ideal place to record your observations about your motives and values and the conflicts that you discover, both within yourself and between your own values and those of other people.

Activity
It might help – and it might be fun – to make a note now about your values regarding helping and then look back at the end of this course to see if, and/or how, your values change.

Discussion points on personal values
How do you react to the statements below?

Suicide and self-harm are wrong. If someone told me they were going to harm or kill themselves, I would do my utmost to stop them.

I could not listen to someone using sexist or racist language; I would tell them that it was wrong and to stop doing it. To listen without comment is to condone it.

I just couldn't sit in the same room as a child abuser. I would want to kill them!

I help people to make them happy. I would always try to end a session on a positive note.

I believe that there is nothing wrong with being gay, but I feel uncomfortable when gay people of my sex come too close to me.

I can't work out what my position on abortion is. I keep changing my mind. If I have an unwanted pregnancy, I suppose I'll work it out then.

For some of these issues, there are no 'right' or 'wrong' stands to take. Counsellors, as a group, don't have a 'position' on suicide, or abortion. These are personal values regarding human life. However, there are some 'counselling values' which are generally held, e.g. counselling isn't about making people happy or cheering them up. Also, if you have conflicts between your values and your behaviour, then the process of personal development should help you resolve these before you start offering your help to others.

Counselling values

Returning briefly to the five models of helping we overviewed in Chapter 2, you will notice that each one carries with it a set of attitudes about human beings, helping and change. The very fact that you are on a counselling course means that your values probably include the notion that helping people is a good thing. Some people, however, believe that helping others makes them weak and dependent – where do you stand on this?

If we look to the 'core' conditions for effective helping proposed by Carl Rogers – empathy, non-judgemental warmth and genuineness (see Chapter 5 for details) – we find that these 'core' conditions are more than just the foundations of good counselling and relationship skills. They suggest that in order to be effective helpers we need a certain set of attitudes and values as well.

These 'hidden' helping values may be:
- completely new ideas to us
- familiar but different from the ones we are used to
- ones with which we totally and enthusiastically agree
- values with which we disagree in part or have difficulty in accepting
- attitudes with which we basically agree but have difficulty in genuinely displaying

Note

In 1957 Carl Rogers proposed six conditions that he thought must be present for therapeutic change to take place and I looked at these briefly in Chapter 2, p. 36. Three of these conditions – those provided by the therapist – are often called the 'core' conditions. It's important to remember, though that there are three other conditions which must be present. I will describe all six conditions in more detail in Chapter 5.

Rogers, CR (1957) The necessary and sufficient conditions for therapeutic personality change. *J. Consulting Psychology,* *21*(2), 95-103.
Reprinted in H Kirschenbaum & VL Henderson (eds) (1990) *The Carl Rogers Reader* (pp. 219-35). London: Constable.

When we begin to learn about helping we might think that counselling is value-free, or perhaps transparent to values or culture. After all, helping is just helping, isn't it? People wanting help is natural, and people offering help to each other is natural. Consider the following examples of possible values that may be implicit in counselling processes:

Activity
What do think the values implicit in your *helping might be?*
✍

- change is a good thing
- change involves struggle and pain
- people are basically good underneath the surface
- cooperation between equals is the best way to structure helping relationships
- people are best helped by someone who has had a very similar experience or problem
- people are not born bad, they're made bad by the world and can therefore be helped to change
- too much thinking about your problems makes them worse: a plan of action and short-term support is all that's needed
- some people are beyond helping
- people are basically weak and vulnerable and need to be protected
- in order to be helped to change you've got to want to change
- counselling is for people with problems
- helping takes a long time if it is to get to the root of the problem

---

Discussion points on counselling values

How do you react to the following statements?

People need help in understanding the hidden meanings in their lives.

People need to be offered a range of solutions to problems so that they can choose an appropriate one for themselves.

People should have control over their own destiny.

Clients have no right to make immoral or antisocial choices when they are in counselling.

We should take responsibility for the consequences of our actions, praise ourselves when we do good, admonish ourselves when we do bad, not praise or seek forgiveness from God.

All people are equal and therefore are equally deserving of my help, regardless of who they are or what they have done.

These discussion points have been chosen to represent issues on which there is no 'party line'. Counselling values may well conflict with your personal spiritual and political values.

Will this conflict distort, or get in the way of, your helping capacity?

Will being open to these conflicts through a commitment to personal development enhance your helping capacity?

What other value conflicts can you identify?

Feelings

That counselling is about, or involves the expression of, 'feelings' might seem obvious to many. Even though it's obvious, the prospect of *working* with feelings in some way can stimulate many feelings in us. It's possibly the realisation that feelings beget feelings that makes some of us so anxious about looking too deeply at them. We might meet feelings or emotions in the following ways on a basic counselling course:

- *Listening* to someone talking about their feelings or emotions, i.e. they might tell us how angry they are.
- *Witnessing* someone express their feelings strongly, i.e. they might cry inconsolably in front of us.
- *Thinking* or *talking* about our own feelings or emotions, i.e. being reminded of how angry we were.
- *Expressing* our own feelings or emotions, i.e. feeling sad and crying on our own account, perhaps remembering some loss we have suffered.

Our general reaction to the expression of feelings and emotions will depend upon our values and beliefs about emotions. We will have acquired these values and beliefs from past personal experiences and from the views passed on to us from our upbringing and culture.

So, the famous British 'stiff upper lip' and the 'passionate Latin temperament' are examples of ideas about cultural influences. Statements like 'she's got her mother's red hair, so she'll have her mother's fiery temper' might indicate family influences. Emotional expression is also linked to sex-role stereotyping. Women are supposed to be more open and free in expressing their feelings than men, who are supposed to 'keep it all in'. Like me, you might think that these stereotypes are too rigid and simple to be applicable in everyday life. But then I ask myself why it is my wife who feels more able to cry than me when we go to watch a sad film?

Helping someone by listening accurately and sensitively to them means being sensitive to their whole person, including their feelings. I need to be able to respond to another person's whole range of expression, not have any blind spots caused by my own fear of expressing my own feelings.

'I would say I'm sorry
If I thought that it would change
your mind
But I know that this time
I've said too much
Been too unkind

I try to laugh about it
Cover it all up with lies
I try and laugh about it
Hiding the tears in my eyes
'Cos boys don't cry'

Boys Don't Cry: The Cure
Words by Robert Smith

'One way of putting this … is that if I can form a helping relationship to myself – if I can be sensitively aware of and acceptant toward my own feelings – then the likelihood is so great that I can form a helping relationship toward another.'

Carl Rogers (1961) *On Becoming a Person*. London: Constable, p. 51.

Activity
What are your emotional blind spots? Are you afraid of feelings?

'Feeling and longing are the motive forces behind all human endeavor and human creations.'

Albert Einstein

'It's all a question of how much a person listens to his body – his feelings. Most people are too battered with rules to be heard, and bound with pretenses so it can hardly move. We cripple ourselves with lies.'

Jim Morrison

Thinking and understanding

There is so much emphasis put on feelings that some people believe helping in a counselling way is *all* about feelings and there is no room for thinking at all. Psychologists call our thought processes 'cognitions' and it is from this word that we get the title 'Cognitive Therapy' (see Chapter 2, pp. 45–9). There are a few approaches to change that put a high value on our thought processes by looking at how we keep ourselves unhappy by saying irrational things to ourselves such as:

- 'I'm unattractive, so no one will ever love me and I will be unhappy for the rest of my life.'
- 'I daren't speak out in the group because everyone will see that I'm stupid and I will get so embarrassed that I'll blush and it would be the end of the world.'

Although we know that these thoughts are daft we have difficulty in trying to change them. We still behave as though they were true, for example, by never talking in a group. These patterns of thought can be really troublesome to many people and we need to be able to enter into their world of thoughts in order to understand. The way I *understand* and *think* about my world is obviously important to me so when you are helping me I want you to see, accept and value my thoughts and understandings, not try to tell me that feelings are the only important bits of me. It is important to value your own thinking if you are to genuinely trust and value the thought processes of the person you are helping.

My personal psychology is a mixture of thoughts, feelings and sensations. Although I might feel unbalanced, i.e. that my mind is dominated by thoughts or that I am overwhelmed by feelings, it is not helpful if you, my helper, thinks that my problem is *just* about feelings, or *just* about thoughts. A healthy mental life is a balance – harmony – between thoughts, feelings, sensations and the meanings I attach to them. A good helper will be able to help me explore all aspects of my mental and physical life without bias or preference.

Personal change

On page 66 we looked at counselling values and the possibility that change is a good thing. Whether or not you view change as a *good* thing, one thing is certain – counselling and helping is inextricably interwoven with personal change.

One way of thinking about change is to see it on two interlocking continua – one from big changes to small changes, and another continuum from high personal content to low personal content.

'… the more I am willing to be myself in all this complexity of life and the more I am willing to understand and accept the realities in myself and in the other person, the more change seems to have been stirred up. It is a very paradoxical thing – that to the degree that each one of us is willing to be himself, then he finds not only himself changing; but he finds that other people to whom he relates are also changing.'

Carl Rogers (1961) *On Becoming a Person.* London: Constable, p. 22.

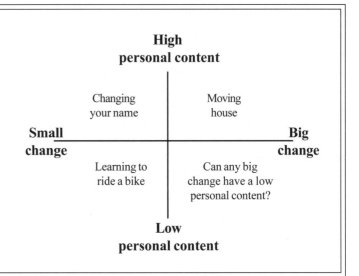

Mapping changes in our lives

This grid will be different for each person, e.g. someone with restricted mobility might put learning to ride a bike in a different place.

Where on the grid would you put the change events in your life over the past 12 months?

High personal content

Changing your name

Moving house

Small change

Big change

Learning to ride a bike

Can any big change have a low personal content?

Low personal content

Psychologists researching the effects of change believe that change and coping with it is very stressful to human beings. I'm sure this will not come as news to anyone! However, you may be surprised to see the top ten most stressful life events include moving house, divorce, bereavement and giving birth – consider whether they involve change, and where on our grid (above) they might fall.

Interestingly enough, psychologists also view learning as change because when we learn something new we have to rearrange all of our previous knowledge to make room for (and make sense of) the new information. Learning that Father Christmas doesn't exist certainly made me review my experience in the light of new information. It was also very painful.

The idea that learning new things is painful is not a new one. Every time we learn something new we have to let go of an old view of things.

Change is involved at many levels when thinking about helping in a counselling way:

- People ask for help because they want change: in simple terms they want to feel settled, happier and problem-free.
- People come to counselling because the want something to change: in simple terms they want to feel better. Or perhaps they are wanting to cope with an unwelcome change such as a bereavement.
- During training, even on an introductory course we want change: we want to know more about helping in a counselling way and we might want to be better at it. Or perhaps we want to change some aspect of ourselves to become a better helper.

In order to cope with change we need support; both clients and those learning about counselling. Our personal reaction to change will affect the way we are able to help others cope with it. This is why, as people interested in helping, we must seek to understand our own thoughts, feelings and behaviour about change.

- If we are afraid of change or believe that change is a bad thing or have unhelpful ways of reacting to change in our own lives, we may distort the helping we offer clients, since change is often what they've come for.

'On our farm we have a row of maple trees that illustrate the mysterious process of adaption. Many years ago these trees were used as fence posts for the stringing of barbed wire around the pasture. Now, fifty or sixty years later, it is possible to look at those trees and observe the way the life process shows itself in adaptation. In some places the trees fought against the barbed wire as a hostile agent, and here the trees have long and ugly scars that deface the bark and inner structure of the trees. In other places, the barbed wire has been accepted and incorporated into the life of the tree. Where this happened, the barbed wire left no mark on the tree, and all that shows is the wire entering on one side and exiting at the other.

It is natural to wonder what makes the difference in the quality of a tree's response to injury. What was there in some trees that made them injure themselves by fighting against injury? What made it possible for other trees to be able to incorporate the injuring object and become master of the barbed wire rather than its victim?'

Edgar N Jackson: *The Many Faces of Grief*, pp. 123-4.

'Can you find a wholeness that includes pain and a readiness to suffer?'

The Religious Society of Friends: *Questions and Counsel*

'Our futile effort at control impedes the flow we might otherwise have in our lives. Once we get out of our own way, we can become ourselves.'

Marilyn Ferguson: *The Aquarian Conspiracy*

'Life is worth living. Not because there is nothing else, but because of what we each may give one another; pain, joy, anguish, peace. It's not an easy journey. You may even call it an adventure. It doesn't matter about the problems, the contradictions. In our hearts we understand everything. We understand it's the struggle that counts.'

Ann Oakley: *Taking it like a Woman*

'Multiple and converging sources of evidence indicate that the person of the psychotherapist is inextricably intertwined with the outcome of psychotherapy. There is a dawning recognition … that the therapist him- or herself is the focal process of change.'

W Dryden & L Spurling (eds) (1989) *On Becoming a Psychotherapist*. London: Routledge, p. 215.

Change in everyday life

Learning a new fact

Learning a new skill

Going to school

Puberty

Leaving your childhood home

Discovering your sexuality

Becoming a parent

Marriage, or deciding to stick with one partner

Separation or divorce

Being ill

Moving house

Getting a job

Losing a job

Joining a counselling course

Being bereaved

Going to live in another country

Which changes do we choose to make?

What feelings arise from such change?

Which changes are we forced to make?

What do we need to support us during change?

It is clear that change is common in our everyday lives and that it can be accompanied by strong feelings. These feelings can be negative or positive, however. Some ways of looking at change emphasise the transition from one state to another and suggest that our strong feelings are associated with the loss of the old (grief) and the shock of the new. Another way of looking at change is to see it as part of the inevitable unfolding of life – nothing stays the same – change is neither good nor bad, it just is.

In the Chinese language the same character stands for both 'crisis' and 'opportunity'.

Some people think about change in yet another way. Rather than see change as a threat, it is possible to look for positive consequences whilst acknowledging the negative aspects. In business it is fashionable to look at the prospect of change in terms of *Strengths, Weaknesses, Opportunities and Threats*. By considering these elements of a change situation it is possible to see what can be gained from it.

It can be helpful to take a moment to consider change in your life and what it means to you.

Keeping a personal journal

Many courses, from basic introductions right up to diploma level and beyond, ask participants to keep personal journals to document their experiences during the life of the course. Courses vary in their requirements, but most agree that keeping a personal journal can be a powerful aid in the process of personal development. Sometimes the keeping of a personal journal can be part of the course assessment.

If the process seems too vague for you, perhaps you could make that the subject of your first journal entry. It might be useful to know that just because it's called a 'journal' doesn't mean that it is just a *written* record using *words*. Use your imagination. Drawings, paintings, tape-recording, in addition to or instead of writing might be used. If your course does require you to keep a personal journal, the course documents will give you any particular guidelines necessary. If all else fails, you might ask the course tutors for guidance.

If you are not required to keep a personal journal, I would strongly suggest that you do. Both as a trainer and a participant, I have found personal journals to be useful, challenging, awkward, contentious and moving in equal measure. (Sometimes all at the same time.) Don't give up at the first sign of it being tough or boring or a waste of time. The process of self-discovery through journal keeping is one that has parallels with the change process in helping – at the very least it will give you insight into the stumbling blocks that beset the people we are trying to help. Stick it out. Challenge and change isn't always easy.

For some people who have never previously kept journals or diaries, the requirement of having to write one for a counselling course can be an irritation or burden. For others it is the start of a rewarding activity that lasts a lifetime. Counsellors sometimes find it very useful to keep a personal journal of their client work, quite separately from a professional log, or notes, of their counselling. A personal journal can be a great help in supervision.

The next page is an extract from a personal journal kept by me when I attended a Person-Centred Expressive Therapy Institute intensive 12-day residential course. I include it not as an example of good practice or model for journal keeping, but to give an idea of what I made out of journal keeping on that occasion. It *is* personal, and records some significant personal struggles of my own. (I wrote the original diagonally across the page.)

'Ever since I
Was a small child
I cannot sleep at night
Without the light on
I am afraid to laugh out loud
Or to stand out of the crowd
I am scared of loving you
I am afraid of losing you
I am afraid to lose control
I am afraid of growing old
I am afraid to die
But it's something I must do
It's not that I'm not strong
It's just that I'm not strong enough for you
It's not that I'm not brave
It's just that I'm not brave enough for two.'

I Am Afraid: A House, words by David Couse

'if you ever get close to a human
and human behaviour
be ready to get confused

there's definitely no logic
to human behaviour
but yet so irresistible

there's no map
to human behaviour'

Human Behaviour: Björk, words and music by Gudmundsdóttir, Hooper and Jobim

'Therapy training programs and their teachers are merely the whetstones on which the novice therapists hone their instruments. Those instruments are the selves of the therapists.'

Ned Gaylin (2001) *Family, Self and Psychotherapy: A person-centred perspective.* Ross-Wye: PCCS Books, p. 131.

January 10th

Day 2 of the Expressive Therapy course and my second journal entry. Although I feel I am writing this mainly out of duty, I do feel quite keen to see what happens as I set pen to paper. Should I give an account of today or just pick up on any-thing that has moved me? We started today with movement, as we will do each day, at 7.30am before breakfast. I have been re-acquainted with my board-like body. Boy was I stiff!! With my arthritis of recent years and my lack of exercise my movement has become very restricted. I think it may be a metaphor for my whole life, since I know I am capable of a wider range in relationships, at work, in play etc. than I currently display. Why is that? How can I loosen up in life? I thought I would find the free movement stuff difficult, awkward and embarrassing. It has turned out to be easier and more enjoyable than my typically conservative expectations. Expressing myself freely by moving around is still difficult for me. I feel stupid, exposed, vulnerable. Maybe people will laugh at me? The whole group movement directed by Shellee was brilliant. Just very moving ... nearly everyone was crying, me too ... simple meeting connecting ... and all the things I can't, don't or won't do in everyday life. I think I was crying for myself and all of the lost opportunities to make connections with people like this. Natalie did a counselling demonstration today which I thought was great. She asked the group to take part at one point which was interesting and, I was impressed. She never lets an opportunity go by without letting us know what she is feeling. She does it in a way that doesn't intrude, direct or push ... drat! I wish I could just experience things without wanting to use them at work as a therapist. I am constantly impressed by her genuineness (in a technical sense) when she is facilitating the group or counselling an individual. She never lets ... It's a very powerful tool ... I must get a handle on it since I would like to be able to do it too.

January 11th 11pm

I have real difficulty in understanding D sometimes. I can't get a handle on why – she seems so airy in the elemental sense of the word, so delicate, so 'other-worldly' that the contact we make is like the landing of a butterfly on my hardest, most insensitive skin. She says words and I simply don't understand the words or the sentences. She and I seem to be from different planets. I think she senses this too, but I don't know for sure, and this is further testimony to our unconnectedness. I shrink from raising the issue for fear of it exploding like a dandelion clock in a puff of wind. She is like a fragile fluttering bird and I fear that she could hurt me.

prejudice, oppression and counselling

When we concentrate so much on the individual and their needs as we do in counselling, we can sometimes lose a certain perspective. That perspective is the one which gives us a glimpse of the wider context of the world and the forces active within it that affect us as individuals. This world of situations and connections that I see is often harsh and brutal with many inequalities. I don't want to lose the harsh 'edge' to this view by wearing de-contextualised rose-coloured spectacles.

Sometimes the world of counselling and helping can be a little like a pair of rose-coloured glasses, through which I see people making choices about their lives in the safety of a helping relationship. The truth is, of course, that the 'real' world gives me – a white, middle-class, able-bodied, heterosexual man with a university education – many more opportunities and choices than almost anyone else. Can a counselling way of helping make any headway against prejudice and oppression?

We should always try be aware of what helping in a counselling way can realistically achieve, both in general terms and for the person we are trying to help. Early on in our training and work as counsellors, there can be a tendency for us to get too enthusiastic about the possibilities and very soon we start to believe that counselling can be a cure for everything.

On the other hand, some people (and indeed some counsellors) think that counselling, with its concentration on the individual person, fails to take into account important social and economic processes. Then, rather than being part of the cure, counselling is seen as part of the disease, since a counselling way of helping can appear to say 'Let's talk about why you are depressed – it'll get better if you share your troubles.' However, talking won't get someone a job and decent housing or stop the racial abuse, if that is the cause of their depression. It is important that helpers and counsellors do not turn away and walk on the other side of the street whenever prejudice and oppression raise their heads.

If basic helping – a counselling way of helping – gives us the privilege of being let into, and understanding, another person's world, we should be prepared to face up to the unpleasant truth that sometimes we (yes, uncomfortably, me too) may be part of the problem.

My purpose in spending time considering prejudice and oppression in an introductory book is to acknowledge that the roots of prejudice and oppression are very deep and we simply cannot start too soon to understand our own attitudes and how we turn them into behaviour. If we put such a premium on self-awareness then we must surely want to become aware of our prejudices, and if we are so keen on self-development, then we must surely try to live our lives in a way that doesn't oppress others.

Many books and courses concentrate on culture and race as the focus of their work on prejudice and oppression. Whilst this is not a bad starting point, it can lead to the idea that cultural/racial oppression is the only oppression we need to look at. In this book, I am going to set the process in motion by looking in more general terms at a wide range of differences between people, e.g. differences in colour, class, gender, age, religion, culture, sexual orientation or whatever, and how we often translate those differences into prejudices.

In recent years some people have become concerned about the effects of global commerce on the 'Third World'. It is interesting that many people refer to oppressed groups as 'minorities', e.g. 'ethnic minorities'. I read a quote some years ago but can never remember who said it. It brought home to me the parochial nature of such terms. Although I can't remember who said it, it helped me put oppression into a bigger picture, 'There is only one minority: rich white men.' It is salutary to appreciate that whether in today's world of globalised commerce, or recent colonial history, elite powerful minorities oppress disempowered majorities the world over.

Prejudice

Prejudice has been defined as, 'an attitude that predisposes a person to think, feel, perceive and act in favourable or unfavourable ways towards a group or its individual members' (Secord & Backman, 1974). This means that our views and beliefs will reveal themselves in the ways we show preferential treatment towards, e.g. ourselves and 'our group' and in the ways we try to disadvantage others and 'their group'.

If we wish to help in a counselling way, we must do something to become aware of our prejudices, at the very least so that we can understand the ways they will affect our helping relationships. And it's worth pointing out that prejudices can be positive or negative (take another look at the definition in the previous paragraph). Feeling overly helpful or positive towards a particular person is just as problematic as negative feelings in a helping situation. We will see in Chapter 5 how important it is to be able to be respectful,

Note

The issue I wish to draw attention to is *difference* or *diversity* and how we deal with it both personally and, in different ways, as a society. I am not, at this introductory level, going to analyse *why* we sometimes have a tendency to respond to differences between us and others in negative ways. I am challenging us all to discover the difference and diversity in humankind, acknowledge our feelings in the moment and offer ourselves a choice to *celebrate* difference and diversity. How does that feel? It must surely be a better starting place for helping someone.

Secord, PF & Backman, CW (1974) *Social Psychology.* Tokyo: McGraw-Hill.

warm and accepting towards the person you are trying to help, whilst also being genuine. This is clearly going to be difficult if you harbour prejudices towards people.

Most of us who are drawn towards helping others like to think that we are a prejudice-free zone. It might come as a surprise to learn that this is not the case. However open-minded we like to think we are, we will have prejudices directing our behaviour. As a white man, I can only think as a white man with all of the views, perspectives and prejudices of a white man.

In some circumstances we tend to focus on the similarities between people, the things that bind us together as humans. Under other circumstances we emphasise the differences. A counselling way of helping tries to capture the positive elements of both similarities and differences; whilst celebrating everyone's uniqueness and their individual qualities, we also want to respect the rights of that person as a human being – to be treated as an equal, with dignity.

What comes into your mind when you think about the word 'prejudice'? The flip chart in the margin illustrates the views of our hypothetical group that we first met in Chapter 1. When you think about this hypothetical group, who do you picture: a mixed group of men, women, black, white, gay, straight? In your mind's eye, who is missing? Did your imaginary group have no black people, no men? What does your mental picture say about your prejudices?

The prejudice I am concentrating on here revolves around a negative view of difference – the differences between you and me. The sort of dimensions on which we judge these differences include:

- race/ethnicity
- nationality
- religion
- class
- gender
- sexual orientation
- age
- dis/ability

Are there any other dimensions you can think of?

Let's look at a few statements to find out where we stand in relation to some of these issues. The questions are sometimes deliberately contentious to get us thinking about our prejudices. We may find that powerful feelings accompany our views on these issues. These feelings are signals that the issues are connected to deeply held views which may be difficult to confront and change.

PREJUDICE

FRIGHTENED   DIFFERENT

HURT   NOT ALLOWED IN HERE

BLIND   NOT LIKE ME   WEIRD

I DON'T LIKE THEM   FEAR

EVIL   NOT NORMAL   INVISIBLE

I'M NOT PREJUDICED BUT ...

PRE-JUDGEMENT   UNFAIR

INSULARITY   BAD INFLUENCE

LOTS OF MY FRIENDS ARE ...

CATEGORISATION   PIGEONHOLING

EVERYTHING IN BLACK AND WHITE

....

Activity
What is it in your experience about these dimensions of difference that causes so much prejudice?
What do you think?

The process must start, however, with raising our awareness. When looking at these statements, try to stay with your first, gut reaction.

- Private clubs should have the right to exclude people on the grounds of gender, disability, race, colour or religion.
- If black people really wanted to get on in life, they would stay on at school and work harder.
- Women have made no real progress in getting equal treatment in recent years.
- I saw a woman breastfeeding her child in the cafe yesterday. It shouldn't be allowed.
- All children should speak English at school.
- I would be very happy if my son or daughter told me they were gay.
- Other people's religious rituals are daft – fancy not eating milk and beef together, or not using a toilet that faces east!
- Young people should be moved on from loitering around street corners, they are always up to no good.
- There are plenty of jobs if you go looking for them, the benefit system is just for scroungers who don't want to work.
- I'm very pleased a mosque will be built close to where I live.
- Everybody over the age of 55 should be made to retire to make more jobs for the younger people.

Power

A counselling way of helping is based on a recognition that all humans are equal. It may seem strange, therefore, to look at power in counselling relationships. We may feel uncomfortable when it is suggested that we have power *over* other people in a helping situation and it would be convenient to think that we are equal to all those we are trying to help, but on at least one basic dimension, there is an inequality – *they* are asking *us* for help.

Gillian Proctor has written about power in counselling and psychotherapy, pointing to four types of power which relate (good or bad) to helping relationships:

- *Power-over*
  In simple terms this is the power to dominate someone. In therapy settings this would include persuading someone, using your authority as a counsellor, to comply with 'treatment', e.g. to get someone to take their medication.
- *Power-from-within*
  This is sometimes called 'personal power' – the power to be your own person, do what you want to do or to resist persuasion.
- *Power-with*
  The power of cooperation or vested in community with equals. This could relate to the helper accompanying the client or joining

Activity
- *What are your reactions to these statements on the right?*
- *Do you disagree and feel angry about them or agree passionately?*

Proctor, G (2002) *The Dynamics of Power in Counselling and Psychotherapy: Ethics, politics and practice.* Ross-on-Wye: PCCS Books.

Note
Proctor takes many of her leads from the feminist therapy movement – a view of helping that emphasises power-sharing and equality, non-victim blaming and validation of client's experiences. Feminist therapy authors have made considerable contributions to our understanding of power issues in therapy.

forces with the client in order to solve the problem.

- *Power-to*
  This is the power of the individual to achieve something, the power of capability or ability. It is also seen by some as a combination of the personal power (power-from-within), and power-with (the power of cooperation).

There is also power in the structures of society – in some jobs in the 'helping professions' structural power vested in roles is very real. This includes the power to control access to services, or funds. The power to take children away from their parents and put them into care or the power to say who is mad and who is sane. If you have ever been in the position of having to ask for help from a statutory service, you will appreciate just how powerless you can feel and just how powerful the social workers or nurses appear to be.

As a volunteer in, for example, a third-sector helping agency, you may feel as though you have little or no structural power in this regard, but someone coming to you for help is likely to see you as a powerful, 'together' person in control of your life. You may also have valuable information which would be of help to them, or be able to help them get access to funding or services. Information and assistance which you could give … or withhold. If they think you are the key to accessing this help, to feeling less miserable and panicky about life, they are quite likely to listen to and do what you say. In short, to be compliant.

I'm pretty sure that's not the sort of power you will want to have. My guess is that you will want to be experienced as more of an equal, a fellow traveller, a companion. The question is how do I present myself as this equal, non-expert, companion? This can be difficult if the people we are trying to help expect effective helpers to be authoritative experts who know more than them. We will see in the next chapter how the core skills of forming a helping relationship provide the foundations of letting go of structural power and power-over.

'Most powerful is he who has himself in his own power.'
Lucius Annaeus Seneca (4 BC–AD 65) Roman philosopher and playwright

'The urge to save humanity is almost always only a false face for the urge to rule it.'
Henry Louis Mencken

'He that has one eye is a prince among those that have none.'
Thomas Fuller

> 'People frequently ask me, "Are you Carl Rogers' daughter?" It has taken women's groups like these to raise my consciousness to give the appropriate answer to that question which is "Yes, I'm the daughter of Helen and Carl Rogers."'
>
> Natalie Rogers (1995) *Emerging Woman: A decade of midlife transitions.* Ross-on-Wye: PCCS Books, p. 170.

Activity

Are there any other factors in your experience that have had the effect of giving you more power or less power?

There are certain factors which shift our sense of power in relation to others; some factors shift it up and some factors shift it down (in the UK, in general):

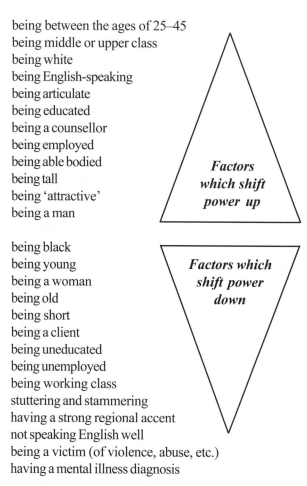

being between the ages of 25–45
being middle or upper class
being white
being English-speaking
being articulate
being educated
being a counsellor
being employed
being able bodied
being tall
being 'attractive'
being a man

Factors which shift power up

being black
being young
being a woman
being old
being short
being a client
being uneducated
being unemployed
being working class
stuttering and stammering
having a strong regional accent
not speaking English well
being a victim (of violence, abuse, etc.)
having a mental illness diagnosis

Factors which shift power down

Note

It is easy to misunderstand cultural references for politeness and courtesy. For example, for some Muslim women, meeting a man unchaperoned would not be acceptable. Others would be comfortable meeting with a man, but feel unacceptably invaded and unsafe if offered a handshake, and eye contact would also be very problematic.

Activity

What specific examples of power differences can you come up with that might give rise to problems in helping relationships?

Differences in power between counsellor and client may have a number of effects. We need to be aware of potential power and status differences in our helping relationships so that they do not get in the way of us offering help.

• Some people are uncomfortable about asking for help unless the helper is seen as equal, i.e. they want a companion or someone to help in a cooperative way.

• Some people are uncomfortable about asking for help unless the helper is more powerful or higher status, i.e. they want help from an expert whom they think will give them good quality help and have some answers to their problems.

• As a helper do you think your helping is only effective if you and your client see each other as equals?

- Some women do not want to receive help from a man.
- Men from some cultures would not ask for help from a woman.
- Some people think that you need to have experienced a problem before you can help them with it, especially if it involves discrimination or oppression.

Oppression

This is one of those words that I think I *know* the meaning of, but I really don't *understand* it. As I mentioned before, I must be one of the least oppressed people around. I looked in the dictionary for a definition and read that oppression is 'prolonged cruel or unjust treatment or control'. Perhaps like me you cannot ever remember being the victim of such cruel treatment and feel fortunate or in some way protected from oppression? This doesn't mean that we should or can do nothing. I wish I could remember who it was that said 'If you're not part of the solution – you're part of the problem'. This phrase seems to catch the feeling exactly and asks me what *I* am doing about *my* attitudes and behaviour.

A good starting place is to understand yourself better in terms of what gives you your own identity and realise that this gives you certain viewpoints and perceptions. So to return for a moment to the list of 'power factors' on the previous page, how do these factors contribute to your sense of identity, i.e. your race, colour, religion, physical stature, gender, education, social class, physical ability and status, etc.? Asking such questions can sometimes be a painful process, so I would not recommend you get too deep without support. Perhaps you could try it with a friend or someone else on your introductory course.

As a white, middle-class, able-bodied, non-gay male, I have a set of perceptions which are particular to that group. I cannot see into the worlds of disabled people, women or black people with ease, if at all. It is difficult or impossible for me to understand and insulting of me to claim to be able to, but I can *try*. If I am sensitive and humble in the trying, then I may be experienced as empathic.

After trying to understand your own position and prejudices better, it can help to try to give oppression some personal meaning regardless of whether you belong to one of the oppressed groups listed above – try the activity in the margin to start you off. And of course another good place to start is with the old proverb: 'Do as you would be done by'.

Finally, let's not assume that because everyone may have experienced oppression at some time in their lives, this means that we can ignore the issue since it all somehow cancels out. There are

---

OPPRESSION

PAIN ABUSE HARASS DO DOWN

MISTREAT SUPPRESS DICTATOR

GHETTO TORMENT INEQUALITY

PERSECUTE NO JOBS NO HOUSING

DISCRIMINATE AGAINST

GLASS CEILING SEGREGATION

HARDSHIP SLAVERY OVERPOWER

APARTHEID MEN OPPRESS WOMEN

SUBTLE, UNSPOKEN SECRET CODE

TORTURE EQUAL RIGHTS FOR ALL

✍ ....

Activity

- *Think about a time when you have experienced oppression yourself. (You may have difficulty in admitting to being oppressed, but most people have been oppressed at some time in their lives; perhaps because of your nationality, religion, accent or bullying during childhood.)*
- *What were your thoughts and feelings at the time?*
- *What did you want to do about it for yourself?*
- *Did your oppressors realise that they were oppressing you?*
- *What did you want the person or people responsible to do about it?*

This last question is important since it seems reasonable to find out what an oppressed person wants from you that would help – and to listen very carefully.

✍

'There are several natural reactions on the part of white Americans which are of no help whatsoever: "I can understand your bitterness because I've been oppressed too"; "Yes, yes, I can understand how you feel, but I have never personally been a part of your oppression. It is the white society which has oppressed you." Whites who are effective seem to learn two attitudes – one toward self and one toward the minority members. The first is the realisation and ownership of the fact that "I think white." For men trying to deal with women's rage, it may be helpful for the man to recognise "I think male." In spite of all our efforts to seem unprejudiced, we actually carry within us many prejudices.'

Carl Rogers (1978) *On Personal Power*. London: Constable, p. 204.

Activity: Mind your language!

It could be said that counsellors (and the profession of counselling) do this by their use of jargon. One way counselling may exclude working-class people or those from different ethnic backgrounds is by using language that only educated middle-class counsellors can understand. What do you make of the following words and phrases?

- *boundaries*
- *empathy*
- *personal limits*
- *defence mechanisms*
- *personal growth*
- *client*
- *counselling skills*
- *sharing*

- *Do you think they are jargon words that may exclude people from understanding the world of counselling?*
- *What other words would you add to the list?*
- *Try to explain helping in a counselling way without any of the above words, just using everyday language.*

many inequalities built into the system in this and most countries. These inequalities oppress both individuals and groups, restricting their freedom to live fulfilling lives. This institutional oppression is familiar to all of those with some of the negative factors listed on page 80. Most of the time institutional oppression or discrimination is invisible. Women describe hitting a 'glass ceiling' when applying for management posts. But all may not be lost, therapists are citizens like everyone else and these oppressive systems are staffed by and voted for by individuals, so we all have a role in maintaining such institutional oppression. We could do well to ask ourselves whether we do anything to oppose oppression when we get the opportunity. This includes voting for certain types of change to make society more equal, and the opportunities which people like me have enjoyed are available to everyone.

Language

One way in which the system oppresses people is in the way language is used to devalue people, to exclude and invalidate their experience. There has been a lot of publicity over the years concerning PC or *political correctness* and the issue of language. My own view is that since, as a counsellor, I try to choose my words with care, I am careful to not contribute to the continuing oppression of others by using offensive or demeaning language.

The current 'backlash' against so-called *politically correct* language just diverts attention away from the real issue. If we are to be respectful towards each other in helping relationships, this must surely include the language we use. Who in the 21st century would say 'n****r' other than someone with racist intent? Our language is a window to the attitudes we hold, so first of all note the words you use, then wonder whether you might find them offensive if used to describe you.

Language can be used in oppressive ways other than being racist or sexist (either intentionally or unintentionally). Language can be used to oppress others by excluding them. This is done by, for example, educated people to exclude the uneducated and by professional people to exclude the non-professionals. Both the words used (vocabulary) and the way they are used in sentences (grammar) can be used to prevent others understanding you, and therefore making them feel left out and inferior. As counselling moves towards greater professionalism, it is important that we do not fall into the trap of excluding people with the language we use.

white comedy

I waz whitemailed
By a white witch,
Wid white magic
An white lies,
Branded a white sheep
I slaved as a whitesmith
Near a white spot
Where I suffered whitewater fever.
Whitelisted as a whiteleg
I waz in de white book
As a master of white art,
It waz like white death.

People called me white jack
Some hailed me as a white wog,
So I joined de white watch
Trained as a white guard
Lived off the white economy.
Caught an beaten by de white shirts
I was condemned to a white mass.
Don't worry,
I shall be writing to de Black House.

Benjamin Zephaniah, 1995

'Psychologists must join with persons who reject racism, sexism, colonialism, and exploitation and must find ways to redistribute social power and to increase social justice. Primary prevention research inevitably will make clear the relationship between social pathology and psychopathology and then will work to change social and political structures in the interests of social justice. It is as simple and as difficult as that.'

George Albee (1996) Revolutions and counterrevolutions in prevention. *American Psychologist, 51*, 1131.

SCHIZOPHRENIA Serious psychological distress or mental 'illness'. Classified in MEDICAL MODEL as 'PSYCHOSIS'. Many very distressing symptoms of confused, chaotic thoughts and feelings, delusions and hallucinations.

MEDICAL MODEL The system used to understand and classify psychological distress in the Western world, based on the similarity of symptoms *not* cause and effect relationships. It is not a disease model although it looks like one, mimicking the medical model of physical disease. It is used by psychiatrists and the majority of mental health professionals.

PSYCHOSIS A medical-model classification of severe distress characterised by loss of contact with reality and lack of insight (person doesn't think they're ill). Types include schizophrenia, clinical depression, bipolar disorder.

PHOBIA Persistent, irrational 'morbid fear' of a situation or object, e.g. spiders, knives or flying, etc.

Read, J (2010) Can poverty drive you mad? *New Zealand Journal of Psychology, 39*(2), 7-19.

Unequal societies may not promote good mental health

It is also rather salutary to move up a 'level' and consider inequalities embedded in the way society is organised and how that might affect our wellbeing in general and mental health in particular. The World Health Organization estimates that one in four of us will have a mental disorder at some point in our lives; see <http://www.who.int/whr/2001/en/>. You may be shocked to learn that in Great Britain, for example, in 2004 one in ten already had a clinically diagnosable mental disorder by age 16; see <http://www.ic.nhs.uk/pubs/mentalhealth04>. The figures seem to be steadily increasing all over the world. Is it time we started to think about what role the societies we live in play in this huge and apparently increasing amount of human unhappiness and distress, and what we can do to prevent the causes of mental health problems?

Of all the societal inequalities, poverty is particularly associated with SCHIZOPHRENIA and it is also strongly associated with of a host of other mental health problems, including depression, PHOBIAS, alcohol abuse, and drug abuse (Read, 2010). For example, a 2007

Fortney, J, Rushton, G, Wood, S, Zhang, L, Xu, S, Dong, F & Rost, K (2007) Community-level risk factors for depression hospitalizations. *Administration and Policy in Mental Health and Mental Health Services Research, 34,* 343-52.

Stansfield, S, Clark, C, Rodgers, B, Caldwell, T & Power, C (2008) Childhood and adulthood socio-economic position and midlife depressive and anxiety disorders. *British Journal of Psychiatry, 192,* 152-3.

EPIDEMIOLOGISTS investigate and describe the causes and distribution of diseases, disabilities, and other health outcomes. They also develop methods of disease prevention and control.

Wilkinson, R & Pickett, K (2009) *The Spirit Level: Why more equal societies almost always do better.* London: Allen Lane. See also the website of The Equality Trust: <http://www.equalitytrust.org.uk>

study covering 14 USA states found that admission to hospital for depression was significantly associated with both poverty and unemployment (Fortney et al., 2007). A 2008 British study that followed nearly 10,000 people since their birth in 1958 found that those who were poor at age 7 were significantly more likely to have a range of diagnosable mental health problems at age 45 (Stansfield et al., 2008).

In addition to this there is very convincing evidence that *relative* poverty is also a strong predictor of poor mental health. In their book, *The Spirit Level* (and on the website of The Equality Trust), British EPIDEMIOLOGISTS Richard Wilkinson and Kate Pickett (2009) report multiple studies demonstrating a far stronger relationship between relative poverty and a range of social, health and mental health outcomes than between poverty per se and the same outcomes. They first explain that in many countries rates of mental illness and levels of inequality have both increased significantly in recent decades. They then report a strong relationship between degree of income inequality and rates of people meeting diagnostic criteria for mental illness over a 12-month period, across 12 countries and this is illustrated in the graph opposite.

The focus on *relative* poverty should not be forgotten when thinking about how to help people with problems. Some problems simply cannot be helped by counselling and to offer counselling would be an insult. Again, we must look at how we act as citizens to get a healthy society, as well as how we act as counsellors to get a good helping relationship. The authors of *The Spirit Level* conclude:

> The solution to problems caused by inequality is not mass psychotherapy aimed at making everyone less vulnerable. The best way of responding to the harm done by high levels of inequality would be to reduce the inequality itself. Rather than requiring anti-anxiety drugs in the water supply or mass psychotherapy, what is most exciting about the picture we present is that it shows that reducing inequality would increase the wellbeing and quality of life for all of us. (Wilkinson & Pickett, 2009, p. 33)

What else can I do?

There are many subtle ways in which we are all racist, sexist, ageist, failing to see the value in other people because of their religion, class or whatever. One way is to think that there are no differences. If I say, 'I'm not racist, I treat everyone the same!' I am failing to acknowledge the important *differences* between people which give each of us our identity. A useful phrase which sprang from the women's movement in the 1970s was 'different but

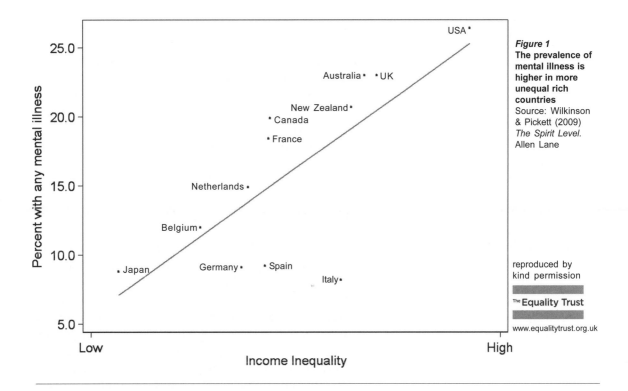

Figure 1
The prevalence of mental illness is higher in more unequal rich countries
Source: Wilkinson & Pickett (2009) *The Spirit Level.* Allen Lane

reproduced by kind permission

™ᵉ **Equality Trust**

www.equalitytrust.org.uk

equal' meaning that women do not want to be seen as the same as men at all (and black people do not want to be seen as the same as white) but as different with valid, useful differences worth celebrating.

If we think that everyone is the same, we are racist and sexist, since we are denying the culture, religion, history and biology that make us different. Does the organisation you work for reflect the community which it serves? How much effort do you personally put in to find out about different cultures?

Actions speak louder than words, and, if you get involved, you will learn about the issues through reading, meeting people and making friends.

- If you work for an organisation:
  - Familiarise yourself with the equal opportunities policy and help monitor the way it is implemented.
  - If there is no equal opportunities policy could you propose one and work with any oppressed groups to write it?
- What can you do to get to understand the issues better?
  - Have you got a list of contacts for local groups for women, gays, lesbians, different ethnic communities, disabled, etc.?
  - Have you made contact with any of these groups for literature, to meet with the staff, to discuss their services?
  - Have you sought out any specific training or personal

development opportunity on race, sexuality, oppression, power?

- Make an effort to learn about different cultural and religious groups in your community:
  - Most agencies, hospital wards and colleges 'celebrate' Christmas. What message does this give to the users of your service?
  - Do you know when the religious festivals of other ethnic groups are?
  - Does your organisation celebrate them or even acknowledge that they exist?
- Oppression is a personal and a political issue, it is *not* neutral (see Kearney, 1996).
  - If you wish to be more active in understanding and counteracting oppression you will have to familiarise yourself with some of the political issues involved. This will take time and patience, since you may well find yourself excluded from some groups and sources of information because you will be understandably seen as one of the oppressing group. It is important to accept and work with this perception. This requires some empathy, effort and willingness to risk an uncomfortable shift in self-awareness, plus a determination to learn and change on your part.

If, like me, you are male, white, and able-bodied, then you are one of the most powerful creatures on the planet. It would be easy to say that I didn't ask to be born a man, white, etc., but this evades the issue. Although I didn't ask for anything, I have used this power every day of my life and continue to, most often even without knowing it. The way our society works is that the sort of power invested in white, middle-class, able-bodied men is the sort of power that thrives by taking power away from others. In other words it is a power used to oppress others. Until I find out how this works for me on a day-to-day basis I will continue to oppress others without even realising it. For my part I feel behoven to do something about my part in it all; not blaming myself, but only if I take responsibility for my part in the world can I change it.

None of these suggestions is going to change the world overnight, but they do give you some power in your own sphere of influence. The process of change in your sphere of influence starts with yourself and then stretches out to include your family, friends and colleagues, and finally your influence as a citizen on how society is organised.

Kearney, A (1996) *Counselling, Class and Politics: Undeclared influences in therapy.* Ross-on-Wye: PCCS Books.

'It is our belief that, to some extent, all individuals are racist, sexist, and classist.

In a setting such as this, some of these will become explicit. It is our hope that everyone will be understanding, respecting, empathic and non-judgmental.

In a setting such as this we should all be allowed to make mistakes.'

Joyce Thompson, 1985

Counselling attitudes or counselling skills?

In Chapter 2 we saw how the different counselling approaches are based upon different principles and to some extent on different values. The foundations of each approach *do* affect the theory and practice of each approach just like the foundations of a building dictate the shape, height and building materials permitted in the final structure.

The practice of counselling is shaped by the founding principles of each approach and you may remember from Chapter 2 that Carl Rogers proposed that his therapist-provided conditions of empathy, congruence and unconditional positive regard had to be held as attitudes. It would not be enough, as far as Rogers was concerned, for these conditions to be just learned as skills and acted out in a mechanical way. That would make the whole act of helping false, a horrendous caricature of real human caring, wherein the helper was, at worst, merely pretending to care, or at best not really believing in the effectiveness of their actions. The client is bound to detect this incongruence in the helper and may not trust the helper or feel safe with them.

Person-centred counsellors use the terms 'principled' and 'instrumental' to talk about the differences between using the core conditions. In 1990 Barry Grant used these terms to mean:

- *Principled* – where something is held as a principle, is part of your belief system and set of values. You *are* this thing, you do not have to *put it on* or *act it out*. You express these values as a natural part of being you because they are held at your core.
- *Instrumental* – *using* something as an instrument or tool in order to achieve a given end, e.g. using empathy to learn about the client's symptoms so you can diagnose them more accurately.

So in terms of the therapist-provided 'core' conditions, 'principled' empathy, congruence and unconditional positive regard (UPR) would mean that you hold these human qualities as core values in your life, i.e. you believe that being empathic, genuine and regarding people positively is the right way to be for you. You would not be being empathic, non-judgemental or genuine in order to get a given effect. As a helper, you would be relying on the client's actualising tendency

Grant, B (1990) Principled and instrumental nondirectiveness in person-centered and client-centered therapy. *Person-Centered Review, 5 ,* 77-88.

to help them, once your helping qualities of empathy, congruence and UPR were provided.

On the other hand, 'instrumental' empathy, genuineness and UPR mean that you would be using human qualities like these as tools or 'instruments' for helping, but you would not necessarily hold them as core values. You would, for example, be *using* genuineness as a tool to get the client to trust you and 'open up'. You would be *using* empathy to get the client to explain their problem or explore it themselves. You may or may not be doing this because you believe that this helping system is effective.

Person-centred therapists would take a principled approach to the holding (and expression) of the core conditions as values, human qualities and attitudes in life. In 1980 Carl Rogers called this a 'way of being'. There can be no clearer indication of what lies at the heart of helping in a person-centred way – a set of genuinely held core values, not the application of the conditions as a set of *techniques* or tools.

Not all approaches to helping take this view. Other approaches may, to different degrees, incorporate Rogers' therapeutic conditions (or something very similar) into their helping framework. These approaches may talk about the importance of the helping relationship or 'therapeutic alliance'. Cognitive, behavioural, psychodynamic and integrative approaches generally *use* a selection of the therapeutic conditions *instrumentally* as tools to further the theoretical aims of the approach in question.

So, for example, a cognitive counsellor will use empathy as a tool to get an accurate understanding of the client's thought processes so that the therapist can suggest the most helpful ways of overcoming debilitating or self-defeating thoughts. In this approach, in order to be effective, the counsellor does not have to be empathic as a 'way of being'.

An eclectic or integrative counsellor will *use* any or all of the core conditions *as tools* if they believe the client will be helped by, e.g. gaining insight into their problem through using them in this instrumental way. The next client seen by an eclectic counsellor may have a different set of tools applied to their problem.

When covering the importance of self-development in Chapter 3, I presented sections on personal values and counselling values. The importance of these sections should now be obvious. It is clear that, in order to be person-centred, you would need to feel comfortable holding the values of empathy, genuineness and UPR as 'good things to be'. Of course, holding these values (as many of us do) would not mean that you *must* be person-centred in your helping style. You could just as easily hold these values and decide, after careful scrutiny of the theories, that a behavioural or cognitive style of helping makes more sense to you.

Note

These counselling approaches are defined and described in some detail in Chapter 2.

Many readers will wish to remain volunteers using basic helping. Those wishing to progress to training as a counsellor will find Chapter 13 useful when we will take a little time to look at the importance of making the right decision about what sort of counsellor you want to train to become. When making that decision, thinking now about whether you prefer the idea of using the conditions as tools, or holding them as core values in life, will have been time well spent.

Counselling and basic helping skills

Most people now look upon counselling as a skilled activity practised by trained people acting in a 'professional' way, i.e. according to a set of agreed standards. This has not always been the case. Indeed when I first started as a volunteer counsellor in 1972 I spent a lot of time defending the skills of counselling (as I understood them then) from the assertions of others that counselling was variously: 'Just chatting'; 'Just listening' or 'Just being someone's friend'. I seem to remember that such put-downs always had the double barb that firstly, counselling is what people do anyway ('chatting, listening or being a friend') and secondly, that it was 'just' or 'simply' that and nothing else. It was not something that had a theory I had to learn, nor something that would benefit by practice, nor that I could get better at by receiving constructive feedback from others. In other words it was not a skill, and could not be learned.

> '**Skill:** an acquired higher-order activity to perform complex ... acts smoothly and precisely.'
>
> *Longman Dictionary of Psychology and Psychiatry* (1984)

The idea that human beings use skills to manage relationships is not a new one. This view gained considerable popularity in the 1970s when the notion of social skills seemed to be cropping up everywhere. Social skills was the term used to indicate that the business of being a social being – having to live a life in the presence of others, in parallel to others and interwoven in the lives of others – was indeed a matter of skill. Some people could be better at it than others. The idea that social skills were important in everyday life soon became accepted and since a skill can be learned and improved with practice, social skills training was set up to help develop the particular type of social skills necessary to have a good marriage, be a good salesperson, be an effective manager, etc.

The idea that helping in general, and counselling or therapy in particular, could be looked at as a set of components which could be learned was made popular by Carl Rogers when he wrote about the 'therapeutic conditions'. Nowadays it is accepted that counselling is skilled and that practice makes better, if never perfect. Most training courses spend a lot of time getting trainees to practise their counselling skills. The question is: 'What are counselling skills?'

This question is closely related to the work covered in Chapter 1:

What is Counselling? In the search for possible definitions of counselling we compared it to other helping roles we are familiar with. So to answer the question 'What are Counselling Skills?' I would ask you to consider other helping roles alongside counselling, e.g. the same ones as in Chapter 1: parent, friend and doctor.

DOCTOR

GOOD AT EXPLAINING MEDICAL
THINGS IN EVERYDAY LANGUAGE

ACTIVE LISTENING

KEEPING PROFESSIONAL DISTANCE

CREATE A SAFE ENVIRONMENT TO
TALK ABOUT PRIVATE THINGS
(CONFIDENTIAL)

....

FRIEND

OFFERS PROTECTION

COMPLETE DEPENDABILITY,
HONESTY AND LOYALTY

GENUINE (NEVER CALLS YOU
NAMES BEHIND YOUR BACK)

IS ON YOUR SIDE

ACTIVE LISTENING

....

PARENT

ACTIVE LISTENING

EVEN-HANDED AND FAIR
WITH DISCIPLINE

SUPPORTIVE

GIVING UNCONDITIONAL LOVE
(NON-JUDGEMENTAL)

UNSELFISH & GENEROUS

ABSOLUTE TRUSTWORTHINESS

....

COUNSELLOR

ACTIVE LISTENING

GENUINE

NON-JUDGEMENTAL

CONFIDENTIAL

EQUAL
(ON THE SAME LEVEL AS YOU)

SUPPORTIVE

....

Activity
Are your ideas similar or very different? How far do you agree with the list of counselling skills on the flip chart?

The flip charts above show a selection of ideas about the kind of helping skills needed in different roles and it is clear that some common helping skills are emerging.

It is not realistic to expect to be properly trained in the use of counselling skills on a course lasting around 100 hours, but it is realistic to expect to raise your awareness to what counselling skills are and to have a go at trying them out to see how it feels. It is in this spirit that I offer the following sections:

- to help you identify the skills you already have
- to back up any skills training you may be doing
- to help you further develop your repertoire of counselling skills
- to give some more detail on the skills you might be encouraged to practise
- to show a range of skills which you may not be able to cover due to time constraints

You will realise by now that all counselling approaches have at their heart the idea that help is best delivered through a relationship. This is an instrumental (see above) way of stating the importance of a relationship. Others might say that a relationship *is* the helping. However you want to understand it, no one says that a relationship (of different complexions) is necessary. Most work on the relationship aspects of helping has been done by Carl Rogers and his associates, so I will start there.

Carl Rogers and Gerard Egan

In Chapter 2 I looked at the origins of theory in counselling, briefly touching upon the work of Carl Rogers and just mentioning the work of Gerard Egan. My own practice has been influenced most heavily by the ideas of Carl Rogers; I describe myself as a person-centred counsellor and I am a member of the British Association for the Person-Centred Approach. Although my own practice did not incorporate ideas from other therapeutic approaches, I acknowledge the influence of the ideas of Egan in developing basic helping skills practice, especially in the voluntary sector in the UK.

Both Rogers and Egan were responsible for developing the idea that counselling was a skilled process, and most would agree that Egan incorporates Rogers' ideas into his framework for understanding the process of helping. Most training courses now emphasise the development of skills as an important, indeed essential, element in training to be a counsellor. At an introductory level we must be content with the basic underlying principles.

The work of Carl Rogers

You may remember from Chapter 2 that Carl Rogers developed his ideas in the 1950s, continuing to refine them until his death in 1987. He proposed that the helper or counsellor needs to provide the right conditions before the natural, positive, self-healing tendency

Activity

In Chapter 2, I looked at where the ideas behind modern counselling approaches have come from and it is useful to ask ourselves where our ideas have come from. What has influenced your ideas on counselling skills? Have your ideas about counselling skills come from:

- *Personal experience of being helped or counselled?*
- *The beliefs of friends and family?*
- *Your wider cultural and ethnic beliefs?*
- *What you've read in the papers or seen on TV?*
- *Someone you know who is a counsellor?*
- *Films?*
- *Someone you know who has had mental health problems?*
- *Books about counselling or psychology?*
- *Other books, e.g. novels or spiritual writings?*

within the client is activated or enhanced. Rogers suggested that the 'right' conditions involved the complete absence of threat to the client. He went on to elaborate his ideas in 1957 and proposed that the six conditions necessary in a helping relationship were:

- that the helper makes psychological contact with the person to be helped
- that the client is vulnerable or anxious
- that the helper is congruent or genuine
- that the helper experiences unconditional positive regard or non-judgemental warmth or acceptance towards the client
- that the helper experiences empathy
- that the client receives the empathy, UPR and genuineness of the helper

Rogers, CR (1957) The necessary and sufficient conditions for therapeutic personality change. *J. Consulting Psychology,* 21(2), 95-103. Reprinted in H Kirschenbaum & VL Henderson (eds) (1990) *The Carl Rogers Reader* (pp. 219-35). London: Constable.

Rogers originally described these conditions in psychological terminology. For a while it became accepted to condense the six into the three therapist provided 'core conditions' (empathy, UPR and congruence) and these form the basis for many skills-approaches to counselling, even though Rogers himself was keen to emphasise the important role of the *whole relationship* in the helping process. He did not see counselling as just assembling a set of skills; rather he believed that counsellors must incorporate the core conditions into their ways of being as people. In recent years, person-centred theorists and practitioners have preferred to remind all counsellors (whatever approach they use) that Rogers wrote about *six* conditions. Moreover that the conditions of psychological contact (condition 1) and the successful communication of the conditions to the client (condition 6) were vital parts of successful helping.

We have looked at how becoming a counsellor involves a good deal of personal change, but now we will identify some basic counselling skills that emerge from the core conditions. Firstly a closer look at the core conditions themselves.

Psychological contact

Just because you are in the same room and looking at the person you are trying to help doesn't necessarily mean that you are in psychological contact with them. Interestingly, if you are offering help on the telephone, you will already know how important it is to keep checking that the person on the other end of the phone is still 'there'. Telephone helpers get used to saying sensitively: 'Are you still there?', or 'I can hear you breathing' during silences. In face-to-face helping it might not occur to you that you will have to *deliberately attend* to making contact with your client.

The key question is: *How do you know you have good psychological contact with someone?*

IF YOU WANT TO KNOW MORE ABOUT
PSYCHOLOGICAL CONTACT

This might be better left to a later stage of training. The best place to find out more is a more advanced book such as:

Wyatt, G & Sanders, P (2002) *Rogers' Therapeutic Conditions: Evolution, theory and practice. Vol 4: Contact and Perception.* Ross-on-Wye: PCCS Books.

The answer is, to some extent, obvious. We all know when we are 'getting through' to someone. They are responsive to what we say or do in a quick and appropriate manner. Looking at us, smiling, talking, etc. In normal conversation we can detect quite easily when this contact is missing. We have colloquial phrases like 'away with the birds' and 'on another planet' to describe it and, for example, when daydreaming, we can quickly come back to the 'here and now' by a noise or a friend clicking their fingers or calling our name. In a basic helping context, however, there might be more silence or less eye contact, so 'natural' checking that you have good contact is more difficult. You might have to deliberately check that, for example, you have been 'received and understood' so to speak, by saying things like 'is that right?', 'did I understand you correctly?', etc.

It might be difficult to maintain psychological contact with:

- someone who is extremely tired or exhausted
- someone who has taken drugs, prescribed or otherwise. Some prescription drugs can have a marked effect on concentration and ability to 'stay with it', especially psychiatric medication
- someone who is drunk
- someone who has taken an overdose
- someone who is extremely agitated or anxious
- someone who is suffering from what psychiatrists call DISSOCIATION
- someone who is having a PSYCHOTIC EPISODE or suffering experiences which could be diagnosed as SCHIZOPHRENIA, MANIA, PARANOIA, or another PSYCHOSIS and has lost contact with our shared reality

As someone offering basic helping, depending upon your situation, you will be able to respond in one of a number of ways:

- there may be agency policy to help deal with someone who is drunk or under the influence of drugs
- if you suspect that someone has taken an overdose of something, or is so drunk that they become unconscious, get medical help immediately
- there may be agency policy to help deal with people who have been diagnosed with a severe mental illness, are having a PSYCHOTIC episode or experiencing DISSOCIATION
- if none of the above apply, you will have to quickly assess the situation to work out:
  - how comfortable you are that you have the personal qualities and skills to see this through
  - if you decide to help, stay calm and make sure you and the person you are trying to help are safe
  - there is evidence from the work of the American psychologist

DISSOCIATION In psychology and psychiatry, a perceived detachment of the mind from the emotional state or even from the body. Dissociation is characterized by a sense of the world as a dreamlike or unreal place and may be accompanied by poor memory of the specific events. <www.medterms.com>

PSYCHOSIS A MEDICAL MODEL classification of severe distress characterised by loss of contact with reality and lack of insight (the person doesn't think they're ill). Types include schizophrenia, clinical depression, bipolar disorder.

SCHIZOPHRENIA Serious psychological distress or mental 'illness'. Classified in MEDICAL MODEL as 'PSYCHOSIS'. Many very distressing symptoms of confused, chaotic thoughts and feelings, delusions and hallucinations.

MEDICAL MODEL The system used to understand and classify psychological distress in the Western world, based on the similarity of symptoms *not* cause and effect relationships. It is not a disease model although it looks like one, mimicking the medical model of physical disease. It is used by psychiatrists and the majority of mental health professionals.

MANIA An abnormally elated mental state, typically characterized by feelings of euphoria, lack of inhibitions, racing thoughts, diminished need for sleep, talkativeness, risk taking, and irritability. In extreme cases, mania can induce hallucinations and other psychotic symptoms.

PARANOIA An unfounded or exaggerated distrust of others, sometimes reaching DELUSIONAL proportions. Paranoid individuals constantly suspect the motives of those around them, and believe that certain individuals, or people in general, are 'out to get them'.

DELUSION A false personal belief that is not subject to reason and is not explained by a person's usual cultural and religious concepts. May be maintained in the face of incontrovertible evidence.

Note

Garry Prouty and his associates developed 'Pre-Therapy', a method of establishing psychological contact with people who were previously thought to be permanently unreachable. If you work with people with learning disabilities, suffering from dementia or who have a brain injury, you might be interested in Pre-Therapy.

IF YOU WANT TO KNOW MORE ABOUT
PRE-THERAPY

The best place to start is:

Sanders, P (ed) (2007) *The Contact Work Primer.* Ross-on-Wye: PCCS Books.

Garry Prouty that slow, extremely basic reflections such as 'we are sitting in the counselling centre', 'you are smiling but not saying anything' and repeating what the client says word for word are helpful.

Don't worry if you don't feel able to do this; just sitting calmly and quietly with them until they are able to make good psychological contact in their own time is probably the best basic helping you can offer. In summary, then:

- don't take psychological contact for granted. Check and think about doing something about it
- if you have not got good psychological contact with the person you are trying to help, see what your agency or workplace policy says you should do

Remember – you cannot really help someone who is not in contact, so simply waiting until they feel able to make contact under their own steam is best if you are at all unsure.

Empathy

This is trying to see the world of another person from their point of view. It involves trying to understand their world, their meanings, their life. It has been described variously as walking in someone else's shoes, understanding how they feel and think, or listening to both the 'words' and the 'music'. The emphasis is on not only understanding, but also on doing this gently and sensitively, then communicating this to the other person – not trampling around their world of personal images and meanings without any care.

Being empathic is:

- listening sensitively – not probing, interrogating or fact-gathering
- trying to make sense of what you hear, but not worrying if it doesn't make sense straight away
- understanding the other person's experiences *in their own terms*
- checking to see if you've got the meaning right with all its subtleties

Carl Rogers describes empathy as the ability to sense the client's world *as if* it were your own, without losing the 'as if' quality. He placed particular emphasis on being able accurately and sensitively to understand the client's *feelings* without getting them muddled up with your own. He makes it clear that we cannot actually put ourselves into the world of others, we can never experience the same things as others. Even if we have a similar experience, we will not have felt exactly the same about it.

A life event that has affected most people is the loss of a parent, close relative or possibly a friend. I can remember when my dad died quite clearly. I was 18 years old and it was three weeks before my A-level exams. I was sure that the pain and loss I felt could not be experienced by anyone else, not even my brother. I knew that his relationship with Dad had been very different from mine (he was 14 at the time), but I had no real way of seeing through my own grief to understand his. This experience of the loss of a parent, close relative or friend is different for everyone. It might come as a shock for certain readers to realise that some people may feel relief or a sense of freedom if their relationship with their parent was abusive, restrictive or burdensome. Others feel conflicted – a person who has devoted many years of their life to caring for an ageing parent might feel sadness, relief and terrible loneliness. Such complex responses can be very difficult to cope with if we expect grief and loss to be a simple, 'pure' emotion, uncluttered by other strong feelings.

It might be tempting to think 'Ah yes, that happened to me too. I know exactly how you feel.' And believe that you may have experienced the same feelings as the person you are trying to help. This is called *identification* and is not empathy. In fact it makes empathy more difficult because your own feelings keep getting in the way of your efforts to understand the other person accurately.

I remember feeling very angry with someone who, on the day of my dad's funeral, came up to me and said 'I know how you feel, I was in a prisoner of war camp. You've got to be strong and look after your mother.' In that one phrase they showed me that although they were trying their best to help, they had got it wrong. What I wanted (but I didn't know what it was called then) was empathy – some reaching out to understand or gain insight into my feelings, thoughts and attitudes, but free of the tangle of the other person's.

Of course what may have been stopping this person from empathising with me was the fact that they were grieving for my father too. Their own feelings were getting in the way of their efforts to understand me. Not only were they grieving for my father but, by their words of 'comfort' to me, it seems likely that my father's death had reminded them of the pain they felt at the loss of their friends in the prisoner of war camp some 30 years before. Not to mention the other terrible ordeals they had to endure then.

This tangle of emotions is not limited to those who have suffered in POW camps. We all have tangles like this just waiting to get activated. This is why self-awareness is so important if we are to try and help others in a straightforward and effective way.

Congruence or genuineness

This involves the helper being open to his or her own feelings as much as possible. It means being my real self – without front or facade, without acting like an 'expert'. Carl Rogers often described it as being 'transparently real', and implicit in the core condition of genuineness is the challenge to us to be ourselves: fallible, vulnerable, imperfect, not knowing any of the answers.

This goes against some of the training we might have received in the so-called 'helping professions' which advises us to keep a professional distance, bluff it out, pretend we know what we're doing (even if we don't) and close ranks. Some of this behaviour *might* be useful when trying to help as a nurse, teacher or doctor (although I must say I'm not too sure about this), but it is definitely not part of a counselling way of helping.

Rogers described genuineness from the client's point of view:

> It has been found that personal change is facilitated when the psychotherapist is what he *is*, when in the relationship with his client he is genuine and without 'front' or facade, openly being the feelings and attitudes which are at that moment flowing *in* him.
> (Rogers, 1961: 61)

Rogers, CR (1961) *On Becoming a Person.* London: Constable.

This doesn't mean to say that the helper lets her feelings gush out in an uncontrolled torrent all of the time. It means that the helper should first of all not deny or avoid, but be aware of her feelings and then, after careful consideration, not be afraid of expressing them if appropriate.

From the helper's point of view Rogers wrote:

> I have come to recognise that being trustworthy does not demand that I be rigidly consistent but that I be dependably real. The term 'congruent' is one that I have used to describe the way I would like to be. By this I mean that whatever feeling or attitude I am experiencing would be matched by my awareness of that attitude. When this is true, then I am a unified or integrated person in that moment, and hence I can be whatever I deeply am.
> (Rogers, 1961: 50)

This means that the whole person of the helper is brought to the activity of helping: feelings, thoughts, attitudes, 'warts and all'. We don't just bring a professional expertise, but all of our humanness. Indeed our expertise *is* our humanness, so if we leave that behind, we will not be effective helpers.

Returning to the example of the person at my father's funeral: they could also have been congruent, that is to say, aware of their own feelings of grief and the links back to their POW experiences and perhaps said: 'Your father's death has taken me right back to the terrible days in the prisoner of war camp during the Second World War. I lost so many friends there. I'm doubly upset because I was close to your father and now I'm reminded of all those years ago.'

Then I could have seen this person as real, as a person with their own grieving to resolve. They might then have said something like: 'I can see how upset you are too, it must be terrible for you today, I know how close you were to your dad.' This last sentence is empathic and would have been much easier for me to hear after the congruent statement above. Genuineness, then, is any expression of the helper's capacity to be in touch with his or her feelings, thoughts or even bodily sensations as s/he seeks to understand the client's world of experience.

Unconditional positive regard (UPR)

This condition is also called non-judgemental warmth or acceptance. It means that we must be able to totally accept the person we are trying to help as a worthwhile human being. The helper must be able to believe that each person is worthy, is OK deep down, or 'all right' underneath it all. Seeing someone as worthy does not mean that you have to approve of their behaviour. It simply means that you see them as a human being of equal value.

I rather like the term 'non-judgemental warmth', since it puts the rather neutral non-judgemental bit next to the very positive 'warmth'. It also helps us break down this core condition into two component elements: firstly, the absence, or suspension of judgement, and secondly, the positive feeling of warmth, and the communication of this warmth to the person you are helping. Many people come for counselling-style helping because they have been damaged by other people's harsh, heavy-handed, unreasonable or unnecessary judgement. It's important that they don't get more of the same from those trying to help mend the hurts.

In 1961 Carl Rogers wrote:

> Can I free him (the client) from the threat of external evaluation? In almost every phase of our lives – at home, at school, at work – we find ourselves under the rewards and punishments of external judgments. 'That's good'; 'That's naughty'; 'That's worth an A'; 'That's a failure'; 'That's good counseling'; 'That's poor counseling'. Such judgements are a part of our lives from infancy to old age.
> (Rogers, 1961: 54)

Rogers, CR (1961) *On Becoming a Person.* London: Constable.

You may wonder whether an honest evaluation of another person might not be quite helpful under some circumstances, and I guess you would be right. Helping styles and roles other than a counselling way of helping could legitimately use judgements in their repertoire of skills. Teachers for example will have to make judgements about a student's work or level of achievement. However, even in this setting, it is important to be careful and respectful in the manner in which the judgement is delivered. In Chapter 3 I looked at the role of feedback in personal development and, of course, feedback is a sort of judgement. The difference is that it is not a judgement about the person and their worth, but feedback about their behaviour.

The two core conditions of congruence and UPR do leave us with a dilemma though. There are potential areas of conflict between being non-judgemental and warm whilst simultaneously being genuine. In simple terms the dilemma is this:

What would happen if you were supposed to be helping someone whom you didn't like because, for example, you knew that they were a convicted rapist?

- Should you be genuine (and judgemental) and say that you don't like them?

Or,

- Should you be non-judgemental and be (falsely) warm and accepting towards them?

This sort of dilemma is often highlighted by introductory courses. It's worthwhile taking a moment to consider how you might resolve this apparent conflict.

Often our worries about not being able to be warm stem from our values or deeply held views. This issue overlaps with personal development, prejudice and the work on personal values we looked at in Chapters 3 and 4. (You might like to remind yourself of the issues we covered.) This illustrates how central self-awareness and personal development are to learning about counselling and how to do it. You may be tempted to think that you could 'hide' your judgemental attitudes from the person you are working with. There will be opportunities during your course to do some active listening practice; it might be useful to ask your partner if they think they could see through any pretence.

Six conditions: Necessary and sufficient

When Carl Rogers described the six therapeutic conditions in 1957, he also said that they were both necessary and sufficient before helpful change was possible. It is easy to forget that there are *six* conditions. It is vital that you, the helper, make *psychological contact* (condition 1) with the person you are trying to help.

By necessary he meant that helpful change will only happen if all six conditions are present. If one is missing, change will either not happen or if it does happen, it may not be helpful change. As we

---

Activity

Do you think you would be fooled? No matter how desperate for help someone is, they usually still have their 'bullshit detector' switched on. Here are some other possibilities for you to consider. In each case the question is how do you experience the conflict between genuineness and non-judgemental warmth – is it more important to be non-judgemental, more important to be genuine or is there a way to be both at the same time? What would you do if:

- *you were asked to help a young woman who had a problem pregnancy and was considering a termination?*
- *you were sexually attracted to the person you were trying to help?*
- *the person you are helping tells you that they were violent to their children when they were young?*
- *the person you are trying to help says that they have thought of killing themselves?*

Rogers, CR (1957) The necessary and sufficient conditions for therapeutic personality change. *J. Consulting Psychology, 21*(2), 95-103. Reprinted in H Kirschenbaum & VL Henderson (eds) (1990) *The Carl Rogers Reader* (pp. 219-35). London: Constable.

Getting to know the core conditions
A self-awareness exercise

Think of each core condition in turn – empathy, congruence and unconditional positive regard. For each condition, think of a person that embodies that core condition. Someone who is the living, breathing personification of that core condition for you. (This should be a real person – someone you know.) Think of a time when you were with this person, perhaps recently, when you 'received' the particular core condition from them.

1. Who is the person – what relationship do you have with them? Write down a brief description of them.

2. What are the qualities of empathy, congruence, and UPR that this person conveys?

3. How does it feel to be on the receiving end of each core condition?

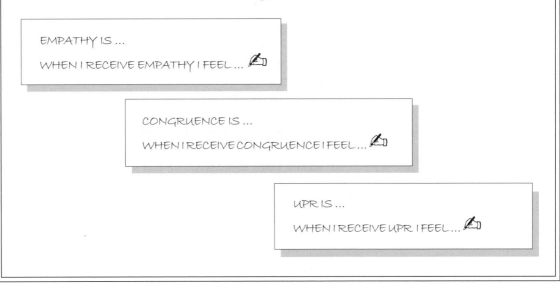

EMPATHY IS …

WHEN I RECEIVE EMPATHY I FEEL …

CONGRUENCE IS …

WHEN I RECEIVE CONGRUENCE I FEEL …

UPR IS …

WHEN I RECEIVE UPR I FEEL …

noted in Chapter 3 there are many types of change, and some of the therapeutic conditions may be present to a greater or lesser degree, but only when all six are present will the change be helpful. It could be said, for example, that brainwashing is change – but we would not consider brainwashing to be 'helpful' change. This means that providing a helping relationship can be quite difficult since we have to provide all conditions, and the three therapist-provided conditions have to be *received* by the person we are trying to help.

By sufficient Rogers meant that if all the conditions are present, then helpful change will take place regardless of any other conditions being met, or factors present – nothing else is necessary. So if the conditions are provided by accident or in an unplanned manner, helpful change would still take place. Have you ever felt that someone was a 'natural' listener or helper? Someone that was sought out by others to share their troubles with? Such people can probably provide the core conditions quite instinctively, without thinking about it or being trained as a person-centred helper. The exercise on page 99 asks you to identify people who can provide these core conditions singly. Occasionally we meet someone who can provide all three instinctively and we experience them as naturally respectful and understanding, deeply caring and very helpful.

Received and understood?

Being the most empathic, accepting and genuine person in the world is of absolutely no use if the person you are trying to help does not perceive these qualities in you. Just as important as you having or 'being' these qualities is the *transmitting* of them and the *receiving* of them by the client.

There are tests used in research to measure how empathic, non-judgemental, warm and congruent a counsellor is being, but it is really not advisable to use them in basic helping settings. The client's view of the counsellor and what they do is crucial to successful helping. The issue of the client's view of the counsellor has most relevance to us because we really should take note of how others receive our helping efforts. In training, you will probably get feedback. If you *intend* to be empathic and warm, but are *experienced* as being well-meaning, but stiff and impersonal, then you should listen to the feedback and try to change the way you express your helping.

The work of Gerard Egan

The next step in learning about basic helping is to see how therapeutic conditions translate into a set of identifiable skills. It isn't enough to just think to yourself 'I'm being empathic, warm and genuine' or chant the words like a mantra. The conditions have to be *experienced by the client* before they are of any use.

Egan, G (1993) *The Skilled Helper: A problem management approach to helping* (5th ed). Pacific Grove, CA: Brooks Cole.

Gerard Egan published the first edition of his popular book *The Skilled Helper* in 1975. He added to the ideas of Carl Rogers by taking the work of other psychologists and constructing a theory of helping based on the skills required at different stages in the helpful change process. (Along with others, Egan thinks that the conditions may be necessary, but are not sufficient – they need some extra elements added to them before helping can be properly effective.)

Many counsellors – those who call themselves 'person-centred' – think that Rogers' ideas were fine as they stood and didn't need anything adding to them – and this is my view too. In short, we think that the core conditions really are necessary and *sufficient*.

However, for the purposes of learning about basic helping in a counselling style, Egan's model of helping is a very handy way of getting across the idea that although certain skills are necessary, it may be that other skills are also involved and that some people want to change the way they offer help in order to improve as a helper.

At this introductory level of training, you will not have enough time to practise the skills in order to become proficient. This takes a different amount of time for each of us, although counselling skills or intermediate courses take around 120 hours over a year and you may wish to continue your training by enrolling for one when you have completed this training. Most people coming to counselling training already have some of the skills necessary, so it's a case of finding out what your skills are then trying to develop a complete or more rounded repertoire of helping skills. In this book, all we can do is find out what the skills are by briefly identifying them, giving examples and maybe putting them in a context.

Gerard Egan (1993) divided the helping process into three stages and suggested that different skills were needed at each stage.

Stage I: Building the helping relationship and exploration

In this first stage, the helper is creating a warm trusting relationship with the client, enabling the client to look at or explore whatever they choose. The helper is trying to step into the other person's shoes and look at the world from the client's point of view.

Stage I skills

This first stage incorporates Rogers' core conditions of empathy, congruence and UPR. The specific skills associated with this stage are:

- Developing a trusting relationship:
  - making and maintaining contact
  - structuring
  - communicating non-judgemental warmth
  - communicating genuineness
- Active listening and communicating empathy:
  - identifying, acknowledging and reflecting thoughts, behaviours and feelings
  - paraphrasing
  - clarifying

Note
Skills development is carried forward in the next book in this series:

Sanders, P, Frankland, A & Wilkins, P (2009) *Next Steps in Counselling Practice: A students' companion for degrees, HE diplomas and vocational courses.* Ross-on-Wye: PCCS Books.

Note
This is a brutal oversimplification of Egan's model and work. The only way to get an accurate picture is to read his latest writing, but do bear in mind that he has developed his model since this version was published in 1993 – it is now in its 9th edition.

Egan, G (1993) *The Skilled Helper: A problem management approach to helping* (5th ed). Pacific Grove, CA: Brooks Cole.

Note
We will look at these Stage I skills in more detail later in this chapter, where I will explain each skill and give examples.

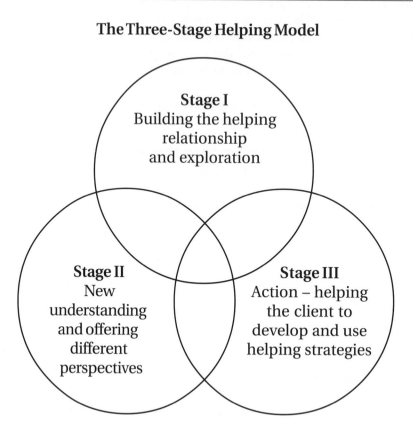

The Three-Stage Helping Model

Stage I
Building the helping
relationship
and exploration

Stage II
New
understanding
and offering
different
perspectives

Stage III
Action – helping
the client to
develop and use
helping strategies

This three-stage helping skills model is derived from the work of Gerard Egan – *The Skilled Helper* (1982). Later editions of the book describe slightly different versions of the same model, using different terms.

The 1993 edition describes the stages as:
Stage I: Helping clients identify and clarify problem situations
Stage II: Helping clients create a better future
Stage III: Getting there – helping clients implement their goals
The Skilled Helper (pp. ix-xiii). Pacific Grove, CA: Brookes/Cole.

Stage II skills
In this stage the client is helped to see themselves and their life from new perspectives, taking into consideration alternative information and other viewpoints. This is done using all of Stage I skills, plus:
- Linking and integrating individual issues and problems into themes:
  - showing deeper understanding and empathy
  - helping the client focus on specific issues

- Challenging the client's views:
  - offering new perspectives
  - sharing the helper's experiences and feelings
  - helping the client move on
- Goal-setting:
  - helping the client identify what they want to achieve

Stage III skills

Now the helper is trying to look, with the client, at possible ways of acting in the situation to help resolve the problem. Possible outcomes will be considered and risks assessed. The client will then be helped to evaluate the effectiveness of their new behaviour. This is achieved using all of Stage I and II skills, plus:

- Helping the client move on to considering action
- Developing and choosing action plans:
  - brainstorming
  - creative thinking
  - problem-solving
  - decision-making
  - planning
- Evaluating consequences of actions:
  - recording events, e.g. diary-keeping
  - evaluation
  - reviewing plans

As the client progresses through the stages proposed by Egan, the emphasis shifts from the client's point of view and their world to a more objective perspective and finally action in and on the client's world to cause change. This may seem far removed from Rogers' ideas of the innate self-healing process. Egan expresses his understanding of the client's ability to direct their own helping process by having the helper as a co-worker, making suggestions or offering ways of tackling issues which the client can use or not as *they* choose.

Person-centred counsellors let the client discover their own new perspectives and make their own action plans by helping them activate their own self-healing process. The counsellor does this by providing the core conditions almost exclusively through Stage I skills.

Basic helping

This extensive range of skills that are used in counselling takes a long time to properly develop, as we shall see in Chapter 13. In this book we can do only a little more than list the skills.

In Chapter 1, I used the phrases 'basic helping' and 'helping in a counselling way' to describe the basic counselling-style helping

Note
In Chapter 13 I look at continuing training and note that professional level training takes years.

that uses a counselling approach, but not a full range of properly developed counselling skills. Basic helping does not use the professional or ethical framework that counsellors use either, but those using this basic helping in a counselling way will have at least considered the positive effects of, for example, the boundaries of helping relationships (see Chapter 1).

Basic skills and attitudes for basic helping

There are some skills fundamental to the basic helping process that you might like to practise as part of your own helping. These are the Stage I skills listed above. You will probably spend an hour or two on your introductory course finding out how difficult it actually is, even though the skills themselves sound quite simple. The ingredients for skills training are repeated practice, evaluation and feedback (we look at feedback in a few places in this book). If your course doesn't give any, or sufficient, time to practise your helping skills you might want to set up a situation in which you can get these ingredients. You may, for example, get together with colleagues from your course, or try it out with friends in your own time. You will need at least an hour – I would recommend two.

The most difficult ingredient to get right in such informal 'training' arrangements is feedback. In Chapter 3, I looked at feedback in a little more detail in the context of personal development.

In a skills training setting it is just as important to be accurate in your observations and honest in your feedback. Since the core conditions have to be communicated to the client, it is the client or, as is sometimes the case in skills training, the person in the client role, whose feedback is most valuable. It is common practice to have a third person acting as an observer who can give the counsellor/helper feedback from a more objective position seeing as they were not on the receiving end of the skills.

Feedback in training is essential, then. It is most useful if it comes from two sources: firstly, the client or person being helped or listened to, and secondly, a 'neutral' observer. You might want to be reassured that you are looking for the right things when you observe and give feedback. In which case it will help to ask your tutor for assistance.

Developing Stage I skills

Developing a trusting relationship

1. Structuring

Every relationship happens in a series of episodes, that is, the times the people concerned actually meet and make contact (this could, of course, be on the phone or by letter, but we will mainly concern ourselves with face-to-face meetings in this book). A relationship

Note: Skills or attitudes – a reminder
Just because we are looking at these qualities as skills, doesn't mean that you should not continue to strive to develop them as attitudes. If you find yourself drawn to a person-centred approach in your helping, you will be trying to integrate these qualities into your self. If you are drawn to a cognitive/behavioural approach in your helping you will be trying to integrate these skills into your repertoire.

begins with the first meeting or episode and the first 'task' in the first episode is to work out what kind or type of relationship it is going to be. This happens pretty quickly and will depend upon the setting, the roles that the people are in, their expectations and the first things that are said. It is called 'structuring':

College classroom

'Hello, my name is Pete Sanders and I'll be teaching you GCSE maths this year.'

Telephone

'Hello, Samaritans, can I help?'

Student services in college

'Hello, my name is Pete, I'm a counsellor here. You must be Sandra. I don't know why you've come to the counselling service, but I'll do my best to help in whatever way I can. Would you like to tell me what's concerning you?'

Telephone

'Hello, my name is Pete and I'm calling from Tele-Marketing Services. We are doing a short survey on car insurance, do you have five minutes to take part?'

Street

'Excuse me, could you tell me how to get to the station?'

Bank

'Don't make a noise or raise the alarm. This is a gun under my coat. Now give me the money! MOVE!'

Some of these are helping relationships and some are not. We can tell because of the setting, the roles, the expectations of the situation or by what is said and how it is said. In everyday life this happens without us having to pay special attention to it. However, in basic helping or counselling, it is important that the structuring is appropriate. The way we behave and speak has to convey the messages, 'I am here to help', 'I am paying special attention to what you say and do', 'This is a helping relationship'.

Sanders, P (2007) *Using Counselling Skills on the Telephone and in Computer-Mediated Communication* (3rd ed). Ross-on-Wye: PCCS Books

2. Making and maintaining contact

Structuring is, of course, one of the essential components of making contact. It signals availability and reaches out to the other person. Signalling availability is important because at the start of each episode of human communication, we need to quickly establish – amongst other things – what is likely to be achieved and how long

Activity
How would you make contact in a way
that indicates you are offering help?
After you've made contact in a helping
relationship, the next task is to maintain
that contact. This is done by doing certain
things (non-verbal communication) and
saying certain things or making noises (you
don't have to actually say words). What
are the methods of maintaining contact
that you use?

Here is another flip chart from our imaginary
group showing some possible answers. Do
you have any to add?

MAINTAINING CONTACT

1. VERBAL METHODS

'YES' 'I SEE' 'PLEASE GO ON'

'RIGHT' 'UH-HUH' 'MMMM'

✍ ....

2. NON-VERBAL METHODS

LOOKING AT THE PERSON

SMILING   NODDING

MAKING EYE CONTACT

LEANING FORWARD IN
YOUR CHAIR

✍ ....

---

it will last. Seeing an acquaintance in the street, waving and calling out 'Hi, how's things?' is not usually an invitation to an in-depth discussion. We expect a simple, 'Fine, thanks, terrible weather!' walk-by greeting. However, a gesture, look and tone of voice can mean the same words are the prelude to a chat-up line. We establish 'contact' with the other person and know pretty soon what the options are likely to be. Buying vegetables, passing the time of day or being asked out to dinner.

Once we have established the purpose and likely end-point of the encounter we have to say and do things to keep us in contact with the other person, and these come quite naturally to most of us. In a helping relationship, however, we want to communicate warmth, genuineness and empathy even in the way we say 'I see' or 'Uh-huh' and 'Aha'. Whether we are successful can only be determined by receiving feedback. In social situations we usually try to read the behaviour of the other people to ascertain whether we have a shared understanding of the nature of the episode. In the more formal situations of both learning about helping and being in a helping relationship, it is good practice to ask for feedback. Saying the obvious is fine, such as, 'What is it you want from this session?' and at the end of the session, 'How did you find the session, was it helpful?' and, 'Is there anything I could have done to be more helpful?'

It is best to actively maintain helpful contact rather than assume things are going OK.

3. Communicating non-judgemental warmth
4. Communicating genuineness
Both verbal and non-verbal methods of communication figure strongly in this section too. Communicating non-judgemental warmth and genuineness is as much about *what you do* as *what and how you say* something. Most of us that are attracted to a counselling way of helping tend to be less judgemental than average, but it can still be a difficult task. It's obvious that if you're striving to be non-judgemental in a counselling way, you don't say: 'Don't you know that having an abortion is killing another human being and is only done by bad, evil people?'

However, many of us do have strong feelings about abortion and may well feel something similar. The question is how do you accept someone who is behaving in what you feel is an unacceptable way? It is necessary firstly to separate the person and their intrinsic worth as a human being from their behaviour, which may be unacceptable. Then secondly, to be aware of your own values and prejudices and be willing to suspend them and withhold judgement for the time being as the person you are helping strives to change. Of course they may not change in a way in which you think is sensible. Skills specific to being accepting are:

Be specific, avoid generalising:
>   *Say*: 'It sounds as though it was really painful for you when your father died.'
>   *Don't say*: 'Everyone feels bad when someone close to them dies, it's only natural.'

Don't debate things – you're not having a discussion, you're trying to help:
>   *Say*: 'So you think it would be best if you went to the clinic for advice on contraception.'
>   *Don't say*: 'I wouldn't go to the clinic, the best place to go is your GP, they know your medical history.'

Don't push the person you are trying to help too far or too fast – accept their pace:
>   *Say*: 'It seems as though you don't want to go any further with this at the moment.'
>   *Don't say*: 'You've spent a long time talking about this topic, don't you think it is time you moved on to what's really upsetting you.'

Don't make guesses or interpretations – you're no expert on the client's troubles:
>   *Say*: 'So you think that the time your boss overlooked you for promotion was the start of this low patch.'
>   *Don't say*: 'Well, you say your boss is responsible, but it sounds as though it's more likely to be the fact that your mother died last year.'

Each one of the 'Don't say' responses above is non-accepting or judgemental in some way. For example: 'Everyone feels bad when someone close to them dies, it's only natural.'

This sounds caring and possibly helpful, but the hidden judgemental message is something like: 'Your hurt isn't specially bad because this sort of thing happens to everybody.' Just as bad is another possible meaning: 'Since *everyone* feels bad at a time like this, if you don't feel bad there must be something wrong with you.'

Activity
It might be useful to try to identify the 'hidden judgements' behind the other responses and you may know of some other ways of being judgemental which helpers might wish to avoid.

ACTIVE LISTENING — WHAT
WE PAY ATTENTION TO IN THE
PERSON WE ARE HELPING

VOICE QUALITY — SOFT, HARD,
CONFIDENT, TIMID, STRONG,
WEAK, ETC

BREATHING — DEEP, SHALLOW,
SOBBING, SNATCHED, RELAXED,
ETC

FACIAL EXPRESSION — RELAXED,
TENSE, AFRAID, HAPPY, DISGUST,
ETC

WHETHER THEY ARE TALKING
OR SILENT

THE 'STORY' THEY ARE TELLING

✍............. ....

Activity
On the flip chart above, our imaginary group have come up with some suggestions to start off. How do their ideas compare with your own? The list is not complete by any means.

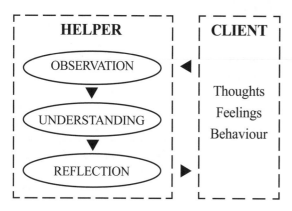

Active listening and communicating empathy
1. Identifying, acknowledging and reflecting thoughts, behaviours and feelings

Active listening is one of the key ingredients in any helping relationship. It is impossible to be helpful if you are not actively listening. Active listening means that you are paying full attention to what the other person is saying. This simple and obvious point needs emphasising, since in most everyday conversations we are only paying partial attention for a part of the time. That's because in day-to-day settings we are trying to manage episodes of everyday human communication which might have many potential functions (remember the earlier section on structuring). When actively listening to someone we are trying to help, we have to attend to all of the signals given off by the person – not only the words, but using your sight to pick up the non-verbal behaviours and your ears to pick up the non-verbal sounds. It should really be called 'active attention' because we are trying to actively pay the most detailed and special attention to the other person using all our senses.

The purpose of active listening, then, is to pay attention to, and try to understand, the thoughts, feelings and behaviour of the other person. How do we do this? If you were the helper, what would you be paying attention to in the speech and behaviour of the other person?

There are three stages to the skill of active listening. In the diagram in the margin the arrows indicate the flow of information. After paying close attention to the other person, comes understanding the meaning of what you are seeing and hearing. In order to do this you need to have achieved some degree of self-awareness. We find it easier to understand another person if we:

- suspend our judgement of the other person
- put our own feelings and experiences to one side while we are trying to understand theirs
- try to put ourselves in their shoes and see the world from their point of view

The final test to see if we do really understand the world of meanings of the other person in all its subtlety, is to check with them. We do this by *reflection, paraphrasing* and *clarifying*. Reflection is the basic skill of empathic understanding and at its most simple involves reflecting the content of the other person's utterances back to them. The purpose is to give the message: 'I am listening carefully to what you're saying and I am trying to understand. I will demonstrate this to you by letting you know that I heard what you just said. Did I get it right?'

The ability to give good reflections without sounding like a parrot is a matter of practice until the activity becomes natural to *you*.

2. Paraphrasing
3. Clarifying

Paraphrasing and clarifying come hot on the heels of reflection and constitute the three basic skills of the therapeutic relationship condition of empathy. When used together they become a powerful method of communicating your care and attention for the person you are trying to help.

Paraphrasing is summarising in a few words what the speaker is saying. Depending upon the circumstances, it may be best to use the client's own words or use your own words. It is a matter of judgement to know how best to paraphrase depending upon the situation. In order to paraphrase effectively we need a reasonable vocabulary, especially when it comes to putting feelings into words. For this reason, I have included the 'feelings vocabulary' activity on the next page.

Clarifying is not quite as obvious as it sounds. It doesn't mean that you clarify the client's muddled thinking, or can see more sense in the client's world than they can. Both of these are rather arrogant positions to be in and would probably be experienced by them as very unaccepting and superior. Rather, it means seeking clarification of your own understanding of the client's world. This can have a number of helpful effects:
- The client will feel that you're trying really hard to understand.
- You will get a better, more accurate understanding of the client's world.
- The client may come to understand themselves better as a consequence of having to explain something in more detail, or in a different way to you.
- Sometimes when a client is in a muddle or fog, you may pick this up by feeling muddled yourself. If you ask for clarification *for yourself*, it can help your client clarify their own thoughts and feelings.

That completes the expanded list of Stage I skills and, as I suggested earlier, it is not appropriate to elaborate the skills associated with Stages II and III any further. Given the number of hours on an Introduction to Counselling Course, there will be hardly any time to practise skills to a level of competence required for a qualification. Practice of this sort is given priority on certificate, intermediate

Developing a 'feelings vocabulary'

Because some of us may not be used to being very expressive where feelings are concerned, we may not have a very large vocabulary of words which we use to describe feelings. It can be very useful to build up the vocabulary of feeling words we use. This is a brainstorming activity for small groups, but you can start it off yourself and then ask your friends to make contributions. Simply think of all the feeling words you know and write them down. You may find that some of the words are alternatives, or indicating a subtle difference in feeling. You could try to group them together under headings if you find it helpful. Then, start using them more often to help you get some 'colour' and richness into your descriptions of feelings.

Angry	**Sad**	**Happy**	**Hurt**	**Afraid**
annoyed	unhappy	elated	upset	scared
enraged	gloomy	cheery	broken	hesitant
cross	choked up	glad	suffering	insecure
sulky	sullen	festive	crushed	panicky
irate	flat	merry	tortured	terrified
belligerent	mournful	jubilant	heartbroken	shaky
✍	✍	✍	✍	✍ ....

Words about intimacy	**Words about interest**	**Other feeling words**
loving	curious	envious
tender	fascinated	jealous
close	inquisitive	bored
sexual	attentive	bold
in-tune	enthusiastic	proud
seductive	absorbed	excited
✍	✍	✍ ....

You may find it useful to look at your feelings vocabulary when observing skills practice.

and counselling skills courses. You may, however, wish to use what course time you do get profitably, in which case the following suggestions may be useful if followed with your tutor's more detailed instructions.

Practising and integrating Stage I skills

It's one thing separating out the Stage I counselling skills for the purposes of illustrating each one; it's quite another to put them back together into a natural piece of real-life helping. I have been at pains to point out that an introduction to counselling course does not prepare or qualify anyone to do any counselling or use counselling skills other than to inform the natural basic helping we all do as colleagues, friends and relatives.

If you do want to practise these helping skills with a colleague, friend or course participant, start off by taking one skill at a time. When you have practised one at a time, you may like to try putting them together in twos and threes. It may help to try them in the order found in this chapter, since this is roughly the order in which the skills are found in an actual relationship.

Never forget that, when practising skills in this way, your prime aim is to learn something. Don't get carried away and begin believing that it is a real helping session. At the same time as realising that this is for the benefit of your learning, you must make sure that you and your friend feel safe enough to talk and listen freely. Practise your structuring to get the ball rolling, introduce yourself and be real, i.e. say 'Hi Paul, thanks for helping me by volunteering to be my client. We're here to practise my listening skills and we've got about ten minutes together. If there's something you'd like to talk about that would be appropriate for this short time, I'll do my best to listen to whatever you have to say.'

It's also essential to make sure you set some ground rules before you start:

- Are you going to make up a story and play the part of someone else or are you going to be yourselves, talking about your own real issues?
- If you are going to talk about real issues, is the practice session confidential?
- Practice is no good without feedback – how are you going to get it?
- It might help to list the skills on a piece of paper and then check them off at the end to indicate those that were appropriately present in the practice session.

Note

Getting your listening skills up to a reasonable standard takes time. For most of us, our conversational style just isn't 'right' for helping. We first have to unlearn certain behaviours – to shut up for long enough to be able to listen. Then we have to learn to make helpful responses. This takes time.

If you are serious about wanting to be a good helper or counsellor, you will have to commit yourself to months if not years of practice and listening to feedback from others. In fact, it's debatable that this process ever stops. However experienced most of us are as counsellors, we are always fine-tuning, learning and developing our skills.

Note

I cannot stress this enough. It is very easy to get carried away. Remember that practice is for learning, it is not real life. It is just as important that your friend or colleague remembers this too – they might also get carried away and try to use the practice session to sort out a real life problem. Some courses recommend this, as long as you strictly stay to small but troublesome day-to-day decisions. Making decisions about important life events, or unearthing past difficulties are not suitable for introductory courses.

I do not recommend 'practising' counselling skills on unsuspecting friends and relatives. Never *use* others as unconsenting guinea pigs. It is neither ethical nor respectful, so is automatically an unacceptable and invalid way of improving your skills. You are likely to find, however, that quite naturally your interpersonal behaviour will change, probably without you realising it. Others may notice and comment. If they do, it might be worth asking them what they think the changes are and whether they think it is an improvement. All feedback is useful!

Important reminder

Finally, remember that the elements of empathy, genuineness and respect, whilst we can break them down into smaller *micro skills,* they are not just techniques. They are qualities, attitudes to being with and helping people. They are the fundamentals of good human helping relationships not a series of disembodied techniques, so remember that, following the chapter on the importance of self-development, it is imperative that we integrate these skills into our very selves. If your approach to basic helping is based on good human relationships, then you will have to integrate these qualities into your whole person. This will mean changing the way you are, not just the way you do things.

'So where might we find information about the human condition which appealed to people's sense of what it is to be human rather than the psychology and psychiatry of diagnosis, drug trials and involuntary treatment? How can we find out about the lived experience of service users, what they want and what they don't? … A further challenge for the pseudo-scientific community of psychiatry would be to embrace the common place wisdom of philosophy, literature and poetry.'

Guy Holmes (2001) in C Newnes, G Holmes & C Dunn (eds) *This is Madness Too*. Ross-on-Wye: PCCS Books, p. 4.

'Science is essentially half an education. Not only does it produce wooden dancers, it puts little to no demands on the individual to know themselves or to develop social skills … or to have any respect for the world of feelings other than to reduce them to biological or cognitive underpinnings.'

Peter Chadwick (2001) *Personality as Art: Artistic approaches in psychology.* Ross-on-Wye: PCCS Books, p. 162.

'Be aware of wonder. Live a balanced life – learn some and think some and draw and paint and sing and dance and play and work every day some.'

Robert Fulghum

what to do when you reach your limits

Referrals and recommendations

When we are helping others in a counselling way, these helping relationships can begin and end in different ways. One particular beginning and ending event in helping that happens – whether you are a professional counsellor, using counselling skills or helping in a counselling way – is called referral. This is when one agency, professional or helper sends a client or patient to another agency, professional or helper for help, treatment or service.

Some trainers in counselling will be wondering why there is a chapter on referrals in a book aimed at basic introductory courses. The answer is that such handing on of people seeking help doesn't only happen in professional settings. In non-professional settings I have come to call these 'handings-on' *recommendations* rather than referrals in order to distinguish between professional links between helpers (such as a GP referring you to a specialist at the local hospital) and non-professional ones. Since I wrote the first edition of this book an increasing amount of helping is done through voluntary agencies, or as they are likely to be known nowadays, 'third-sector organisations', and these voluntary agencies are staffed with well-trained volunteers. Many such third-sector organisations are used by statutory agencies for expert advice and help. For example, Childline is acknowledged as a leading agency in work with child abuse. As a consequence, professional referrals increasingly happen in voluntary settings, when one agency will pass on a client to another agency, so I will use the terms together where appropriate in this chapter.

Professional referrals are nearly always followed up and checked by the person making the referral. This wouldn't necessarily happen with a recommendation. Also, the person making the referral (e.g. your GP) will get a report back from the person she has referred you to (the hospital specialist will send notes back to your GP).

- You don't have to be a professional counsellor in order for another helper or agency to *recommend* a client to you for helping. And in this circumstance, you will probably not be expected to make any report back on the client.
- Similarly you may be trying to help a friend or a colleague at work with a problem and think that it might be better if someone

else helps them rather than you. You would *recommend* that they go to their GP or Social Services for example.

It doesn't matter whether you are a professional or a volunteer, qualified or unqualified, making and receiving recommendations should be done with the utmost care and consideration for the person you are helping.

Receiving a referral or recommendation is when:
- someone is recommended to see you for helping/counselling by the helper/counsellor they are currently seeing
- a person comes to see you after deciding themselves that you are the helper/counsellor that they want to see (this is called *self-referral*)

Making a referral or recommendation is when:
- you feel that the person you are helping/counselling would be better helped by another helper/counsellor
- your client feels that they want help/counselling from someone other than you

There are many reasons why we have to pass people on from one helper to another and all of the reasons are to do with *limits* of one sort or another. Instead of a short activity in the margin, the next few pages are an extended activity where I ask you to think more actively about your own responses as we go along. Here is a list of some of the limits involved (there may be some of your own that I haven't thought of):

Extended Activity
When you see this symbol in the margin it is an invitation to

✍ MAKE A NOTE OF YOUR OWN, ADDITIONAL IDEAS

- Limits of the situation:
  - legal limits
  - service/agency limits
  - of counselling itself
  - ✍ … time/timetable limits
- My personal limits:
  - confidence limits
  - ✍ … emotional limits
- The limits of my competence:
  - no expertise in specialist area
  - skills limits
  - ✍ … qualification limits
- The limits of the person I am helping/counselling:
  - lack of confidence in me
  - doesn't like me
  - wanting a different style of helping
  - wanting a different type of helper, e.g. male, female, gay,
  - ✍ … black, white, etc.

It's possible in our enthusiasm for helping people, that we try to help everyone, in every situation, all of the time, regardless of their problem. This way of working is always dangerous. It's obvious that no one can do this, but it's easy to get seduced into thinking that we can.

- sometimes it happens *because the people we are trying to help expect it of us*
- sometimes it happens *because we expect it of ourselves*
- sometimes it happens *because we haven't got enough experience to understand the limits of the situation*
- sometimes it happens *because our boss tells us that we must do it – or at least suggests that it's the done thing if you want to get on*

It's dangerous to work beyond our limits because:

- beyond our limits we cannot be of any help, we will probably *do damage to the person we are trying to help*
- beyond our limits we will put stress on ourselves and possibly *do damage to ourselves*
- beyond our limits we will be seen as acting irresponsibly and *do damage to the reputation of helping or counselling or the agency we work for*

In order to avoid working beyond our limits we need to understand where those limits are. It will be a little early in your learning about counselling for most of you reading this book to think too deeply about what your limits might be, but it's important to know that as helpers of any kind we must know our limits and stay within them. We will look at each of these sets of limits in a little more detail, but before we do it's important to remember that with referrals and recommendations, as with everything else in a counselling way of helping:

- each situation is different
  - each client unique
    - each referral or recommendation requires special consideration leading to its *own* solution

We will tackle the problem of understanding limits by asking some questions. By now you will realise that the questions we ask in training in counselling do not always have fixed right or wrong answers. They're much more interesting than that – there's room for opinion, discussion and disagreement. These questions are no exception, but if you already work in an agency, or do a job such as teaching or nursing where there will be well-established protocols which determine when and how you make referrals or recommendations, you must always follow those protocols. These

Note: Always check the law

The Government Equality Office guide *Equality Act 2010: What do I need to know?* provides the following advice and vignette. I include it here to illustrate how voluntary agencies and counsellors need to keep abreast of the law. It can be viewed at <http://www.equalities.gov.uk/pdf/14314%20EDF%20Gender%20Quick%20start%2011th.pdf> 🖎 ...

'In general, if you are an organisation that provides separate or single-sex services for women and men, or you provide your services differently to women and men, you should treat transsexual people according to the gender role in which they present.

Service providers are allowed to encourage transsexual people to use their facilities or services if they think transsexual people have been disadvantaged in the past because of discrimination, or if they have a low rate of participation.'

A women's sexual abuse crisis centre receives a request for support from Alice, a transsexual woman. The centre usually provides group support sessions, but Alice is still in the early stages of gender reassignment and the centre is concerned that other female service users might feel that her presence 🖎 ... affects the benefit of the group sessions for them. The centre decides to offer one-to-one support to Alice at home. This different treatment is likely to be lawful because it enables the crisis centre to fulfil its legitimate objective of providing all service users with a safe 🖎 ... and supportive counselling environment in a fair and reasonable way.

activities and discussions are for exploration and learning. There *are* right and wrong ways to behave in most professional and third-sector helping settings.

Understanding the limits of the situation

- Are there any legal requirements which mean that I cannot help this person?

  Examples: it may be illegal to offer certain kinds of help to children – e.g. issue contraceptives or advice about family planning. It is currently illegal to help someone to commit suicide.

- Does my agency have a policy which prevents me from helping this person?

  Examples: An alcohol counselling service may not help someone unless they stay 'dry'. A women's counselling centre may not help male clients or people who have undergone a gender reassignment operation from male to female (see note in margin). *In some settings (teaching or residential social work), it may be inappropriate for the helper to be alone with the person needing help.*

- Counselling cannot help everyone in every situation. Am I trying to use a counselling way of helping in a situation in which it cannot be effective?

  Example: Counselling is ineffective in solving 'concrete' problems like being homeless or having no money because you're unemployed or being denied a service because you're disabled or being refused admission because you're black. (Counselling can help to make people feel stronger, less downtrodden and more worthwhile as a person, but can't get you a house, a job or human rights.)

- Do I have enough time to help this person effectively?

  Examples: Someone may want help when it's inconvenient – during your lunch hour or five minutes before you're due to go off duty or when all appointments for the week are filled. What would you do in these situations?

- Do I have the right physical resources to offer a safe helping environment?

  Examples: Sometimes there isn't an appropriate space available for helping of a confidential or private nature. 'Safe' also means safe for the helper, so on other occasions agency policy or common sense may mean that you would not work on your own in a building with a client.

What counselling is not for

'When someone decides to attend counselling sessions, they are, by definition, distressed. It is, therefore, particularly important that the client doesn't have either their time wasted or their distress increased by attending something that we might reasonably predict would be of no help.

It is difficult to honestly predict whether counselling will definitely help in a particular circumstance. Nevertheless there are times when counselling is clearly not the first or only appropriate intervention. It is doubly difficult to appear to turn someone away when they arrive because sometimes:

- part of their distress might be that they have difficulty feeling understood and valued
- they may lack self-confidence and a rejection would damage it even more
- they have been to other types of helper and they think that counselling is their last hope
- they are so desperate they might consider suicide

However difficult it might be, we have to be completely honest with clients if we think counselling is not going to help. It would be wrong to let them find out after a number of sessions, after which they might feel that they are to blame for not trying hard enough. The use of counselling should be questioned if it is likely that their symptoms of distress are caused by:

- poor housing or homelessness
- poverty
- lack of opportunity due to discrimination or oppression

Problems of this nature are best addressed by social action. The counsellor as a citizen shares responsibility with all other members of society to remove these blocks to peoples' physical and psychological wellbeing.

It would be convenient if we could divide problems up into two neat categories: those of psychological origin (and amenable to counselling) and those of non-psychological origin (and therefore not amenable to counselling). However, there are some other causes of distress which, although they will not be *solved* by counselling, will undoubtedly be helped by counselling in that the person concerned will be able to function better with the kind of support that counselling can provide. It may also be that the client experiences repetitive patterns of self-defeating thoughts and behaviour which renders them less effective in dealing with problems which do not have a psychological origin. It might also be that a person would be better able to challenge an oppressive system if they felt personally empowered, and counselling can sometimes achieve this. Such problems include those caused by:

- poor health or a physical illness
- oppression and discrimination, including bullying
- living in an abusive relationship'

Pete Sanders (2006) Series Introduction. In *The Person-Centred Counselling Primer*. Ross-on-Wye: PCCS Books, pp. 3-4.

Understanding my personal limits

- What 'tender spots' do I have emotionally? (There is more on self-awareness in Chapter 3.)

  Examples: Some people say that they could not work with, for example, rapists or abusers. You may feel very emotionally sensitive to certain situations after recent upsets, e.g. bereavement.

- How confident in my helping abilities and skills am I?

  Examples: I might be overconfident in my ability to help someone because I've been told by my friends that I'd make a brilliant counsellor or, I might be frightened of trying to help someone in case I mess it up, even though I have the necessary skills.

Understanding the limits of my competence

- Does this person need help in a specialist area that I know little or nothing about?

  Examples: Clients might need medical attention, welfare rights information or help from a specialist counsellor, e.g. a drug rehabilitation counsellor.

- How far do my helping skills go?

  Examples: It would not be appropriate to try to help distressed or disturbed people with only a smattering of rudimentary skills. Counselling is a skilled and ethical profession requiring lengthy training. If you think your skills are not up to it – you're almost certainly right. Get ready to refer your client on.

  Your client may need what is sometimes called 'formal' help. By this I mean help provided by statutory services such as the health service, social services, etc. How will you know if your client needs this kind of help?

- What do my qualifications permit me to do?

  Examples: Obviously only doctors can make a medical diagnosis, but you'd be surprised the number of times clients expect you to either be a doctor or be able to give them medical advice, like how many tablets to take or why their baby is crying. Clients may ask for all kinds of advice from helpers. If you give advice you're not qualified to and something goes wrong, you or your agency may be liable.

Important Note: Formal help
In this context, 'formal' means the whole pattern of statutory services that are available to help individuals whose emotional distress is so pronounced that they would seriously stretch the resources of any counsellor. If you are helping in a counselling way you may be either on your own – helping in your family, community or at work – or working for a service or agency. It is important to know that your helping should not extend to very disturbed people without some kind of backup. An agency or service can provide this backup in the form of support from a more experienced person or medical advice from a doctor on hand. If you are on your own, there's no need to feel completely isolated. GPs, social workers or in an emergency the Accident and Emergency department of your local hospital are all there to help and support you if you are trying to help a relative or friend. Do not try to go it alone.

Lack of qualifications should not stop you from helping within your limits. The best sort of helping you can offer is *accurate active listening*. This will be a novel experience for many people seeking help – to be sensitively listened to is deeply comforting. It will also have the added benefit of assisting you to make the decision as to whether your client needs any more highly qualified help.

Understanding my client's limits

The next type of limit also needs some active listening from you. Your task is to understand why your client wants to be referred on, since sometimes a client themselves will identify the need for referral. The questions that follow do not require answers from your point of view. They might, however, give you some idea of the reasons that clients wish to be referred on to another helper. Make a note of any reasons you come up with yourself.

- Does my client lack confidence in my ability?

  Vulnerable people quite often need to be reassured that the person helping them is up to the job. Don't be offended if they don't have confidence in you. Accept it and help them find someone they do have confidence in. If you soldier on, you'll always be trying too hard to convince them they were wrong about you. ✍ …

- Does this client dislike me?

  There is no rule that says we must be able to be liked by all of our clients. Some people just don't hit it off from the moment they meet. Such instant dislike would inevitably get in the way of the client being able to receive help from you. ✍ …

- Does this client require a different style of helping?

  Your way of helping, whether it's your own personal style or the counselling approach that you use, may not suit the person you are helping. They might find it too laid-back or maybe too intrusive. ✍ …

- Does the person you are helping want a different type of helper?

  Working this out can be tricky. You will need to know a little about what is available locally or, of course, your client might be telling you loud and clear that they need a different type of help – will you be able to hear? ✍ …

When not to make a referral or recommendation

Whenever we consider referring a client on to another helper we must make sure we also know *when not to make a referral*. By this I mean that we should carefully consider our motives for making or receiving a referral or recommendation. What possibly questionable motives could there be?

- You don't like a client very much and you would rather refer them on because you cannot bring yourself to say so.
- A client's problem is awkward to handle, so you would rather refer them to another helper than try to work with the awkward problem.
- A client is inconvenient, so you would rather refer them on than bear the inconvenience.

Important Note: How do you know if I need formal help?

Persistent symptoms: I may have symptoms such as physical sensations, breathlessness or pains, sleep disturbances or eating problems which persist more than a week or so: these are common symptoms of grief or anxiety. Talking the problem through will help and the symptoms should ease after a short time. If the symptoms persist or get worse, get yourself backup and me some professional help – my GP is probably best.

Unusual or extreme symptoms: Hearing voices in my head, thinking that someone is controlling my thoughts, seeing things that aren't there, are all unusual symptoms which you are not equipped to deal with and must be drawn to the attention of my GP. Extreme depression (e.g. thinking that I am responsible for all evil in the world) or fear which makes it impossible for me to go out of my house also means that I should see my doctor. If you notice that I am harming myself by cutting or burning myself or if I threaten to kill myself, again, I should be encouraged to see my doctor.

What to do: Ask me if it's all right if you contact my doctor or social worker. Ask me if I want you to come along to give me moral support. You could encourage me to go and then check up to see if I kept the appointment. Don't take control and act for me without checking unless my behaviour is likely to cause harm to myself and/or others. Making this decision is not as easy as it might seem so the most important thing to do is *get support and backup for yourself.*

✍ YOU MIGHT LIKE TO WRITE DOWN ANY MORE MOTIVES THAT COULD BE BEHIND YOUR OWN REFERRALS.

Note
See Chapter 8 on *Support and Supervision in Basic Helping and Counselling* for more help with this.

As we learned in Chapter 5, one of the therapeutic relationship conditions of a counselling way of helping is *genuineness* or *congruence*. This condition requires us to be open about our feelings and reasons for doing things. In some situations it might be better to be honest and open about our feelings towards the person we are trying to help, rather than trying to avoid the feelings by off-loading the client on to someone else. This is, however, a tricky decision to make. It is not always helpful to be honest and open, nor is it always helpful to keep such feelings to yourself. Experienced counsellors would normally seek help from a colleague to resolve such problems.

Making a referral or recommendation: How to do it

Having looked at the 'whys and why-nots' of making referrals, the question is, how do you do it? Most people would think that it's just a matter of passing your client on and that the process should be simple and obvious. Even if this is the case (I don't think it is quite that simple), *basic helping in a counselling way is often about understanding and refining the art of the obvious.*

I have adapted the following checklist (originally for counsellors) for use by anyone using basic helping or counselling skills. As soon as the possibility of making a referral or recommendation occurs to you, go through the checklist to explore what action you feel it would be appropriate to take:

- Has anything been said about referral yet?
  - either by me or my client? (*It is unusual and inadvisable to consider making a referral without the permission of your client. Seek further support and advice if this is not the case.*)
- Who has identified the need for referral?
  - my client (or the person I am helping)?
  - me?
  - my colleague, supervisor or line manager?
  - someone else?
- What is the purpose of the referral?
  - to get properly qualified help
  - to get more expert help
  - so that I don't go beyond my limits
  - a different type of helper is wanted
  - a different style of helping is wanted
  - any other purposes … ?
- Do I have enough information about possible referral agencies?
  - if not, do I know how to go about getting it?
- What do I want to say to my client?
  - going in to a meeting with a client you have decided to refer requires preparation. Don't fly by the seat of your pants.

- What backup or support do I need for this referral or recommendation?
  - Can your supervisor or line manager help? Some agencies have medical advisors who might assist volunteers.

At the heart of each onward referral lie the following aims:

- to pass the person on as though they were a precious gift rather than an awkward bundle
- to pass the person on so that their life and experience is added to rather than taken away from
- to make sure the person understands that the 'passing on' that I'm doing is not a rejection of them, but my best attempt to help them meet their needs better
- to make sure that the person knows that even though they are being referred on now, they will be welcome to seek help from me or the agency I am working for at any point in the future, at which point I will again do my best to help them meet their needs

Receiving referrals and recommendations

It can be a great feeling to be asked to help someone. They may come along themselves (called a 'self-referral') or someone else may suggest that they come to see you. It can be flattering to think that someone thinks you might be able to help. It's easy to get caught up in the good feelings and say 'Yes of course I can!' before you've considered the implications.

There are several situations in which it is entirely appropriate to offer help to another person and do the best you can. Elsewhere in this book I look at how having a rudimentary awareness of basic helping in a counselling way can make you a better parent, neighbour, friend, colleague or citizen. It would be a sad day if we all had to go away and think about it before we responded instantly, from the heart, as a fellow human being to the distress of others. Being called upon to offer basic helping as an ordinary human being is a wonderful opportunity for us to feel fulfilled as a person.

However, someone asking you for help because they know you have been on a basic counselling introduction or skills course is a different matter. If your *only* training is this introductory course then you will have to think very hard before offering help *since you are not qualified to offer help.* You must make sure that the person asking for help understands that you are not a qualified counsellor. You need to think which hat you're wearing when you respond to the request. It is quite possible that you might be too close to someone to help them effectively. If your son or daughter asks for help, it's probably best that you be their mum or dad, rather than try out your basic helping skills on them. If your best

YOU MIGHT LIKE TO WRITE DOWN ANY MORE CHECKLIST IDEAS THAT MIGHT AID YOUR OWN REFERRALS.

YOU MIGHT LIKE TO WRITE DOWN ANY MORE AIMS YOU MIGHT HAVE FOR YOUR OWN REFERRALS.

Contact details for BACP:
British Association for Counselling and Psychotherapy
BACP House, 15 St John's Business Park, Lutterworth, Leicestershire LE17 4HB
Tel: 01455 883300
Email: bacp@bacp.co.uk
Website: www.bacp.co.uk

Note
Each of these professions has its own set of rules and protocols for who you are or are not allowed to take referrals from or make referrals to. If you are not familiar with those that apply to you, you should get the information as soon as possible.

friend asks for help, being their best friend will almost certainly be what is needed.

If your employer has sent you on this introductory course and expects you to go back to your workplace and act as 'the counsellor', you may have a problem. You should point out to your employer that you are not qualified to counsel people and the tutor on your introductory course will support you with that explanation. If in any doubt contact BACP who will be able to help you clearly explain the ramifications of the situation to your employer.

If you are working as a volunteer or in a service where you do take referrals to help people in a counselling way, you must be sure you can figure out if the person being referred to you falls within the range you can help. If you work as a volunteer in a drug project – is their problem a drug problem? Again, regardless of the expectations of the managers of the service, you must not work beyond the limits of your competence or qualification. Get more information and support from BACP if you are in doubt.

If you are a qualified teacher, nurse, social worker or support worker, the situation is somewhat different. Your qualifications and experience will mean that you will be expected to receive referrals within your professional competence in the normal line of your work. This still doesn't mean that you can claim to be a fully-qualified counsellor unless you have gained a Degree or Higher Education diploma-level qualification (see Chapter 13).

Regardless of the setting in which you are offering help, some special considerations might apply.

- Are you prepared to see clients who are sent to you against their will? Sometimes this is a normal part of your helping work if you are, for example, a tutor in a school or college – students may be sent to you because they are not attending their course – yet you may still wish to use a counselling way of helping.
- You will have to be clear about how much information you pass back to the person making a referral. In other words, if a tutor has suggested to a student that they come to you for help, what will you do if the tutor wants to know how the student got on? It is at times such as these that differentiating between a referral and a recommendation is useful.

Finally, we must be prepared to say 'No, I am not able to help you'. This can be difficult because we all like to think we can help others, but we must not get out of our depth. If this should happen, both the helper and the person we are trying to help will suffer. The chances of you taking on too much or getting out of your depth is lessened by getting support and supervision for your helping activities. This is true whether you are an unpaid volunteer or a professional helper, and we will look at this in Chapter 8.

Why bother with ethics at an introductory level?

Not for the first time do I find myself having to explain the inclusion in this introductory text of an area of understanding which might be seen as the responsibility of higher-level training. The purpose of this chapter is twofold – firstly, to let readers know of the effort put into the development of ethical frameworks by the counselling profession. We are, of course, all potential clients and the British Association for Counselling and Psychotherapy (BACP) *Ethical Framework for Good Practice in Counselling and Psychotherapy* is there to inform and reassure all members of the public, both actual and potential clients, who seek the help of counsellors and helpers whether or not they are members of BACP. It can be viewed on their website and printed for personal use. I strongly recommend you look at it as soon as possible.

Secondly, it is important to cultivate an attitude of responsible helping regardless of the perceived level of the helping activity. We should not subscribe to the view that 'low-level', voluntary, community-based or otherwise 'amateur' helping should be seen as beyond morals, not worthy of rules of conduct, or somehow not important enough for ethics.

The question is 'How should the issue of ethical behaviour be interpreted at this level of basic helping or helping in a counselling way?' We'll never find out unless and until we have a go at identifying the issues, so this chapter is a starting point for beginning helpers learning basic helping in a counselling way and their trainers.

Note
To view and/or download the BACP Ethical Framework, visit: <http://www.bacp.co.uk/ethical_framework/>

Ethics – What are they and what are they for?

Ethics can be defined as a set of moral principles or rules of conduct. Most people are familiar with the idea of ethics in medical practice: that doctors must keep their patients' details confidential, and must always act to save life, extend life or improve the quality of life. These and other rules of conduct for doctors are enshrined in the 'Hippocratic Oath'.

Our appreciation of medical ethics is sharpened because doctors deal literally with life and death, and it is when life-and-death decisions are made that we understand the importance of seeking the support of a good set of rules. That is why there is such vigorous debate over such issues as whether to turn off life-support machines, should terminally ill people be 'assisted' to die, or at what age is a human foetus considered 'alive', etc. Many of these ethical decisions have a direct relationship with our values, spiritual beliefs, political views and other deeply held convictions.

The profession of counselling has its own 'rules of conduct' and in the UK they have been in a process of development through the professional body, the British Association for Counselling (then BAC, now BACP) since before the first Code of Ethics and Practice for Counsellors was published in 1984. Equivalent codes are provided by all counselling and psychotherapy bodies in other countries in Europe and North America. Although counselling and helping doesn't concern itself directly with life-and-death decisions in the same way as medicine, there are several ethical dilemmas which counsellors and helpers can find themselves caught up in and some of them do lead to life-and-death consequences. This is because counselling concerns itself with damaged, distressed, or otherwise vulnerable people. From my own experience of needing help, I know that in some desperate circumstances I would do almost anything to put an end to my distress. At such moments, the 'rules of conduct' or ethics of the helper, whether they are a doctor, lawyer or counsellor, will go some way to protect my interests as a client.

Note

Counsellors might be involved in life-or-death decisions when a client is so distressed that they are contemplating killing themselves or others. You will probably be aware from recent news items that it is extremely difficult, even for qualified professionals such as social workers and psychiatrists, to assess how dangerous a person is, and what risk they present to themselves and others. As a provider of basic helping in a counselling way, you must immediately seek advice and support if decisions like this occur in your work.

Ethics in counselling and helping

As I mentioned on the previous page, BACP published the *Ethical Framework for Good Practice in Counselling and Psychotherapy* which became active from April 2002 and replaced four older codes of ethics and practice. The current *Ethical Framework* and the old codes cover the work of:

Note

The BACP has other information sheets and publications relating to ethical practice. Take a look at the BACP website <http://wam.bacp.co.uk/wam/Search.exe?SRT>]. BACP

BACP House,
15 St John's Business Park, Lutterworth, Leicestershire LE17 4HB
Tel: 01455 883300
Email: bacp@bacp.co.uk
Website: www.bacp.co.uk

- those working as counsellors
- those using counselling skills alongside other professional skills in a helping role other than 'counsellor'
- those who provide supervision and support to counsellors
- those providing training in counselling and counselling skills

Other organisations concerned with counselling and psychotherapy also take a view on ethics and good practice (although BACP is by far the biggest). The United Kingdom Council for Psychotherapy (UKCP) makes statements about ethics and good practice, but rather than publish a national code, it works through its member organisations.

Note

To learn more about UKCP, visit their website: <www.psychotherapy.org.uk>

For those counsellors and therapists who do not feel comfortable with the professionalisation of helping (see pp. 187–92, Chapter 12), the Independent Practitioners Network (IPN) exists to promote and maintain good practice. Like the UKCP, the IPN also works through its constituent groups. Each group is responsible for the practice of its members and each group is networked with other groups to make practice accountable. The members of IPN, just like the members of BACP and UKCP, think that their particular method of establishing and maintaining standards (and protecting clients) is the most effective. IPN was founded in 1994 and is independent of all other professional, regulatory and training organisations. Its members were centrally involved in the opposition to the proposed regulation of the helping professions.

Ethics in helping is very much a matter of 'horses for courses'. Different types and levels of helping activity have different ethical requirements. If we want to understand what ethical considerations we might wish to take into account as beginning helpers offering basic helping in a counselling way, we could start by looking at the ethical framework developed by professional counsellors.

My first suggestion is that you obtain a copy of the BACP *Ethical Framework for Good Practice in Counselling and Psychotherapy*. In addition to helping understand the BACP perspective on ethical issues, it is a useful resource for the future should you or any of your friends or colleagues seek counselling or training. You will know what kind of conduct to expect from counsellors, helping professionals using counselling skills, and trainers. It is also, of course, a reference point for professionals to inform and guide their practice. It is interesting to note that professional therapists still debate difficult cases and ethical dilemmas through the pages of the BACP magazine *Therapy Today*. It is clear that there are many grey areas in the ethics of helping.

What topics do you think should be covered in a code of ethics for counsellors? If left to our own devices, we might get as far as confidentiality and not wanting to damage clients, then dry up. After many years of continual development, the main issues considered by the BACP in their *Ethical Framework* are divided into:

- values
- principles
- personal moral qualities

You will find that all of these headings have links with the material covered in several chapters of this book. The current chapter concerns itself with the issues in a more direct way.

As I have already explained, at this introductory level my aim is to raise awareness and get you thinking about the ethics of helping in general ways. There is no better place to start than the three headings used by BACP. It is not appropriate to go into the BACP *Ethical Framework* in a great deal of detail here. In the margin you will see plenty of links to the relevant sections of the BACP website for you to read more, and BACP provide lots of supportive material.

IF YOU WANT TO KNOW MORE ABOUT
IPN

You will find a little more information on pages 190-2 in this book, or you can visit the IPN website <www.i-p-n.org>

Note
After a little consideration you will appreciate how easy it is to aim for high ethical standards yet how difficult it is to put rules in place to achieve them. All of these bodies and groups are doing the best they can to ensure a secure setting in which helpers can work and safe practice methods so that clients are protected and receive the best help possible. You have to choose which is best for you.

Note
To view and/or download the BACP Ethical Framework, visit: <http://www.bacp.co.uk/ethical_framework/>

Extract from the British Association for Counselling and Psychotherapy Ethical Framework

The fundamental values of counselling and psychotherapy
include a commitment to:
- Respecting human rights and dignity
- Protecting the safety of clients
- Ensuring the integrity of practitioner-client relationships
- Enhancing the quality of professional knowledge and its application
- Alleviating personal distress and suffering
- Fostering a sense of self that is meaningful to the person(s) concerned
- Increasing personal effectiveness
- Enhancing the quality of relationships between people
- Appreciating the variety of human experience and culture
- Striving for the fair and adequate provision of counselling and psychotherapy services

Values inform principles. They represent an important way of expressing a general ethical commitment that becomes more precisely defined and action-orientated when expressed as a principle.

The ethical principles of counselling and psychotherapy
- Being Trustworthy: honouring the trust placed in the counsellor
- Autonomy: respect for the client's right to be self-governing
- Beneficence: a commitment to promoting the client's well-being
- Non-maleficence: a commitment to avoiding harm to the client
- Justice: the fair and impartial treatment of all clients and the provision of adequate services
- Self-respect: fostering the practitioner's self-knowledge and care for self

Personal moral qualities
Empathy: the ability to communicate understanding of another person's experience from that person's perspective.
Sincerity: a personal commitment to consistency between what is professed and what is done.
Integrity: commitment to being moral in dealings with others, personal straightforwardness, honesty and coherence.
Resilience: the capacity to work with the client's concerns without being personally diminished.
Respect: showing appropriate esteem to others and their understanding of themselves.
Humility: the ability to assess accurately and acknowledge one's own strengths and weaknesses.
Competence: the effective deployment of the skills and knowledge needed to do what is required.
Fairness: the consistent application of appropriate criteria to inform decisions and actions.
Wisdom: possession of sound judgement that informs practice.
Courage: the capacity to act in spite of known fears, risks and uncertainty.

BACP (2010) *Ethical Framework for Good Practice in Counselling and Psychotherapy*, pp. 2–4.
Retrieved 11/05/2011 <http://www.bacp.co.uk>

More detailed consideration and discussion of these issues at the level appropriate for you is best conducted by tutors on courses. It is essential that you consider how each of these headings is of relevance to basic helping in a counselling way and relate them to the setting in which the helping takes place. This takes time and is best done in discussion with tutors, agency managers, line managers, and supervisors.

Basic ethics for basic helping

So, where can we make a start to consider appropriately ethical basic helping? The following topics are a starting point to stimulate thinking and debate regarding ethical issues.

- Issues of competence:
  - Do I have enough training?
  - Do I have enough personal and other resources?
  - Do I monitor my competence, e.g. through supervision?
  - What am I doing to stay effective, e.g. further training, support and supervision?
- Confidentiality:
  - What should limit the confidentiality I offer to clients?
- Issues of responsibility:
  - What responsibilities do I have towards my clients?
  - What are my responsibilities to myself as a counsellor?
  - Do I have any responsibilities to other counsellors and other helping professionals?
  - What are my responsibilities to the wider community?
- Advertising:
  - How should I advertise any help that I can offer?

Every time that we offer help to someone, we should consider the way we conduct ourselves. Throughout this book there have been pointers to the issues:

- *In Chapter 1* we asked: 'What sort of help are we offering?'
- *In Chapter 2* we asked: 'What gives us the idea that our helping will be effective?'
- *In Chapter 3* we asked: 'What are our motives for helping?' and 'Will our own feelings and thoughts get in the way?'
- *In Chapter 4* we asked: 'Do we have any prejudices which will bias our help?'
- *In Chapter 5* we asked: 'How do we improve our helping skills?'
- *In Chapter 6* we asked: 'Will we keep within the limits of our expertise?'
- *In Chapter 8* we will ask: 'Do we have enough personal support to offer effective help without hurting ourselves or those we are trying to help?'

You may see some similarity between the issues raised in the chapters and those included in the BACP *Ethical Framework*. They might be considered to be the 'core ethical issues' of *competent and responsible helping practice*. The answers arrived at as you work through this book will have a strong personal element because, as I have pointed out, ethics are to some extent based on our personal values and beliefs. There are, however, some common strands to ethical conduct as you can see from the BACP extract on p. 126, and we might summarise these as follows:

- We try to act within the law
- We respect human rights
- We respect people's autonomy and ability to control their own destiny
- We keep promises, contracts or agreements we have made with those we are trying to help, even if they are informal, and we try to draw attention to such unspoken agreements and bring them into the open
- We try to act in a fair and reasonable way
- When faced with a dilemma we try to do the most good and the least harm

If there is any central strand which draws together these ethical issues, it is the welfare of the person we are trying to help. Underneath it all, helpers are trying to help someone rather than exploit them; to increase someone's options not narrow them down; to help someone make emancipated autonomous decisions not to manipulate them into doing what we want. We find that these ethical issues also manifest themselves in the kind of basic helping that we might be involved in at an introductory level.

For example, if we were to help a colleague at work, or our next-door neighbour, we should not abdicate ethical or moral responsibility. We should do our best to ensure good ethical conduct:

- How might you behave unethically in the case of helping your colleague at work? Although you are not a trained counsellor, a colleague has come to you for support because his wife has just left him. It was a sudden and unexpected separation and he is distraught. How might you behave 'unethically'?

✍ MAKE A NOTE OF YOUR OWN ANSWERS & EXAMPLES

The greatest danger is that the person you are trying to help is exploited by you either wittingly or unwittingly, for example:

- In your enthusiasm to help, you may help more than you are qualified to:
  - e.g. you might give him some of your mother's sleeping tablets to help him sleep.
- You may exploit your colleague for personal gain:
  - e.g. you may see an opportunity for promotion and break

confidentiality by telling your boss that your colleague's work is suffering.

- Your own problems might get in the way:

    e.g. you may identify very strongly with his problem because of a recent separation of your own. This may lead you to suggest solutions you wish you had tried yourself, rather than ones which might genuinely benefit him in his situation.

- You may have a vested interest in a particular outcome:

    e.g. you believe that families should stay together for the sake of the children and try your best to manipulate a reconciliation against everyone's wishes.

- You are overenthusiastic and friendly in a way that cannot be maintained:

    e.g. you see that he is lonely and become his friend when in other circumstances you would have kept him at arm's length.

Clearly these ways of acting will not be in the best interests of the person you are trying to help. There are many more ways of behaving 'unethically' in this situation. You may be working as a volunteer in a helping service already. If the agency does not have a code of conduct and you think it would be helpful, why not draw up your own set of guidelines for ethical conduct in basic helping. Get other volunteers and management to help.

The question of monitoring the conduct of helpers is partly dealt with in Chapter 8 and again in Chapter 12. Any code of practice must have the power to sanction when it is broken. There is a complaints procedure operated by the BACP for the benefit of clients, supervisees and trainees. Where basic helping is concerned, however, there is no governing body to protect us (some would say, rightly so). Everyone doing basic helping must assume the mantle of responsibility to help in a principled and ethical way.

Note
The BACP complaints procedure comprises pages 11 to 19 of the BACP Ethical Framework, see: <http://www.bacp.co.uk/ethical_framework/>

support and supervision in basic helping and counselling

Support

Most of us nowadays are familiar with the idea of support. Many people recognise that human beings need various types of support in order to function effectively. Whether you are a single parent, business executive or volunteer, you will understand the need for support. It is often assumed that counsellors and helpers are the ones that give support, but in this chapter I am looking at the notion of giving support to the helpers. Caring for the carers, in other words.

Helping other people can be exhausting work, and the helpers need to be restored. As the UK wrestles with the financial cost of caring for ill, distressed and disabled people, the need for and reliance on carers has been brought to everyone's attention. More often than not this work is done by family and friends, but it still takes its toll. As the parent of a daughter with special needs, I have known the value of support for my wife and myself, e.g. a weekend of respite care for our daughter, so that we can take a break. It does not seem strange, then, for carers to need support. Counsellors and those offering basic helping are carers too, and as such we must make sure that when we offer helping in a counselling way, we have the support we need to continue to do a good job.

There are various ways of looking at support:

- *Physical support*: crutches or a plaster cast on a broken limb, holding someone up when they're weak or unwell, using your physical presence as support by going along with someone to the doctor's, for example
- *Verbal support*: speaking up in agreement with someone, being an advocate for someone unable to state their case
- *Financial support*: a loan for a business venture, a grant for a charity, social security benefits
- *Emotional support*: a shoulder to cry on, someone to share your troubles with, someone 'rooting' for you during exams, someone believing in you
- *Just being there*: we all know what this means, and how incredibly comforting it is to know that someone will be there, on call if needed

'We often noticed that we had an argument every time that I had reconciled another couple. The couple had invested their violence in me, and I was investing it in my wife. I have always been aware my workshop provided a place where I could discharge my violence. Working on wood, steel or gold with hammer, saw or file, I could invest the violence which my patients had poured out on me in the consulting room.

Paul Tournier (1978) *The Violence Inside* (Edward Hudson, Trans). London: SCM Press, p. 71.

Activity
Can you think of any other types of support?

We've all received support of some kind or another in our lives, both as children and as adults, at work and at home, and would probably have failed without support at some time.

Burnout

Any person's ability to help in a counselling way needs to be maintained rather like a car needs to be maintained between journeys. The oil and water need checking along with the tyre pressures, and we need to make sure there is enough fuel in the tank. We need to assure ourselves that our car is fit for the journey and will not break down. Helping and counselling are, as I have said in previous chapters, responsible activities for which we need to maintain ourselves in a kind of peak form. The helper equivalent of a car breaking down due to poor maintenance is *burnout*.

Burnout is the word we use to describe the damage we might do to ourselves if we don't get sufficient support. We may also, of course, do damage to our helping relationships and/or the people we are trying to help if we don't get sufficient support. Since counselling takes a lot of effort, concentration and a clear mind, we need to be in peak form to be effective helpers or to do our best counselling. For many people, being satisfied with our present level of effectiveness is not enough, we also want to continuously improve our abilities in counselling and helping.

So as helpers we need to do three things:
- restore ourselves and recharge our energy to do our helping work
- maintain ourselves to prevent burnout or damage to our clients
- develop and improve our helping abilities and our resilience

How can we as helpers or counsellors achieve these aims? Support for helpers and counsellors comes in many forms, from informal, on-the-spot support to formal supervision required by a professional body. In the same way that the more time and effort you put into maintaining your car, the better and more reliably it runs, the more time and effort spent on establishing and maintaining yourself as a helper and counsellor, the better off you will be.

Training and professional development

You will have taken the first step to becoming a more effective helper by undertaking a basic Introduction to Counselling course. You will be helped to make up your mind about how far you wish to go with training. You will get an idea about the limits of counselling and the helping you can offer at different stages of training.

However far you proceed with training in counselling, you will find that your development as a helper never feels 'complete'. Practising professional counsellors attend training events to update their knowledge or gain new expertise in specialist areas. The BACP monthly magazine *Therapy Today* carries details of a wide range of training events open to all participants regardless of qualifications. Local 'alternative lifestyle' magazines also carry advertisements for events in your area.

Personal development

From your reading of Chapter 3 you will know that personal development comes in many forms. The main purpose, in addition to believing that self-development is intrinsically good for its own sake, is that in this context we understand that it will contribute towards making us better helpers. However, whatever you choose to do to increase your self-awareness, in addition to being challenging, will probably have the effect of increasing the range of distressing stories you are able to tolerate and making you more resilient without hardening you.

One of the many conundrums facing helpers is to be more resilient without being hardened. We need the right blend of toughness with tenderness. That is a different balance for everyone and one way to achieve it is through personal development.

The other way personal development can be supportive is to directly address any distress we experience as a result of our helping work – in other words take it to our own therapy or counselling. Maybe a client's problems remind us of things that have happened in our past, perhaps completely out of the blue we find ourselves unable to cope with a particular disturbing experience, or it could be something as apparently trivial as not getting on with a particular client.

Fun, etc!

Before we get too serious, do remember that it is essential to have balance in your life. There must be room for the things that you enjoy – art, music, sport, watching TV, having a massage, or everyday activities from cooking to DIY. And the 'etc' in the subheading is a reminder to not forget the contemplative or spiritual side of yourself. To be a good helper it goes without saying that you will need to be focused and concentrating on the task, but you will also need to be relaxed, and bring your sense of humour, varied experiences and spiritual connectedness to your helping too.

This is a very small subsection in the book, but a very important one!

Support you can give yourself

There are many contexts in which helping and counselling take place. The one common element in the various settings is *you*. There are some simple things we can all do to support our helping endeavours. The following are some suggested questions you could ask yourself before you start any helping activity:

- Make sure you're fit to help:
  - Are you physically well enough to give good quality help (i.e. not ill)?
  - Have you been drinking or taking drugs?
  - Are you alert or are you feeling tired?
- Prepare yourself to help:
  - Do you have the right amount of time to help?
  - Do you have the right kind of space you need to help? (Do you need it to be private, quiet or confidential?)
- After you've done your helping:
  - How do you feel?
  - What do you need to do before you can continue work or go home? Talk to someone?
- Have you made any notes that may be necessary?

My rough rule of thumb is – if you're not fit to drive, you're not fit to help anyone properly. By 'fit' I mean physically (e.g. not exhausted, or overexcited) and mentally (e.g. not distracted) up to the task. There is increasing awareness regarding the *responsibility* attached to driving a lethal machine. Although not lethal in the same sense, if a suicidal person comes for help and we appear irritated because we are stressed, bored because we are tired, or joyful because our football team has won the cup, the consequences could be tragic.

Similarly after a helping or counselling session you may need to sit for a moment to gather your thoughts or maybe talk to someone before you can carry on or drive home. Try not to arrive home burdened by your client's troubles. Remember that counselling and helping take more out of you than you think, and you may feel preoccupied with someone else's problems if you don't take a minute or two to recover your sense of who you are, and to separate yourself from them.

Basic support for basic helping

At this stage of training, you will be offering basic help and for this you will need to establish some basic support. It is not necessary to set up formal supervision sessions, although this may be done for you if you work for an agency or service as a volunteer.

HAVE YOU ANY OTHER IDEAS?

Note

This is not meant to be taken absolutely literally – people with certain sensory impairments and physical disabilities may not be able to drive, but are perfectly well able to help in a counselling way, or be a counsellor.

There are some simple ways of getting the support you need to be an effective helper:

Debriefing: This is when there is a set time after a critical incident, perhaps at work, for talking the incident through, getting any feelings off your chest. During the debriefing, normal work is suspended whilst the aftermath of the emergency is dealt with. In a helping setting this can be of use after a distressing session with a client, maybe one that has been verbally or physically abusive.

Co-worker support: This happens when two helpers agree to pair up to support each other. They may make this a formal relationship where they agree to meet at set times, e.g. once a week. During these support sessions they may talk about the personal and learning issues that have arisen during their helping work that week. It can help if one takes the role of 'supporter' and the other the role of 'person supported'. This can stop the session becoming a general chat.

Sometimes this co-worker support can be in the form of an agreement to be available in emergencies, e.g. perhaps being willing to be contacted at home on the phone to help someone off-load stress.

Support groups: Sometimes, a number of helpers agree to get together to talk over the difficulties of their work. They don't have to come from the same place of work, indeed, sometimes it can be an advantage to talk to someone who is not a work colleague, since they can give you a different perspective on a situation because they are not so closely involved.

Support network: You may agree to exchange telephone numbers or addresses with a group of helpers. Then they offer 'spot support' if something arises out of our helping work on the spur of the moment. This works well in rural or less well-populated areas where people live a long way apart or where people don't have access to transport.

Special training events: Many services and agencies run special training events every month or two months where people get together to learn about a new or developing aspect of the helping professions. The discussions afterwards give opportunities for informal support or may help you set up one of the support systems mentioned above. BACP also run regional events and meetings on an occasional basis.

BACP is a good place to start looking for details of activities in your area, either online, or in the magazine *Therapy Today.*

Contact details for BACP:
British Association for Counselling and Psychotherapy
BACP House, 15 St John's Business Park, Lutterworth, Leicestershire LE17 4HB
Tel: 01455 883300
Email: bacp@bacp.co.uk
Website: <www.bacp.co.uk>

Some ground rules for basic support

Co-worker support (above) can be a formal arrangement in some agencies. If so there will be a set of rules to follow and, hopefully, a little training to help prepare you. It is also, of course, a spontaneous, natural and casual offering of help. If you are called upon to support another helper, whether they are a colleague and/or a friend, try following these rules. Don't be afraid to offer support; if you intend to be supportive by providing a safe environment, you won't go far wrong.

- Support and helping are very similar. Use what you know about helping in a counselling way to give support to other helpers.
- Use active listening skills to listen carefully to what the other person is saying.
- Don't be afraid if they get upset when they're talking. It's quite natural for helpers themselves to get upset when they need support. It's often just a matter of letting your colleague off-load some of the feelings that have accumulated when listening to very distressing experiences.
- Setting limits to the time and type of support you are offering will help both of you.
- Be ready to find that technical or ethical issues regarding your colleague's work might arise. Don't be caught cold – think this possibility through and make sure you and your colleague have a strategy for dealing with this eventuality.
- Remember, though, that support is *not* the same as helping; it is similar.

Backup

So far I've been talking about support for helpers in terms of how to off-load the feelings we all get when we have to listen to other people's troubles on a regular basis.

There is, however, another kind of support which is invaluable, if not essential. I call it *backup*. You will know what backup is if you work for a service or agency such as The Samaritans. There they have more than one person on duty at most times and each volunteer on duty is backed up by a day leader – someone on call at home or work who can give information, advice, guidance, and support to the volunteer if something crops up that's beyond their limits. Samaritans branches usually have backup from a local doctor who can help volunteers if the client has a problem which might have a medical element.

Backup is great if you've got it, but very difficult, if not impossible, to organise if you're working or helping on your own in a casual setting. Perhaps you want to use your counselling style at

---

Activity

If a colleague asks if you can talk through a difficult helping session on the spur of the moment:

- *What sort of ethical issues might arise when you support your colleague?*
- *Even though it might be casual, informal support, do you feel obliged to do anything if you are not a member of a professional body?*
- *What could you do?*

IF YOU WANT TO KNOW MORE ABOUT
SUPPORT AND SUPERVISION

Take a look at the information sheets provided by BACP. There is a small charge for each one, and they are constantly revised and added to. There are some that focus on support, supervision and ethical decision making. Visit <http://wam.bacp.co.uk/wam/Search.exe?SRT>

home with your family and friends, in your neighbourhood or at work. There's no need to feel completely isolated, since we have looked at ways of getting basic support. It is also possible to *feel* backed up even though you haven't any proper backup. There are plenty of professional helpers such as doctors and social workers who can back up the emergency or 'first-aid' helping you might do – but it is you who must prepare by contacting them first.

When helping someone, you may decide that it's best if they get help from someone better qualified or you might want to help them get some detailed information about their problem. Here's a short list of possible steps to take *with the permission of the person you are helping*:

- Find out who their GP is and how to get in touch
- Do they have a social worker, home help or health visitor?
- The Citizen's Advice Bureau near you is another source of information, advice and backup
- Go back to look at Chapter 6: *What to Do When You Reach Your Limits*

Supervision for professional counsellors

As I have mentioned several times, practising professional counsellors are required to be supervised by various codes of ethics and practice, e.g. British Association for Counselling and Psychotherapy *Ethical Framework for Good Practice in Counselling and Psychotherapy*. I decided to look briefly at supervision for counsellors to give readers an idea of the responsibilities involved in being a counsellor and the safeguards in place to ensure that clients get the best quality help.

You may be familiar with the term 'supervisor' when used in other settings. For example a supervisor at work may be your line manager or someone who oversees or checks your work. Sometimes a supervisor is someone who takes overall responsibility for a job or chases the job's progress. Counselling supervision means none of these things.

- As a counsellor your supervisor should not be someone you work with or for. Your supervisor should not be your line manager.
- Your supervisor should not be someone you are, for example, related or married to.
- When either of the above situations arise, it is called a *dual relationship*, i.e. you have two relationships running alongside each other, a work or friendship alongside a supervision relationship. This can lead to conflicts of interest and when this happens either one or both of the relationships may be compromised.

It has been accepted practice, though, for experienced counsellors to be in co-supervision with colleagues. This is where two counsellors offer each other supervision, one is the

Note

There is also a huge amount of information available online. You must only take information from trusted sources, since there is also an awful lot of unreliable or simply wrong information on the Internet too.

- For issues concerning some technical and legal aspects of helping, the BACP website is a good place to start: <http://www.bacp.co.uk>
- For medical information try NHS Direct: <http://www.nhsdirect.nhs.uk/>
- For benefits, rights and other legislation, try the huge UK Government website: <http://www.direct.gov.uk/en/index.htm>

Note

To view and/or download the BACP Ethical Framework, visit: <http://www.bacp.co.uk/ethical_framework/>

Note

It is best practice that your supervisor should not be your boss or line manager. Some agencies require line management supervision so it is sometimes not possible to adhere to this best practice recommendation. It will mean that your supervision is not independent. Some practitioners arrange and pay for their own independent supervision in these circumstances and sometimes the employer will pay for it.

'7. All counsellors, psycho-therapists, trainers and supervisors are required to have regular and ongoing formal supervision/consultative support for their work.

8. Regularly monitoring and reviewing one's work is essential to maintaining good practice. It is important to be open to, and conscientious in considering feedback from colleagues, appraisals and assessments. Responding constructively to feedback helps advance practice.'

BACP (2010) Maintaining competent practice. *Ethical Framework for Good Practice in Counselling and Psychotherapy,* p. 6.

'It is a breach of the ethical requirement for counsellors to practise without regular counselling supervision/consultative support.

   Counselling supervision/consultative support refers to a formal arrangement which enables counsellors to discuss their counselling regularly with one or more people who have an understanding of counselling and counselling supervision/consultative support. Its purpose is to ensure that efficacy of the counsellor-client relationship. It is a confidential relationship.'

Code of Ethics and Practice for Counsellors, BAC (1992) Amended AGM September 1993, par. B.3.1 & B.3.2.

supervisor and the other is the supervisee, then they swap roles. It is still vital that your co-supervisor will put counselling supervision before friendship or comfort when working with a colleague. If in doubt, don't do co-supervision.

- Your supervisor should be someone who is a qualified counsellor with some years' experience of counselling, although it is not necessary for them to be more experienced than you.
- Your supervisor should be someone who can challenge your comfortable assumptions about your work. This is particularly important when you have a co-supervisory relationship. Your co-supervisor must never feel that they should not challenge you on an aspect of your practice because they are afraid that they might lose you as a friend.

'[The question] "What ought I to do?" is not equivalent to the question, "What is the consensus of my colleagues about what I do?" ... What makes [a given action] right has nothing to do with the numbers of people who take it to be so. Therefore the fact that professional colleagues have agreed to put a rule in your code does not *make* this the right action.'

Dale Bayerstein (2011) The functions and limitations of professional codes of ethics. Cited in R House & N Totton (eds), *Implausible Professions* (2nd ed). Ross-on-Wye: PCCS Books, pp. 350-1.

'I don't know what I would do without my individual supervisor. I've worked with him for six years. He has been my sounding board, my guide, my inspiration and mentor. I have often come with quite difficult issues and stressful concerns yet he's been supportive, helpful and astute in his supervising.'

'Sally' (1999) in L Buchanan & R Hughes, *Experiences of Person-Centred Counselling Training.* Ross-on-Wye: PCCS Books, p. 71.

In the next few chapters I am going to be trying to place counselling as an activity in the world in which we live. There will be some echoes back to Chapter 1: *What is Counselling?*, Chapter 2: *Where Do Ideas in Counselling Come From*, and also the pages in Chapter 3 on personal values and counselling values. As we have seen, counselling is a particular kind of helping, no better or worse than any other kind, but with its own ideas, values, skills, limits and ethics. Where does counselling as a helping activity fit in the early 21st century? What is the context in which it operates and what other human activities might counselling be connected to?

A short time ago whilst on holiday I struck up a conversation with a fellow traveller. Upon learning that I was a counsellor, she launched into a monologue complaining that there were counsellors everywhere nowadays and that when she was young she didn't need counselling. Not even when two of her school friends were killed in a road accident; she and her other friends just got on with their lives. In a similar vein, the principal of a college I worked at fretted about introducing a counselling service because he believed that if the students found out that there was a counsellor available they would start having problems that they would not otherwise have had.

These ideas are not as odd as they might initially seem. Many people wonder why there seems to be such a great need for, and emphasis on, helping nowadays. They also wonder if the help on offer might in some way make us weak or cause us as a society to become dependent upon counselling. There are two questions suggested by this, firstly: 'Where has this apparent need for counselling, and the increase in people wanting to be counsellors, suddenly come from?' And secondly: 'What is the *meaning* of helping in the 21st century?'

The next two sections will look at some possible answers.

We didn't need counsellors in my day so why do we need them now?

People who ask this and similar questions are most likely appealing to a remembered notion of how life once was, but looking back into the past through our own experience is a process that is fraught

Note

My old principal's idea is not so far removed from the notion that the media have some effect upon what people want and expect from life. This includes what we think good mental health is and how we think it is achieved.

As we go through this chapter, I will mention the media occasionally and it might be interesting to ask yourself what effect the media (TV, magazines, newspapers) have on what we think leads to living a fulfilling life.

Activity

What do you think? Take a moment to think about how our society has changed in the way we help people.
- *Have there been any changes?*
- *What might have caused them?*

✍

Note

This list will inevitably go out of date very quickly. The point is that we have an ever-changing idea of what we need in order to be fulfilled, and that idea is usually supplied by 'lifestyle' media and the gadgets they want us to buy. Our identity and happiness are increasingly bound up in the brand-named goods that we own.

Note

Another factor affecting our expectations of care and help is that the world has become more 'customer-centred' and we expect certain levels of service. We have been encouraged to think of ourselves as 'customers' of, for example, the NHS and social services. If we don't get what we think we are due, we complain.

Note

How we categorise certain experiences changes over time. In the First World War, shell-shocked troops were thought to be suffering from a character flaw, 'cowardice', and were dealt with by being shot. It has also been known, at different times, as 'hysterical NEUROSIS', 'battle fatigue', and 'post-Vietnam syndrome'.

NEUROSIS Mental 'illness' characterised by a 'normal' human quality, like anxiety, being amplified to unpleasant and debilitating levels. Includes phobias and panic attacks.

with difficulties. Our memories are notoriously inaccurate and as we develop and change, so does the way we perceive the world. For example, I remember that Burton's Wagon Wheels were much much bigger when I was a child. The chances are that Wagon Wheels are just the same size that they always were, but I have grown relatively bigger. Set against this is the indisputable fact that some aspects of our world *are* changing markedly. How do we sort out the real differences from the imagined ones? For the purposes of this book, I am simply going to leave you with the dilemma, rather than provide any answers.

My own view is that it is highly likely that there has been a change in the needs of people today compared with the needs of people, say, 40 years ago. The reasons for this are likely to be far from simple, but I offer the following guesses for your consideration, so that you can carry the debate further yourselves:

- Perhaps we keep raising our expectations regarding what constitutes the 'good life'. Nowadays, people are not satisfied unless they have satellite TV, a mobile phone, laptop computer and a dishwasher. I can remember my mother thinking she had arrived when we had a refrigerator. As each year goes by we *demand* a better quality of life, and our psychological wellbeing is part of it. We demand that we are cared for to a higher standard in all ways – we expect more of doctors, nurses, dentists and social services, requiring them to be more supportive and sensitive. The 'pull your socks up' approach to care is no longer enough, we demand a more up-to-date model.

- It has been suggested that the old community support systems are breaking down – gone is the extended family and neighbourhoods where everyone knew each other. Partly because of the effect of some forms of town planning, increased mobility, different communications technology enabling remote contact, etc., we no longer access the person-to-person face-to-face support that was such a strong feature of our neighbourhood community groupings.

- It is possible that, years ago, people just weren't 'tuned-in' to psychological distress as we are today. Soldiers suffering from shell shock were often shot for cowardice in the 1914–18 war. By the Second World War it was just about recognised as a condition, but many were still thought to be malingerers. Nowadays we have a different appreciation of psychological suffering and the same behaviour is likely to be diagnosed as the mental illness 'post-traumatic stress disorder'.

- Some people believe that at the start of this new millennium there is a general disillusionment in our 'developed' Northern European/Anglo-American culture regarding the failure of technology to make the world perfect. To some extent, people are turning away from science as a method of progressing human living, and biological solutions to psychological distress such as drug treatments, and turning towards what they believe to be more 'natural' treatments such as counselling.

- It could be that our technological culture has separated us from our 'souls' or 'spiritual selves' and that counselling offers the hope of rediscovering or renewing this spiritual connection. A connected idea is that the self-awareness and self-affirmation that is a feature of all counselling approaches serves to fill the spiritual void in modern life.

- Finally, counselling is not solely aimed at 'unhappy' people or 'the worried well'. It is increasingly demanded by people for whom the psychiatric services have failed. Psychiatric treatment is still based on drug treatments and some patients are increasingly suspicious of drug treatments as public concern grows over side effects and addiction to PSYCHOACTIVE DRUGS, and evidence mounts to show that many drugs are no better than PLACEBO. Counselling is seen as offering a more gentle, natural way of alleviating the distress of mental illness.

What is the meaning of helping in the 21st century?

You have decided to embark on the first stage of learning about counselling – a particular form of helping relationship. It is vital that at an early stage in your learning and development as a helper, you ask yourself what it means to be a helper. There are two important questions to ask. Firstly, 'What does it mean to be a helper in the 21st century?' Secondly, 'What does it mean for me to be a helper?'

If you remember, in Chapter 2 I suggested that the people responsible for developing the founding ideas behind modern counselling approaches could not escape the cultures in which they lived. The culture at the time informed their thinking one way or another. The same is true of you and me. Our ideas about what helping means to us as individuals cannot be divorced from cultural notions about the meaning of helping.

The following are some ideas about helping that are representative of our modern culture:

- Some people believe that we need to be tough in order to get along in a tough world.
- Along the same lines is the view that only the strong will survive and in the law of the human jungle, the weak will go to the wall.
- On the other hand, plenty of people hold another set of views regarding helping – namely that the strong should help the weak; that helping people enables them to live to their maximum capacity and become full and active members of society; that

Note

As with almost everything else in the text in this chapter, this is debatable. Whilst sections of the public turn away from science, we see the pharmaceutical industry selling record levels of drugs, particularly psychiatric drugs. And many people feel reassured by biological explanations of psychological distress.

Activity

What thoughts do you have on the apparent increase in the 'need' for counselling?

PSYCHOACTIVE DRUGS Drugs which alter mood and mental state.

PLACEBO A treatment that is intended to have no therapeutic effect or power, e.g. sugar-pill with no active ingredients. Used in research as a dummy-treatment.

Activity

Ask yourself these questions now and note down your answers.
Discuss your answers with other members of your training group to see what variety of responses you get.

> 'I did not have a counsellor; it was only months later I realised how much pain such a person would have saved me, and how much more pain it would have saved my family.'
>
> Brian Keenan, *Daily Mail*

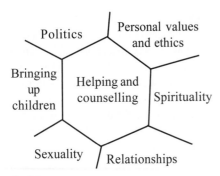

Activity

How would you arrange counselling so that it fits into your life, alongside those other elements of your life which are driven by sets of values?

IF YOU WANT TO KNOW MORE ABOUT
SPIRITUALITY AND COUNSELLING

Read:

Thorne, BT (1991) *Person-Centred Counselling: Therapeutic and spiritual dimensions.* London: Wiley.

West, W (2000) *Psychotherapy & Spirituality: Crossing the line between therapy and religion.* London: Sage.

IF YOU WANT TO KNOW MORE ABOUT
POLITICS AND COUNSELLING

Read:

Cooper, M, Proctor, G, Sanders, P & Malcolm, B (eds) (2006) *Politicizing the Person-Centred Approach: An agenda for social change.* Ross-on-Wye: PCCS Books.

Kearney, A (1996) *Counselling, Class and Politics.* Ross-on-Wye: PCCS Books.

Proctor, G (2002) *The Dynamics of Power in Counselling and Psychotherapy.* Ross-on-Wye: PCCS Books.

Samuels, A (2001) *Politics on the Couch: Citizenship and the internal life.* London: Profile.

helping can be a cooperative partnership of equals, not the strong bestowing charity or protection on the weak. Furthermore, helping others is good for us, it makes the helper a better, more rounded, happier and fulfilled person.

- Still others may hold the view that it is divine will that we help those less fortunate than ourselves and that in doing so we get closer to heaven, nirvana or spiritual completion.
- Another view might be that those suffering misfortune in their lives are doing so because they have been bad, either in this life or a previous one, and that the sort of help they need is either spiritual guidance or to be left to learn their lesson.

I have included these sets of ideas because they illustrate an important point about counselling and contemporary life. Counselling as a helping activity impinges upon or shares a boundary with many other values in the modern world. The way we choose to help someone says something about us as people.

Political contexts and spiritual connections

Talking about our personal values is often tricky. For some of us it goes too close to the things we are often urged to never talk about at dinner – politics and religion. (How do you feel about talking about the other topics in the diagram in the margin?) However, I am going to do just that and I will ask you to do the same.

How we think about helping and what we actually do are *not* neutral. They are shot through with personal, political and spiritual values. As you have been working through this book, and in particular the last section, you may have noticed that most of the things we do in our lives are governed or at the very least informed by the values we hold. There can be no spiritual or political tradition that does not have something to say about helping and what it means to help another human being. Some readers may believe that counselling is apolitical or has nothing to do with 'soul' or 'spiritual self', but I think there is no disputing the close links over the years, from the work of Freud, Jung, Skinner and Rogers, who all acknowledged such connections, through to more contemporary work listed in the margin. In Chapter 3 there are short sections looking at personal values and counselling values in which I ask the reader to think about and try to identify links between the two. There are activities presented in these pages to help explore your thoughts and feelings around these issues.

This section is primarily concerned with wider contexts as they affect the person of the helper. Elsewhere (Chapter 12) I look briefly at the meaning of helping and counselling in the 21st century for the clients and those seeking help.

Which sorts of help do you think are best?

1. A homeless person begging on the streets
- £5 for a good meal
- Giving money for a homeless shelter charity
- Saying a prayer for them
- A prescription for 'antipsychotics'
- Trying to change local and national housing policy
- Counselling
- A kick up the backside

2. An 80-year-old woman grief-stricken after the death of her husband who is terrified of being taken into a nursing home
- Someone to go round to cook her a meal each day
- Giving money to Help the Aged
- A prescription for TRANQUILLISERS or antidepressants from her GP
- Saying a prayer for her and her husband
- Trying to change the government's policy towards pensioners
- Counselling
- Being told to pull her socks up; what else does she expect at her age?
- A referral to a psychiatrist

3. A male colleague at work whose marriage is on the verge of breaking up because he spends too much time at the office
- Suggesting that he talk to the vicar at the church he goes to
- Counselling
- Saying a prayer for him
- Buying him a self-help book on positive thinking
- A stiff drink
- Organising other workers to petition management about the unreasonable hours people are expected to work
- Offering to take on some of his workload
- Lifestyle coaching
- Telling him that everyone's in the same boat and that if he can't stand the pace to get a different job

- Make a note of your responses then discuss them with others in your training group.

- What feelings came up for you when looking at each of the options you were offered?

Medical contexts

Counselling and alternative or complementary medicine

Some recent media coverage of counselling has presented it as part of the 'therapy' boom, or what some believe is a reaction against traditional scientific Western medicine: the flight into (or possibly [re]discovery of) alternative healing arts.

There may be some similarities between the social and political positions of counselling and alternative medicine therapies. Firstly, some counselling approaches are holistic. They treat humans as integrated working systems – change one element of the system

TRANQUILLISERS A type of drug which has a mood-flattening effect, often popularly referred to as 'downers' or sedatives. Sometimes referred to in medical literature as either 'major' tranquillisers such as Largactil (*chlorpromazine*) or 'minor' tranquillizers such as Librium and Valium (*diazepam*). Many of these drugs cause serious dependency and all have 'side' effects, some serious and permanently debilitating.

Note

Some 'alternative' medical treatments were, in fact, 'mainstream' until the advent of the NHS. They lost out politically, at least in the UK, when the National Health Service was established and the closed-shop monopoly was handed to the scientific medical physicians. Amongst those who lost out would be, most notably, medical herbalists (often local, community practitioners who were disenfranchised thus favouring the new drug companies).

It is the case that drug companies use herbal sources for many drugs, changing the molecular structure slightly in order to patent it.

Note

At time of publication, the government continues to publicise IAPT and announce funding. The whole project is contentious, with many practitioners dismayed at the mono-cultural provision (little is available beyond short-term cognitive behavioural therapies). It remains to be seen whether IAPT will deliver distressed people a choice of effective treatments. (See Chapter 11, p. 169.)

IF YOU WANT TO KNOW MORE ABOUT
IAPT

Take a look at the information sheets provided by BACP on their website:
<http://www.bacp.co.uk/iapt/>
and on the IAPT website:
<http://www.iapt.nhs.uk/>

Activity

Where, as newcomers to the counselling world, do you stand?
• *Do you have a view about alternative medicine?*
• *Do you think that counselling is associated with the boom in alternative medicine?*
• *How has media coverage of counselling affected you?*

and the whole system is thrown out of balance. Secondly, if we look at the types of alternative therapy we can see that some alternative therapies are based on 'ancient', 'lost' or ethnic healing systems and some on more recent ideas such as homeopathy. The reason some of these methods are 'alternative' is political. As I said, I don't think it has anything to do with whether they work or not. The medical profession is one of the oldest 'closed shops' in history. Anything that rivals the closed world of medicine is labelled 'quackery' and dismissed as useless, exploitative and dangerous. Because of this, many worthwhile treatments have been withheld for years because they were not within the domain of the medic and some ineffective and dangerous treatments have been offered by the medical profession in the guise of 'scientific' treatment.

As far as counselling is concerned, the helping approaches described in Chapter 2 do have echoes back to ancient healing systems, since we must concede that the ideas of Freud, Rogers and the rest are almost certainly not new. The theoretical formulations in their present state, however, are only 50 to 100 years old. Also, the counselling and psychotherapeutic models described in Chapter 2 have all had difficulty in gaining acceptance within the conventional medical system at one time or another. It is difficult to say whether more are accepted today in the places of power where decisions are made, even though the UK Government has said that it is committed to 'Improving Access to Psychological Therapies' (IAPT).

A section of the counselling community is trying to put 'clear blue water' between alternative medicine and counselling. They are uncomfortable with the idea that counselling is part of the alternative therapy boom and fear the trend in some newspapers, magazines and television to cast counselling in the same category as what some media like to portray as 'quackery', i.e. alternative therapy such as using crystals, aromatherapy, reflexology, etc.

Although I spend a little time in Chapter 12 looking at the thorny question of whether or not counselling works, I don't think the current interest in counselling and alternative medicine is to do with whether it works or not (even though the media sometimes try to portray it as such). What does seem to be important is that the media like to be seen as the readers' or viewers' friend and will make a show of tracking down quacks and charlatans on our behalf. The reporters and editors are so eager to get a good story that accuracy, integrity and, therefore, the real interests of the people they are serving, are either distorted or lost.

Counsellors in GP practices

Most readers will be aware that counselling is available from a number of GP surgeries in the UK. Some of you will have been referred by your GP to such a counsellor, and that might be why you are reading this book. This provision of counsellors in primary healthcare is relatively recent (gaining ground over the past 25 years) and there are still some GP practices without counselling as a treatment option. Sometimes the practice employs its own counsellor(s), sometimes the practice will 'buy in' a service provided by the local psychological services team or another source. The way psychological services are funded at GP practices changes frequently and will not doubt change with each change of government.

This picture changes year by year, as does the type of counselling you might be offered at a GP practice. Twenty years ago I believe the majority of counselling at GP practices would have been person-centred, but there has been a shift in recent years towards cognitive behaviour therapy. This may be because cognitive behaviour therapy is thought to be quicker (although it's difficult to find good evidence for this). There is good scientific evidence to show that both person-centred and cognitive behavioural therapy are *equally effective* with a range of problems, and both are better than routine GP care for anxiety and depression.

Counselling and psychiatry

In Chapter 11, I explain what a psychiatrist is and does. The version I give there is the 'official' one. It may help if you read that first if you are unsure about who does what in the helping professions.

Although most readers are taking literally their 'first step' into helping and counselling, I have tried really hard not to protect you from many of the rather awkward disputes and debates which characterise the helping professions in the 21st century. Some of

Note

At the time or writing, it is intended that IAPT (see margin, previous page) will have a role in providing the majority of this sort of service.

Readers should note that GP funding is currently under review and should make sure they keep up to date if counselling in primary care is their goal.

IF YOU WANT TO KNOW MORE ABOUT EFFECTIVENESS RESEARCH

There is some further information in Chapter 12, pp. 182-3 and a very good comprehensive, accessible book is:

Cooper, M (2008) *Essential Research Findings in Counselling and Psychotherapy: The facts are friendly.* London: Sage.

Your political and spiritual beliefs and your helping approach

- What political beliefs do you hold?
- What spiritual beliefs do you hold?
- How did you come to have these beliefs?
- How do you think these beliefs affect your views on helping?
- How would you behave as a helper if you *fully* acted out your political and spiritual beliefs?
- Are any of the approaches described in this book, or elsewhere, that you have read about or been told about by your tutor, in harmony with your political and spiritual beliefs?

- Make a note of your responses then discuss them with others in your training group.
- What feelings came up for you when looking at each of the options you were offered?

We are taught to expect strong feelings to come up when we talk about these topics. Did that happen for you? Were there strong negative or positive reactions from others when you shared your beliefs?

MEDICAL MODEL The system used to understand and classify psychological distress in the Western world, based on the similarity of symptoms *not* cause and effect relationships. It is not a disease model although it looks like one, mimicking the medical model of physical disease. It is used by psychiatrists and the majority of mental health professionals.

> IF YOU WANT TO KNOW MORE ABOUT THE MEDICAL MODEL OF MENTAL ILLNESS

Take a look at:

Lemma, A (1996) *Introduction to Psychopathology.* London: Sage.

For a critical view, try:

Newnes, C, Holmes, G & Dunn, C (1999) *This is Madness: A critical look at psychiatry and the future of the mental health services.* Ross-on-Wye: PCCS Books.

Neither are recommended for *absolute* beginners, but the following book, whilst critical, is a good, accessible read and evidence-based:

Bentall, R (2009) *Doctoring the Mind: Why psychiatric treatments fail.* London: Penguin.

NEUROSIS Mental 'illness' characterised by a 'normal' human quality, like anxiety, being amplified to unpleasant and debilitating levels. Includes phobias and panic attacks.

Note

There should be a 'Fairness Warning' here, since I would remind you that this list of landmarks is written by a counsellor, trained in the early 1970s, active in the anti-psychiatry movement. I do not apologise for the lack of balance for you will get the other side of the story almost everywhere else you look.

Note

Some are concerned that the increases in psychiatric diagnosis mark the 'medicalisation' of diversity, and cite the medicalisation of sexuality, pregnancy, disability, etc. as evidence.

these disputes and debates go back many years. As you read this you must bear in mind that psychiatrists are *primarily* medical practitioners. This bears on the debate in a number of ways, but particularly because psychiatrists are medical practitioners, they use what is known as the 'MEDICAL MODEL of mental illness' to describe the full range of human psychological distress and disturbance. Although it is actually no more than a system of naming things (e.g. the term 'NEUROSIS' [literally meaning an infection of the nerves] is just a list of symptoms; it actually *explains* nothing), it gives an air of authority to any psychiatric 'diagnosis'.

The MEDICAL MODEL of mental illness is a contentious subject. It is supposed to work in the same way as the system for naming physical ills, and we need to bear in mind that first, it was developed at a time when there wasn't any other way of naming distress available that seemed coherent, and second, it was developed by doctors, and because of their training (i.e. as specialists in *physical disease*) they genuinely believed that psychological disturbance was rooted in physical causes.

The relationship between counselling as a psychotherapeutic form of helping and psychiatry goes back many years, but I am not going to relate the history of psychiatry here. I will, instead give a few landmarks in the development of the contemporary dispute between therapeutic counselling and psychiatry.

1920s Freud was a physician by training, who until late in his career was shunned by the medical profession.

1950s Carl Rogers used the label 'counselling' for the whole field of non-medical helping for those with psychological disturbance because he was not allowed to use any terms that alluded to psychotherapeutic or psychiatric practice by the American medical profession. Those without a medical qualification were not allowed to practise psychotherapy.

1960s The 'anti-psychiatry' movement was founded, on both sides of the Atlantic, by people who strongly objected to the 'medicalisation' of psychological disturbance and all that comes with it. By this I mean that a whole range of human emotions, distress and disturbance became labelled as 'illness' according to the social mores of the time. In partnership with the law, doctors became (and remain) extremely powerful agents of social control, since you can be locked up and treated against your will for a variety of 'illnesses'.

The following 'medical conditions' were (historically – not necessarily in the 60s) treatable by force by psychiatrists:

Sexual Deviance: any kind of socially disapproved sexual feelings or practices, including masturbation and being gay, or having an

Counselling Skills for Nurses

In the normal course of a nurse's job (whatever the specialisation), he or she will be 'helping people' in the classic sense. It's why people become nurses. The ability to form good relationships is central to the nursing role. It may even be the case that people get better more quickly from physical illness when they have a good relationship with their carers. However, as with so many jobs, it has traditionally been assumed that the 'working with people' or 'people skills' part of the job is *natural*. It was assumed that everyone could do it just by dint of will, and that it was quite obvious how it should be done. After working through the first eight chapters of this book, I hope you can see that, although some people might be naturally good at forming effective relationships, there are some things we can all learn from the world of counselling.

The meaning of illness
People vary in how they respond to illness, whether it be mild or severe. Illness has *emotional* meaning for us – some of us behave as though death is imminent when all we have is the common cold, whilst others are stoical despite great pain and disability. Helping ill people endure and recover from illness is not just a matter of tending to physical needs – psychology plays an important part. *Understanding* the meaning of illness for each patient is the key to good nursing, since some patients exaggerate symptoms whilst others hide them. Being non-judgemental and respectful are also essential to the patient's feeling of wellbeing. These are the key elements of healing relationships, both physical and emotional.

Relatives of ill people
We don't need to be reminded that when someone is ill, the whole family is affected. When the illness is serious or requires lifestyle changes for the patient and their family, nursing takes on a wider supportive function. For example, patients with organ failure awaiting transplants need to adapt their lifestyle, maintain a recovery-oriented way of thinking and feel supported by their families. These expectations (and a natural wish to be supportive) can soon become burdensome and the carers need to sustain themselves and feel supported. When a nurse is the only point of contact, basic helping and counselling skills are the most appropriate qualities on which to base support for patients' families.

Terminal illness
Palliative care is a medical specialisation in its own right; however, general nurses on medical wards and district nurses are the 'front line' when it comes to routine care and support for people with a terminal illness and their families. However experienced, it is still distressing and draining work. If nurses become inured or hardened to the work, it will show and they will damage their patients and themselves. The self-awareness and self-support qualities of counselling-skills helping, the ability to be almost infinitely understanding and respectfully protect the patient's dignity, can be enhanced through counselling skills training.

Specialist support
Many patients with chronic (long-lasting) illnesses require support beyond the physical (changing dressings, tests, and administering repeated treatments). Having a chronic illness is debilitating psychologically as well as physically and relationship skills are essential to help the patient get the best out of life.

If you are a nurse, what areas of *your* work and specific tasks do *you* think would be helped by a better understanding and implementation of counselling skills? ✍

Note

The American Psychiatric Association produce a diagnostic manual that is used by all American psychiatrists to help diagnose mental illness. It is called the *Diagnostic and Statistical Manual of Mental Disorders*, or DSM for short. It is now in its fourth edition (so you will know what people are referring to when they use the term DSM-IV) the fifth edition is due in 2013. It is the 'bible' for psychiatric diagnoses. If it's in there, it's an 'illness'. If it's not in there, it's not.

You may (or may not) be shocked to know that until 1973 'homosexuality' was in there as an 'illness', in the complete absence of scientific evidence (you would imagine that psychiatry is 'scientific').

'A notable gay physician, Howard Brown, aptly commented upon the DSM Board vote deleting homosexuality as a diagnosis. He stated, "The board vote made millions of Americans who had officially been ill that morning officially well that afternoon. Never before in history had so many people been cured in so little time."' (Minton, 2002, p. 261)

Minton, HL (2002) *Departing from Deviance*. Chicago: University of Chicago Press.

Laing, RD (1969) *Self and Others*. London: Penguin.

American Psychiatric Association (1994) *DSM-IV.* Washington DC: American Psychiatric Association.

ELECTROCONVULSIVE THERAPY (ECT) See margin notes on pp. 171 or 184.

IATROGENIC Damage caused by procedures intended to heal most often used to mean illness caused by medical treatment.

Activity

You are likely to already have views on the subject of psychological and psychiatric services.
• *Have you received psychiatric care, or do you know anyone who has?*
• *Have you received counselling, or do you know anyone who has?*
• *Were these experiences positive or negative?*
• *How has this affected your views on helping?*

illegitimate child. These 'illnesses' led to people being incarcerated and 'treated' against their will in mental institutions.

Drapetomania: A disease which caused black slaves to run away. The prescribed treatment was beating.

The anti-psychiatry movement rails against what they considered to be brutal psychiatric treatments such as ELECTRO-CONVULSIVE THERAPY (ECT) and enforced drug treatments, many of which lead to IATROGENIC illness. With patients suffering tremors, cramps, mood swings and permanent disability caused by psychiatric treatment (drugs), it soon becomes difficult to tell the effects of the cure from the symptoms of the original complaint.

The anti-psychiatry movement fails to deliver alternative treatment methods that seem to 'work' (see Chapter 12), and those offered, e.g. Laing (1969), are subjected to ridicule by psychiatrists. Few, if any, of the alternative treatments for psychological distress are funded by the NHS, and so have to be offered privately.

1970s Counselling in various forms is established in education (in university and further education student counselling services) and voluntary helping agencies such as the National Marriage Guidance Council (now Relate) and gains rapidly in popularity away from the disapproving gaze of the medical profession.

1980s From various sources comes the message that counselling is only suitable for helping 'the worried well' and that the really disturbed people are only safely treated by psychiatrists. This is said even though psychiatric treatment has become only marginally more sophisticated and still causes great suffering with IATROGENIC conditions through overprescribing of drugs.

New, non-invasive, treatments for very disturbed people begin to emerge, pioneered by psychologists and counsellors.

1990s Psychiatrists still maintain that some of the most chronic, long-term forms of mental problems cannot be treated. These conditions are evidence that mental 'illness' is rooted in physical causes and can only be corrected by physical (i.e. chemical or electrical) treatments. The best example of this type of disturbance is 'schizophrenia' where the sufferer hears voices.

Cognitive psychologists and counsellors mount a concerted effort to demonstrate that much chronic 'schizophrenia' and voice hearing can be relieved at least as much by the sensitive application of new findings and development of new 'talking cures' or psychotherapy as by drug treatments and ECT. A self-help action group is formed by voice hearers called 'Hearing Voices Network'. These people are far from 'mad'; they organise meetings and conferences to discuss treatment options and life in general (some meetings are open to people who *cannot* hear voices.)

2000s Research increasingly shows that counselling approaches (a) are as effective as routine GP care and some drug treatments for anxiety and depression, (b) cognitive and person-centred therapies are equally effective, and (c) the criteria for empirically supported treatment embrace many counselling conditions and skills – even including such apparently esoteric qualities such as empathy.

There is still vigorous disagreement in many circles over the 'proper' roles for 'talking cures' like counselling and psychotherapy, and on the other hand, physical treatments such as drugs within psychiatry and the helping professions. There is, however, real public debate about how best to care for people with enduring serious mental health problems, particularly concerning whether disturbed people should be cared for in the community or in specialist places of safety.

Educational contexts

In the 1960s, the ideas of Carl Rogers began to infiltrate education in the United Kingdom. Initially, the idea that university and polytechnic students (away from home for the first time) would find it useful to talk over their problems took hold in a handful of higher education institutions. Amongst the first wave of counselling services in the UK were Keele University, Preston Polytechnic and Portsmouth Polytechnic. These services often were 'generic', that is to say that a student might be helped with a financial problem, changing course or a career choice upon leaving. Indeed, many counselling services grew within or in close association with the careers service.

Postgraduate courses were developed at the Universities of Keele, Swansea, Exeter, Reading and Aston to meet a small but growing need for counsellors in education, and the usual course requirement was that applicants be qualified teachers with two years' teaching experience. Again, these courses were often closely associated with careers officers' courses.

In the 1970s and 1980s, counselling services in higher and further education grew in popularity and became commonplace. It was taken as read that students, whether at the local tech or at Oxbridge, should have someone to go to for a confidential chat. Problems taken to such services ranged from getting the bus fare home through to dealing with a problem pregnancy or surviving an abusive home life.

Over this period a few counsellors were appointed to work in schools. A very small number of innovative educational authorities had county-wide schemes to place counsellors in schools, but the

Note

The literature describing studies on the effectiveness of counselling is not an easy read for people without a psychology background, but if you enrol for diploma training, you should become familiar with it. An excellent and accessible book by Mick Cooper is a good starting place:

> **Cooper, M (2008)** *Essential Research Findings in Counselling and Psychotherapy: The facts are friendly.* London: Sage.

Note

Some practitioners, whilst committed to evidence-based practice, are disappointed by what they see as the partial way the evidence is treated and included/excluded when it comes to setting the criteria for NICE. NICE is the National Institute for Health and Clinical Excellence – see also p. 183, Chapter 12.

Counselling Skills for Teachers

All of us at some time have been pupils, so we know how we personally rate the qualities of a good teacher. My favourite teacher at secondary school treated me like an adult, my least favourite teachers were those that were bullies. I would be very surprised if the qualities of being a good teacher did not include the qualities necessary to make good helping relationships, i.e. empathy, acceptance and genuineness. Of course it is not *simply* a matter of helping skills. Teachers must be good communicators, good motivators and be able to administer fair discipline. These are the professional skills of the teacher, alongside which the skills of good basic helping sit very nicely.

Being a good tutor
In the last years of secondary school, especially when pupils are preparing for work, or further/ higher education, many schools operate a tutorial system. Small groups of pupils will meet daily or weekly for a session where social and personal education is the focus. Tutors will also be available for one-to-one support, and it is primarily in this role that the skills of basic helping come to the fore. Here the adult is less of a teacher and more of a mentor, so respect, understanding and being a good role model are the important qualities.

Helping the bullied and the bullies
Specialist knowledge and skills are only occasionally needed when dealing with the problem of bullying at school. The theories and plans that have been developed to combat bullying draw heavily on basic helping skills. Almost every reader will have some experience of this, either as a victim or a bully, and probably as both. So will the vast majority of teachers. Our personal experience should help develop our sensitivity and awareness of the situation, not cloud our thinking, making us less understanding. Being open, non-judgemental and genuine will enable the teacher to help both the bullies and the victims. Primarily victims need to be believed and bullies need to be understood – this facilitates the next step of resolving the situation, protecting the victim if appropriate and stopping the bully.

When home life comes in to school
This is an occasion when the concept of boundaries comes to life. Although we might like to compartmentalise life, events at home will inevitably affect life at school – for both pupils and teachers. It is often the form teacher who notices something first and sensitive intervention, with the qualities of basic helping early on, can prevent the distress being compounded at school. Likewise, if the teacher is to leave their own worries at home, and not visit them upon their pupils, increased self-awareness and an ability to attend to their own needs are essential. Respectful understanding and self-awareness are key helping qualities that help us separate our own emotional baggage from those we are trying to help. Since our experiences at school are a rich source of feelings – good and bad – it is no more than good sense to make sure that we do not bring any leftover feelings to our work.

> If you are a teacher, what areas of *your* work and specific tasks do *you* think would be helped by a better understanding and implementation of counselling skills? ✍

majority used the schools' welfare service or educational psychologists in the schools' psychology service, since the only time a pupil was deemed in need of extra help was if they were underachieving academically or disruptive. The overstretched welfare officers and educational psychologists were usually too busy to deal with all but the most serious of cases, so 'everyday' problems from bereavement through to bullying were left for the form teacher or pastoral team in most schools.

It is not difficult to argue for counselling in schools. Greater levels of awareness regarding the experiences of children in general and the problems of violence and bullying at school mean that an increasing number of people can see the value of counsellors working independently of the teaching staff in schools. The key here is the *independence* of counsellors. That counsellors can be seen by everyone as different from the teaching staff is both an advantage and a disadvantage. School pupils may disclose more to someone who is believed to be independent of the teachers, but the teaching staff can sometimes view the counsellors with suspicion because they might see them as being on the 'side' of the pupils. Getting the balance right and being experienced with integrity by all groups in a school is part of the challenge of the job – a good school counsellor is a wonderful asset to any school.

The good news is that there is a definite trend towards increased provision of counselling in schools in the UK. At the time of going to print, the Welsh Assembly Government (WAG) had committed to extending schools counselling and research projects to evaluate the provision. The WAG project is ongoing in conjunction with BACP and various research establishments. Also, the University of Strathclyde Counselling Unit was funded by Glasgow and Clyde NHS Board to evaluate schools counselling, again with a view to rolling out provision to a larger number of schools.

Social work contexts

The role of social workers as helping agents in our society has been the subject of media criticism in recent years. Social workers are expected to cover a huge range of care functions, from the fair allocation of access to services (deciding who gets what service) through to managing individual cases, carrying out care plans and working in residential settings with children and adolescents. When the system fails to deliver the best care, the social worker is the person at hand who will bear the brunt of the criticism.

At one end of the job, the management and administration of care services may appear to be a mechanical task, but as a parent of a disabled child, I have seen at first hand how decisions regarding funding that affect the quality of life of my family are made by

Note

The BACP has a thriving division, Counselling Children and Young People (CCYP – for decades known as Counselling in Education), and you will find details of their activities on the BACP website <http://www.ccyp.co.uk/>.

IF YOU WANT TO KNOW MORE ABOUT
COUNSELLING IN SCHOOLS

Take a look at:

BACP (2006) *Good Practice Guidance for Counselling in Schools* (4th ed). Rugby: British Association for Counselling and Psychotherapy.

Note

Preliminary research results in both Scotland and Wales are very promising and the schemes are being rolled out to more schools. Details of the Welsh Assembly Government funded research and the preliminary results can be accessed by looking at the BACP Research website <http://www.bacp.co.uk/research/School_Counselling.php>.

Counselling Skills for Social Workers

Nearly all of the tasks involved in social work pivot upon good 'people skills', but not all social work training pays sufficient attention to the development of such qualities and abilities. The relationship skills at the core of social work practice are practically identical to those presented in this book as basic helping. There are, however, crucial contextual differences between social work and counselling – one of the main differences involves the legal responsibilities of the social worker. Qualified social workers will have no trouble in understanding the concept of confidentiality; however, a counsellor will not have the same statutory duty of care.

Advocacy
One of the key roles for social workers is to act as an advocate for, for example, a child, older person or person with a learning disability who is not able to represent themselves. This role requires sensitivity, empathy, acceptance and courage, as the social worker tries to discern the wishes and needs of their client, and then press the client's case on their behalf. Basic helping skills will help the social worker understand their client (and their needs) better.

Needs assessment
Social workers are frequently called upon to assess what a person or family requires in order to have a reasonable quality of life. A typical scenario would be when a person is disabled, either at birth or by accident or illness. There will be lots of people in the client's life who all have vested interests, family and friends, but the social worker has to take a view that embraces all of these whilst putting the needs of the individual first. My experience as a parent of a child with special needs taught me that, after years of thinking I knew best for my child, I had to admit that the social workers brought a new and challenging view. Basic helping in a counselling way helps everyone avoid being defensive and work towards the best solution.

Crisis intervention
When certain crises hit our lives, social workers are the people who have to pick up the pieces. If a family is made homeless, for example, social workers will have to place the children in care. Rapid responses are needed, but the caring elements of the work must not be overlooked. Confidence in one's basic helping qualities of empathy, acceptance and genuineness will help make a difficult situation as least distressing as possible for all concerned.

Residential care
This challenging sector of social work requires, in effect, being an active helper without respite for hours at a time. Coffee breaks, mealtimes, 'relaxing' in front of the TV – all become therapeutic possibilities. Having a secure foundation of basic helping qualities, empathy, acceptance, respect and genuineness, is the key to survival, let alone good practice. Being able to look after yourself and remain an effective helper requires a high level of self-awareness. An increasing number of social workers in this setting train to the level of counselling skills and beyond in order to better prepare for the rigours of this work.

If you are a social worker, what areas of *your* work and specific tasks do *you* think would be helped by a better understanding and implementation of counselling skills?   ✍

social workers at some cost to themselves. There is great stress involved in trying to fairly allocate insufficient funds, and there is a high turnover of social workers in some settings.

It would be reassuring to think that counselling skills should be a part of the professional repertoire of social workers who manage and provide care, for example:

- helping older people as they struggle with a senile partner
- supporting a family with a disabled child
- working in residential homes with children taken in to local authority care
- supporting the same young people when they leave care to live independently
- monitoring adoption and foster parents and supporting where necessary
- providing respite care and support for carers

Few would argue that listening, accurate understanding, acceptance and genuineness are essential qualities for such work, yet counselling skills are rarely built in to social work training. It has been the case in the past that it was simply assumed that social workers would be natural helpers, even though the major part of the training involved the administration and legal aspects of the job. Some social workers complete counsellor training as a supplement to their work and go on to offer dedicated counselling services within their team, but this nearly always depends upon funding. Increasingly, social services departments use the voluntary sector to deliver counselling and support to clients.

Commercial contexts

Two views of human nature are frequently presented in management texts. These were described by Douglas McGregor in 1970 as 'Theory X' and 'Theory Y'.

McGregor, D (1970) *The Human Side of Enterprise.* Maidenhead: McGraw-Hill.

Theory X
- People have a natural dislike for work and will avoid it if they can.
- Therefore people must be controlled, directed, threatened and cajoled to get them to put in enough effort to achieve the organisational objectives.
- People prefer to be directed like this, they dislike and avoid responsibility, have little ambition and want security above all.

Theory Y
- It is as natural for humans to work as it is for us to play or rest.
- People will exercise self-control and self-direction in order to

Activity
What do you think about these different viewpoints on human nature and work?
• *What is your experience of yourself and other people at work – is there a difference?*

CONTAINMENT A term from psychodynamic counselling meaning keeping negative or destructive personality traits and forces under control.

Coaching

The International Coach Federation (ICF) defines coaching as 'partnering with clients in a thought-provoking and creative process that inspires them to maximize their personal and professional potential.' The Federation casts a professional coaching relationship as essentially a business agreement bound by a set of ethical codes.

This is particularly appropriate for coaching in a business context, but as can be seen from the definition, coaching as a generic term and practice has a much wider application including helping people to achieve a more fulfilling personal life, quite independent of any occupation they might have.

BACP established a Coaching Division in June 2010 and that should prove to be a good information resource when established.

The ICF Code of Ethics can be found at <http://www.coach federation.org.uk/welcome/icf_code_of_ethics.phtml> and the BACP Coaching website at <http://www.bacpcoach ing.co.uk/index.php>

---

meet organisational objectives to which they are committed.
• People will, under proper conditions, not only accept but seek responsibility.
• The majority of people are imaginative and creative when faced with organisational problems.

You may have worked in organisations which ran as though the managers believed either Theory X or Theory Y. You may also see that these approaches to human nature have some elements in common with some of the ideas that underpin the approaches to helping we looked at in Chapter 2. Theory X is very roughly equivalent to a psychoanalytic view of human nature where the assumed antisocial aspects of human nature need CONTAINMENT and direction. Theory Y has more in common with humanistic approaches to helping.

Management ideas like this become the style, ethos or culture of the company and will to a large extent determine the company attitude towards employee welfare. Welfare officers used to be employed in personnel departments of the vast majority of medium-sized and large companies. It was their job to visit sick employees, take care of the families of deceased employees and even run social activities. My uncle was employed for all of his working life at a car components manufacturers in the Midlands and I vividly remember the popular company social club and annual sports days. Company welfare officers have long since gone and personnel departments have been 're-envisioned' as 'human resources management' and employee welfare is now likely to be attended to by one of the many Employee Assistance Programmes.

Employee Assistance Programmes (EAP)

Since the mid-1980s, private companies (EAPs) have provided some of the welfare and assistance services previously provided by welfare and personnel officers, including a range of advice and support, including counselling. EAPs will provide a service tailored to the needs of the company and their employees. So, for example, employees may be given a card with the telephone number of the EAP to be called for legal assistance or personal problems. Legal assistance may be delivered via a telephone helpline, and personal problems may be received firstly on the telephone, where a counsellor will assess the situation before attempting to either deal with the problem on the phone or refer the employee to an EAP counsellor close to where they live.

EAPs also offer critical incident debriefing in situations where people require support and counselling, both after major disasters such as train crashes, and after accidents at work.

Research done with Post Office employees in the 1980s showed

Counselling Skills for Managers

A few years ago I would have been laughed at for suggesting that the qualities of good helping would be useful for managers in industry, commerce and the public sector. The 'world of work' may be so called because we are supposed to believe it is somehow separate or different from our other world at home. It is not, even though we have many unpleasant phrases to describe it: 'cut-throat', 'the rat race' and others just as colourful. There are several areas of management that require the skills and abilities of counselling. If a key function of any manager is to unlock the potential of those that they manage, then the essentially *enabling* qualities of basic helping in a counselling way are nothing short of essential.

Mentoring/Coaching

Many managers are called upon to mentor or coach employees new to a job, or manage a mentoring scheme. Mentoring or coaching are not simply teaching or instructing. (Most adults have varying memories of teachers and many might not appreciate being cast in the role of 'pupil' especially if they are older than you.) The ability to build a good enabling relationship is at the heart of mentoring and coaching at work – being non-judgemental, respectful, empathic and genuine combine with being a good motivator and educator. Both the workplace competencies *and* the personal needs of the mentored person are developed in this process. Starting from the point of view that the person being coached has potential, the task is to help them discover this and use it for themselves and the company to live a more fulfilling life at work and at home. Coaching is a term that is growing in use to describe collaborative enabling relationships, aimed at helping people fulfil their potential at work and in life in general.

Bullying at work

Recently identified as a major problem in some workplaces, bullying at work (including harassment) is no easier to prevent and resolve than bullying at school. Recently highlighted in the media, bullying and harassment at work can be a major cause of unhappiness and stress at work, as well as leading to poor work performance. Although some specialist training will be required, there is no doubt that the skills of basic helping will serve you well when trying to understand the *people* involved, rather than simply seeing it as another problem to be solved.

Stress and burnout

As the pace of life in general, and the world of work in particular, increases, we are all more susceptible to stress, overload, or just simply 'the pressures of life'. Some workplaces expect employees to work over and above their paid hours in the mistaken belief that an overworked stressed-out employee is more efficient than a happy, relaxed one. The line manager is often the person best able to spot individuals vulnerable to stress, either because of work schedules or personal worries. Knowing your employees well and having a good relationship is the start. Listening, respectfully valuing them as people and genuinely caring for their welfare completes the picture. Stress, though debilitating, can be reduced if the causes are attended to and the person concerned learns new ways to constructively deal with the ordinary, reasonable stresses of work and home life.

If you are a line manager, what areas of *your* work and specific tasks do *you* think would be helped by a better understanding and implementation of counselling skills? ✍

that workplace stress and staff turnover were reduced as were sickness and absence rates, when employees had access to workplace counselling services.

Counsellors employed by EAPs will be fully qualified to diploma level or beyond and will also be accredited or registered with UKRCP (United Kingdom Register of Counsellors/Psychotherapists) or UKCP (United Kingdom Council for Psychotherapy).

Community contexts

Most approaches to psychotherapy go beyond the individual to groups and communities. Almost all of the major theorists found it unsatisfactory to end their theorising at the level of the individual. Freud and other psychoanalysts were concerned about political movements in Europe in the 1930s. Skinner wrote a novel *Walden Two* depicting a utopian behaviourist society where all were in charge of their own destiny. Carl Rogers expanded his ideas to large groups and communities, spending the later years of his life working for world peace. Aaron Beck has written extensively on aggression in contemporary society (Beck, 1999).

At the most simple level, regardless of the approach you take, the more people there are with highly developed basic helping qualities, the more caring a society we will have. The values implicit in counselling, from the individual helper up to BACP, are the values of care, mutual understanding and respect, cooperation and sharing. A community based on these values should thrive.

Classical Freudian theory and more contemporary psychodynamic theories take a somewhat darker view of human nature and therefore would expect that the destructive parts of human personality would need CONTAINMENT, or, in community terms, active policing. The qualities of good psychodynamic helping, though, are still seen as good foundations for a healthy community.

Most of the theories of counselling place at least some of the blame for human psychological distress with the community or society so it is sensible that we should look to improving mental health by improving our social and material environment – in short the society in which we live.

Note

There is a little more information on UKRCP in Chapter 12, p. 190. The website is <http://www.ukrconline.org.uk>.

Skinner, BF (1966) *Walden Two*. New York: Macmillan. (Original work published 1938)

Some of Carl Rogers' large community and peace work is published in the last five chapters of:

Kirschenbaum, H & Henderson, VL (1990) *The Carl Rogers Reader*. London: Constable.

The history of this work can be found in Kirschenbaum, H (2007) *The Life and Work of Carl Rogers*. Ross-on-Wye: PCCS Books.

Beck, AT (1999) *Prisoners of Hate: The cognitive basis of anger, hostility and violence*. New York: HarperCollins.

CONTAINMENT A term from psychodynamic counselling meaning keeping negative or destructive personality traits and forces under control.

Activity
- *What sort of community would you like to live in?*
- *What values are the foundation blocks of this community?*
- *Are the principles and values of basic helping in a counselling way in accord with this?*
- *Do you think it is sensible to understand human distress and healing in terms of communities?*

'In every community, there is work to be done. In every nation, there are wounds to heal. In every heart, there is the power to do it.'

Marianne Williamson

'Our mission in this new century is clear. For good or ill, we live in an interdependent world. We can't escape each other. Therefore, we have to spend our lives building a global community of shared responsibilities, shared values, shared benefits.'

Bill Clinton

Counselling Skills for Volunteers

Involvement in voluntary work has been one of the most popular ways of expressing community-mindedness or citizenship. There is a huge list of voluntary agencies in which the volunteers require a sensitivity to others that, in some circumstances, can be called 'counselling skills'. The abilities to not judge the other person, to listen patiently and to be authentic are at the heart of much volunteer work both secular or faith-based. Some voluntary organisations provide services which have particular resonance with helping in a counselling way, indeed some provide services that are, to all intents and purposes, counselling, or the offering of counselling skills. Many of these organisations do not use the term counselling to describe their work, sometimes because they were founded before the word was used in its modern sense. If you want to do counselling-related voluntary work, here are a few organisations which you could consider. Many have short specialist training which has to be completed before you begin.

Samaritans
Phone: 08457 90 90 90 <http://www.samaritans.org/>
Famous listening service for people thinking of committing suicide founded by The Rev. Chad Varah in 1953. Volunteers staff phone lines and in some places offer face-to-face befriending and other appropriate services.

Rape Crisis
http://www.rapecrisis.org.uk/
A feminist support service for the victims of rape and sexual violence, male or female. Each Rape Crisis centre is independent – the website is for the umbrella organisation.

(Lesbian, Gay, Bisexual, Transgender) LGBT Switchboards
There are several LGBT Switchboards dotted around the country, each one autonomous, providing locally appropriate services for people who are not certain about their sexuality, are worried about stigmatisation or are afraid to come out. Started as telephone services, but provide many other outreach and education services as well.

Cruse Bereavement Care
http://www.crusebereavementcare.org.uk/
Founded in the late 1950s, the charity provides grief counselling and bereavement support for people of all ages and circumstances. Telephone helpline and face-to-face counselling.

Working with young people: Youth Access
http://www.youthaccess.org.uk/
An umbrella organisation representing youth counselling agencies. If you want to work with young people in your area, contact Youth Access to find out more.

Relate
http://www.relate.org.uk/
Started as the National Marriage Guidance Council by Rev Herbert Gray on 1938. Was instrumental in the spread of counselling in the UK in the 1960s and 70s and centrally involved in the founding of BACP (then BAC). Dedicated to helping people with relationship and sexual difficulties through national network of centres. Rigorous training and commitment is required for volunteers.

> Your local library is a good place to find out about local voluntary organisations if you can't get online.

Counselling Skills for Citizens

I hope it doesn't sound too grandiose to suggest that the qualities of basic helping should be a natural part of good citizenship. In the last years of his life, Carl Rogers devoted much effort to furthering world peace. In fact, he was to be nominated for the Nobel Peace Prize but he died before he could be told. Rogers believed that the qualities necessary for good therapeutic relationships would apply to a wide range of settings including conflict resolution and the building of communities. He conducted groups in South Africa at the height of apartheid and in Northern Ireland at the height of 'the troubles' – going to the heart of political hot spots. Empathy, UPR and congruence in everyday parlance turn out to be understanding, acceptance and genuineness. Who could argue that these would not be included in a list of the essential characteristics of citizenship?

I am not suggesting that we all dive in to try to resolve conflict or solve local problems in our neighbourhood. I am suggesting, though, that as citizens we all have roles and responsibilities. On the preceding pages I have very briefly looked at where counselling skills might fit in to work. Work, however, is only one part of life. Although communities are dependent upon work, other personal and social factors are just as influential. 'Family' and 'neighbourhood' may appear to be concepts that have passed their sell-by date, but the human needs for love, development, protection and community cannot be neglected. We would do so at our peril.

As partners, parents, friends and neighbours we have connections and responsibilities that would be enhanced by better self-awareness and the qualities of basic helping in a counselling way. That does not mean that we should 'play the counsellor' for all and sundry. Far from it. Children need parents to love them in ways that counsellors never can. Neighbours need to give and take, live together in ways that counsellors cannot live with their clients. Respect and understanding for, and valuing of, each other regardless of race, class or creed, are the foundations both of counselling and of healthy communities.

It is clear that neither counselling nor counsellors have all the answers. Counselling theories are flawed and incomplete, and counsellors get things wrong. However, counsellors *do* appreciate the value of being non-judgemental to others and one's self. We could be kinder to ourselves and each other by not being so afraid of failure that it distorts our every natural movement. We could be not so ready to find someone to blame that it strangles our natural inclinations to get involved and help. It might appear that these projects would need coordinated effort in order to succeed. However, action at the level of the individual citizen *does* have an effect, and then these individual actions can be organised.

How will you use the learning you have made in your introduction to counselling? Whatever reasons and objectives you may have had when you started the course, how might you enhance your contribution to society as a citizen?

As a citizen, what areas of *your* life and specific contribution to *your* community do *you* think would be helped by a better understanding and sharing of counselling skills? ✍

clients

This chapter is an opportunity to turn the focus completely on *clients*. I'll do this by looking at what clients bring to counselling in terms of both problems and resources. I'll deal with the last one first and briefly describe some recent ideas about what clients contribute to the counselling process. Then I'll offer a few illustrations of who seeks and receives counselling in the UK. How they do it and what is likely to happen. Neither section is intended to be a comprehensive list. As with other parts of this book, they aim to be both informative and a starting point for further exploration.

What do clients bring to counselling?

In the 1940s, Carl Rogers suggested that the client was the expert in their own problem and that they, by and large, had the solutions within them, if only they could be helped to find them. As a general principle this seemed to make sense to many professional helpers, but the idea that clients were intrinsic self-healers was not developed until relatively recently. Books on helping traditionally concentrated almost exclusively on what the helper was doing, ignoring the client almost completely.

Art Bohart and Karen Tallman were the first therapists to systematically assemble the evidence that clients are active self-healers in their 1999 book, *How Clients Make Therapy Work: The process of active self-healing.* They explain how clients have a surprisingly wide range of ways of managing their own healing, or 'self-righting', in and out of therapy. This idea that clients actually do something active proved to be challenging, since it seems that clients also make positive use of 'mistakes' that helpers make in the helping process. They found that clients do two things in therapy to make it work for them:

- They look beyond the superficial things (like individual therapist responses) for the underlying stable factors such as the attitudes and values of the therapist and how they think therapy is going.
- They look for things to make positive use of, i.e. practically anything the therapist says or does, including suggestions or advice from the therapist.

Note

This is not *strictly* accurate, since CBT practice has acknowledged the creative ways in which clients cope with the symptoms of distress. CBT practitioners work to make the clients' own coping strategies safe and to enhance them.

Bohart, AC & Tallman, K (1999) *How Clients Make Therapy Work: The process of active self-healing. Washington* DC: American Psychological Association.

Note

The above 1999 book is difficult to get hold of in the UK (you could try used-book websites). The same work is updated in a briefer chapter in:

Cooper, M, Watson, JC & Hölldampf, D (eds) (2010) *Person-Centred and Experiential Therapies Work: A review of the research on counselling, psychotherapy and related practices. Ross on Wye: PCCS Books.*

Bohart, A & Tallman, K (1999) *How Clients Make Therapy Work: The process of active self-healing. Washington* DC: American Psychological Association.

Note

Many of us are happy to pay gym membership fees, so paying for regular therapy sessions may not sound so strange and the sessions don't have to be weekly.

IF YOU WANT TO KNOW MORE ABOUT
CO-COUNSELLING

There are two variations of co-counselling: Co-Counselling International (with an active UK network) and Re-evaluation Counselling (developed by Harvey Jackins – worth a look on wikipedia). Both websites are packed with useful information. Look at both before you decide:
CCI<http://www.co-counselling.org.uk/>
RC<http://www.rc.org/>

Bohart and Tallman found that the client will use everything in their own way, *regardless of what the therapist may have intended.*

Although these results suggest that even poor responses from the helper can be turned to positive effect by the client, they do not give licence for shoddy helping in practice. It is clear that this relates to occasional *lapses* or *mistakes* rather than consistently bad helping. The fact we must not forget is that clients are not passive recipients of helpers' interventions, they are active seekers of positive factors.

Furthermore, Bohart and Tallman suggest that this explains why clients get better even though they don't seem to be doing what the theories of therapy say they should be doing. They conclude that clients are running their helping process themselves according to their own rules.

Why do people seek basic counselling-style helping?

Many people accept that talking through problems is beneficial. The word *counselling* comes readily to the lips of anyone seeking such an opportunity to talk and be listened to. A glance at the notice board in your public library or a flick through the front of your telephone directory will give you an insight into the range of local problem-related counselling services available. It may seem all too obvious that counselling is for people with problems. An increasingly popular use for counselling in the 21st century has nothing to do with problems as we would normally think of them.

Personal growth

It may be less obvious that a growing number of people in this country seek counselling as a route to self-improvement. In a similar way to seeking self-improvement through yoga classes, sport, arts and crafts, or adult education such as writing for pleasure, people seek self-improvement through counselling. Although this may seem to be a solitary and costly leisure activity, it needn't be. There are several peer-support networks around the country where people get together in pairs and larger groups to offer help and counselling to each other. The most well known of these networks is called *co-counselling communities*.

Embedded within this 'counselling-for-self-improvement' activity is a dimension of counselling and helping that is only recently getting the attention it deserves. That is the spiritual dimension. The search for self-improvement and self-fulfilment inevitably touches upon the spiritual side of humanness. Not only is this spiritual dimension present for the seeker, but also for the helper/counsellor. Forming helping and therapeutic relationships by being empathic, non-judgemental and authentic five days a week the year through is a deeply spiritual process, similar to many spiritual disciplines throughout the world. Many helpers and those seeking help make direct links between helping and spiritual life by doing their helping in a religious context. Counselling fits well into many spiritual traditions, although there can be clashes of culture between faith-based systems of help and restoration and counselling ways of helping, sometimes focusing on being non-judgemental.

Lifestyle coaching

Coaching is becoming more popular as a method of helping people live more fulfilling lives. The term 'lifestyle coaching' helps us understand that the activity is not 'problem-centred' in the same way that counselling is. Here coaching is a method of personal growth and development, a way of helping a person achieve goals and ambitions to live a more fulfilling life, and the key word is 'more'. Coaching is not the best option for dealing with grief, addiction, trauma, mental health problems, etc. It is a lifestyle choice.

The link between coaching and counselling in the UK has been growing in recent years, but in terms of formal links, the BACP inaugurated a Coaching Division in June 2010 and as the division becomes established it should be a good source of information.

The International Coach Federation (ICF) lists core coaching competencies as including:

- *co-creating the relationship*, which involves 'establishing trust and intimacy with the client'
- *communicating effectively* which involves 'active listening', 'powerful questioning' and 'direct communication'
- *facilitating learning and results*

The full list of ICF competencies can be found on their website, and I encourage readers to visit if they have an interest in coaching whether as a coach or potential client.

Problem-centred and context-centred helping and counselling

The term 'counselling' sits quite comfortably alongside information, advice and guidance when it comes to thinking about helping strategies for problems. People in great need often do not care what the process is called, nor what comes along with it, as long as it is not coercive or abusive. However, most agencies offering information, advice and guidance will explicitly offer counselling, or acknowledge that counselling skills are used in the delivery of their other helping services.

Perhaps it is because we have a keener sense of the need for support at times of personal crisis and a better understanding of

Note
There is more on coaching in Chapter 9, pp. 154, 155 & 161.

Note
The BACP Coaching Division webpage is at <http://www.bacpcoaching.co.uk/>. The International Coach Federation (ICF) defines coaching as 'partnering with clients in a thought-provoking and creative process that inspires them to maximize their personal and professional potential.' The ICF have a code of ethics for coaches at <http://www.coachfederation.org.uk/welcome/icf_code_of_eth ics.phtml> and a very useful webpage detailing core coaching competencies at:
<http://www.coachfederation.org.uk/credentialing/coaching_core_compet encies.phtml>

what good helping is, or perhaps it is because of the breakdown of support systems like the extended family in our society, but there has been an explosion of agencies and services offering support and counselling in the past 30 years. As seekers of help we have become accustomed to looking for, and more often than not finding, help tailored to our specific needs, and if we don't find it, we are more likely than ever to start a self-help group and become a provider of help as a result of our distressing experience. Some of the critical life events that take us to counselling are listed below with a word or two of explanation.

Bereavement, grief and loss

Bereavement is the one life event which is universally accepted as a time when humans need support. Much work has been published on the grief process, how unresolved grief can lead to more serious distress and how counselling can help. Grief support and counselling is popular as a peer activity through organisations such as Cruse (nationally) and many local organisations. It is a specialism offered by many professional counsellors.

Note
There is more about Cruse on p. 157, Chapter 9.

Unresolved grief can lead to more complicated and long-lasting symptoms, so good support through bereavement is sometimes literally a life-saver and invariably improves the quality of life. Importantly, the term 'grief and loss' usually encompasses the reaction to *any* significant loss in a person's life, including becoming unemployed, having a limb amputated, losing a faculty through illness or accident, or separating from your spouse, and so on.

Relationships and marriage

The well-deserved reputation for excellent counselling gained by the former National Marriage Guidance Council, now known as Relate, has done much to associate relationship problems with counselling in the minds of the general public. Many people turn to relationship counselling before the relationship breaks down, whilst some want support after the event.

Note
There is more on the history of Relate on p. 157, Chapter 9.
and more on LGBT counselling on p. 164 and also on p. 157, Chapter 9.

Lesbian, gay, bisexual or transgender (LGBT) couples with relationship problems are catered for within Relate, by other specialist LGBT counselling services and through professional counsellors in private practice. People from ethnic minorities with relationship problems have some, though limited, opportunities to get more culturally sensitive help from specific agencies.

HIV and AIDS

It is a requirement that all those requesting an HIV test receive 'counselling' before the test and on hearing the results. The purpose of the pre-test 'counselling' is to obtain informed consent from the patient. However, the post-test counselling is sensitive and important work regardless of the outcome of the test. In the early days the quality of the counselling offered was variable and an attempt to address the problem was made in the report of the BAC and Department of Health Joint Project on HIV Counselling by Tim Bond (1990).

The need for counselling and support related to HIV and AIDS is not limited to those that are HIV positive or suffering from an AIDS-related illness. Partners, relatives and friends need support too along with people who worry that they might have been infected.

The history of the spread of the HIV infection in the UK and USA is that gay men and IV drug users represent the largest groups of infected people. Although this is, of course, not the picture worldwide.

For this reason, most specialised agencies are oriented towards the needs of these groups. However, many people not in these groups are needing support – there is an increase in HIV infection in heterosexuals of all ages. In some areas a befriending scheme exists where people that are HIV positive are befriended by a 'buddy'. There are yet few opportunities for black and ethnic minority people to get culturally sensitive help; however, organisations like the Black Health Agency (BHA) in Manchester and other similar local groups are addressing this issue.

Victim support

Now officially the title of a national, government-funded organisation with local branches, victim support can also mean the help and counselling offered to any victim of crime. There is a growing concern that victims of crime have had their needs neglected and the provision of such schemes attempts to redress that imbalance.

The national organisation offers a set of co-ordinated services for victims of crime and, where counselling is offered, the counsellors are fully qualified. Counselling for shock is offered alongside more concrete help with form-filling, insurance claims and other everyday things that need doing after traumatic crime, through to support during court appearances. Local schemes do try to meet local demand for minority languages and cultural minorities.

Trauma: Surviving and witnessing terrible things

Post-traumatic stress disorder, or PTSD, is the term used to describe the very distressing aftereffects suffered by people who have survived trauma such as disasters. The events at Hillsborough football ground, the destruction of the World Trade Center Twin Towers, the Dunblane tragedy, aircrashes and other disasters have prompted the provision of specific post-trauma counselling.

Note

At the height of the government drive to publicise the risk of HIV, some people became excessively worried about AIDS or HIV infection, despite being known to be uninfected or at little or no risk; these so-called 'worried well' people took up a lot of time and resources of AIDS advice agencies. This particular health worry simply highlighted a more general type of mental distress where people develop debilitating anxiety that they have a physical illness. They are best catered for through the usual channels of psychological help – clinical psychology or counselling at a specialist service.

Bond, T (1990) *HIV Counselling: Report on National Survey and Consultation 1990.* London: BAC/Dept of Health.

> **IF YOU WANT TO KNOW MORE ABOUT**
> **BLACK AND ETHNIC HIV SUPPORT**

Try:
• BHA <http://www.thebha.org.uk/home> and their specific HIV information: <http://manchester.enquira.co.uk/family/counselling-advice/black-hiv-aids-forum-l2050.html>
• The African AIDS Helpline:
0800 0967 500, and their website: <http://africaninengland.org.uk>

> **IF YOU WANT TO KNOW MORE ABOUT**
> **VICTIM SUPPORT**

Try their website:
<http://www.victimsupport.org.uk/>

Post-trauma counselling is specialised work and is offered to a wide range of people including, for example, building society staff after armed robberies and members of the emergency services who witness horrific scenes in the course of duty. Anyone surviving a trauma (car crash, mugging, or witnessing horrific accidents) is vulnerable to PTSD and should be encouraged to seek help, whether or not a specific scheme is offered. Post-trauma counselling is now offered as a specialism by counsellors in private practice and counselling at major incidents is often provided by commercial organisations such as Employee Assistance Programmes (see Chapter 9, p. 154 and *Counselling at work* on page 166, Chapter 10).

Surviving abuse, rape and sexual violence

Rape and abuse are sometimes looked upon as separate issues, but I have put them together here to indicate that the victims and survivors are mostly women who have been subjected to male violence. This reflects the pattern of provision of support, help and counselling which is frequently by women for women. There has been an increase in the attention given to child sexual abuse recently and the national agency Childline is a point of first contact for children.

Much long-term counselling work is done with the adult survivors of such abuse. This is specialist work and the effects of remembering past abuse are frequently very traumatic and debilitating. This group does include men and it is thought by some that the degree to which it affects men has been underestimated. Local organisations, rape crisis centres and women's groups should be able to give initial support and make referrals where necessary. There is limited specialist provision for men or ethnic minority groups.

Sexuality

Here I am using the term sexuality to refer to sexual orientation, i.e. heterosexual, bisexual, gay, lesbian and transgender. Sexuality also covers sexual attraction to children, cross-dressing, wanting to hurt or be hurt by others, having less usual objects of sexual desire such as items of clothing or machinery.

Our culture is not very flexible when it comes to accepting sexuality or sexual practices which differ from the perceived cultural norm of heterosexual sex. The problems that most people have regarding their sexuality arise from this societal or family pressure to 'be normal'. Some sexual practices are illegal, such as paedophilia (sex with children) which may make it difficult for an active paedophile to seek help to change.

There are specialist self-help/support groups both nationally and regionally that offer help for people wanting to explore, come to terms with or change their sexual orientation. A mixture of information, advice, group support and counselling may be available.

IF YOU WANT TO KNOW MORE ABOUT
RAPE CRISIS

See Chapter 9, p. 157, and run an Internet search for local services. Each service is autonomous and has its own specialities.

IF YOU WANT TO KNOW MORE ABOUT
CHILDLINE

Try their website:
<http://www.childline.org.uk/Pages/Home.aspx>

IF YOU WANT TO KNOW MORE ABOUT
WOMENS' AID

Try their website:
<http://www.womensaid.org.uk>

IF YOU WANT TO KNOW MORE ABOUT
LGBT COUNSELLING

Pink Therapy is a good resource:
<http://www.pinktherapy.com>

Sex

'Sex' refers to problems with 'normal' sexual functioning – often called sexual dysfunction. Popular terms describing these problems are 'impotence' in men (including premature ejaculation) and 'frigidity' in women. The problems include a wide range of incomplete, absent or inappropriate sexual responses and cause great distress and shame to the sufferers. Counselling approaches pioneered in the UK by the then National Marriage Guidance Council (now Relate) are effective in a large proportion of cases. This specialist area requires counsellors with specialist training. Some professional counsellors in private practice offer sexual dysfunction counselling.

Medical conditions

Illness is another crisis point in a person's life where support is needed, not only for the person themselves but also for their family. Many medical conditions have long-term debilitating effects and a wide range of support groups offering a range of services from information, advice, guidance to counselling and befriending have grown out of the need for such support. From arthritis and asthma to tinnitus (noises in the ear) there are organisations offering help, sometimes on a local basis – some employ specialist counsellors.

Some NHS specialist areas employ counsellors. You may find counsellors offering support and advice to patients before, during and after diagnostic procedures and treatment for several conditions including:

- amputees
- prospective parents who may be worried about their chances of having an abnormal child
- infertility and associated treatments
- sterilisation and vasectomy
- terminal illness

Palliative care and the hospice movement

Palliative care is the term used for treatment to help make people with terminal illnesses more comfortable. The hospice movement was at the forefront of palliative care in the UK and counselling is frequently provided for the patients and their relatives. Psychological support in the form of counselling is less frequently available for relatives who want to care for the patient at home.

Having cared for my mother at home as she died I found little or no structured provision to support me and my family. Our GP and District Nurse were, however, wonderful and a few words of comfort from them went a long way. I worry about the single person wanting to do the best for their child, parent, husband or wife. A little

Note

By 'normal' I mean any legal lone sexual practice or sex between two or more consenting adults. The previous section looked at services helping people with the effects of stigmatisation of sexual preferences. Here I'm looking at services offering help when sex doesn't happen the way we want it to.

| IF YOU WANT TO KNOW MORE ABOUT RELATE |

See Chapter 9, p. 157 and try their website: <http://www.relate.org.uk/home/index.html>

appropriate emotional support would be invaluable at such a distressing time.

Suicide and despair

Probably the most famous telephone helping agency, the Samaritans was set up to listen to people who were so desperate that they may consider taking their own life. Samaritans branches offer listening and befriending and are reluctant to call their basic helping 'counselling'. Undoubtedly, many Samaritans volunteers are proficient in the use of counselling skills. Volunteers are trained, but remain anonymous so ongoing helping relationships are difficult unless a client is 'befriended' by a more experienced volunteer.

A few Samaritans branches offer minority languages and a service which takes into account local ethnic groups. Samaritans now offer email counselling.

> IF YOU WANT TO KNOW MORE ABOUT
> THE SAMARITANS
>
> See Chapter 9, p. 157 and try their website: <http://www.samaritans.org/>

Problem pregnancies

Trained counsellors are widely available to help a woman make the decision as to whether she wants to terminate a problem pregnancy or not. Counselling at this important decision point was pioneered by the British Pregnancy Advisory Service (BPAS) and is now commonplace in other agencies offering a similar service. Some other agencies are tied to a world-view or faith-based view which makes a prejudgement about the morality of terminations and so the 'counselling' they offer is not likely to be neutral. It is important that potential clients get the help they want, so it pays to look carefully at the values of the service before making an appointment. Information and advice are available in addition to counselling.

Counsellors are trained by mainstream agencies like BPAS and do an excellent job often under great pressure of time. Some limited after-event support is available, but a client may have to go elsewhere for this. Information and sometimes help is available in minority languages, but there are powerful cultural issues in the area of pregnancy and women's rights.

> IF YOU WANT TO KNOW MORE ABOUT
> BPAS
>
> See their website:
> <http://bpas.org.uk/bpasabout>

Counselling at work

An increasing number of employers are offering help, support and counselling through the workplace. Whether the problem is work-related or of a more personal nature, employers are beginning to realise the cost-effectiveness of counselling since research suggests that, when counselling is provided, fewer days are lost due to sickness and stress. The current trend is to offer Employee Assistance Programmes (EAPs) rather than permanent on-site counsellors. These give different levels of service to different grades of employee. Most start with telephone support to be followed by face-to-face counselling only if absolutely necessary.

> IF YOU WANT TO KNOW MORE ABOUT
> COUNSELLING AT WORK
>
> Visit the BACP Workplace Division website: <http://www.bacpworkplace. org.uk/>
>
> See Chapter 9, p. 154 for a little more about EAPs.

Counselling at your GP surgery

An increasing number of GPs employ counsellors in their surgeries to offer help with a wide range of problems from bereavement through to eating disorders and drug dependency. Some surgeries may have help and information in minority languages. The counsellors should be well qualified and available on an appointment-only basis. Ask your GP for information.

Counselling in education

Colleges and universities have been providing counselling for students for many years. It is often provided under the heading 'student services', 'student support' or 'advice and guidance'. Information and advice, as well as counselling for a wide range of academic, financial and personal problems, is usually available. It is usual for the service to be offered to both full- and part-time students.

Counsellors are usually well qualified and available on an appointment basis, with some limited provision for emergencies. Limited effort is made to provide a culture-sensitive service and information in minority languages, even though higher education institutions attract overseas students in large number.

The recent attention paid to violence and bullying in schools hasn't yet led to widescale provision of counsellors in schools. Counselling in schools is generally less available than in further and higher education, but provision does vary across the UK. In England, some education authorities have policies to provide school counsellors but this tends to be the exception rather than the rule. In Scotland, there has been funding for research which has led to good provision in some areas, and the Welsh Assembly Government has funded bold plans to research the effectiveness of schools counselling and roll out more comprehensive provision.

IF YOU WANT TO KNOW MORE ABOUT COUNSELLING IN EDUCATION

See Chapter 9, pp. 149-51 for more information, including counselling in schools. Also visit the BACP Association for University and College Counselling website: <http://www.aucc.uk.com/> and the BACP Counselling Children and Young People website: <http://www.ccyp.co.uk/>.

Faith-based counselling

The word 'counsel' does have religious associations and many people seek help from their church or community elders when life presents them with crises. Bereavement is a time when people naturally turn to priests for support and guidance.

People resident in the UK belong to many religions and it is not the case that counselling values are shared by all cultures and all faiths. The help offered by priests and elders may not be in harmony with the counselling values espoused in this book.

Basic helping and counselling skills on the telephone

A number of agencies offering basic helping and counselling do so via the telephone – either exclusively or as a part of their service. There are several benefits to such provision, particularly if you are serving a client group who have difficulty attending a centre for

Note

There have been recent news items about faith-based organisations offering psychological treatments to 'cure' sexual orientations and preferences other than heterosexual. Clearly these are not offering counselling as portrayed in this book. Sexuality is an expression of human difference and diversity to be celebrated, not medicalised, stigmatised and changed.

IF YOU WANT TO KNOW MORE ABOUT
TELEPHONE COUNSELLING

Read:

Sanders, P (2007) *Using Counselling Skills on the Telephone and in Computer-Mediated Communication* (3rd ed). Ross-on-Wye: PCCS Books.

BACP pamphlet: *TELEGUIDE Guidelines for telephone counselling.*

Telephone Helplines Association website <http://www.helplines.org.uk/>

IF YOU WANT TO KNOW MORE ABOUT
INTERNET OR E-COUNSELLING

An Internet search for 'Internet therapy' will keep you up to date in this developing area. A good source of information and advice on good practice is:

BACP Information Sheet P6 *Introduction to online counselling and psychotherapy.* And the relevant BACP webpage <http://www.bacp.co.uk/media/index.php? newsId=386& count=165&start=159& filter=&cat=2&year=>

For further information
about any application of counselling in the UK, BACP runs a website called *It's Good to Talk* which has an A–Z of counselling applications. It can be found at this address: <http://www.itsgoodtotalk. org.uk/>

face-to-face interviews, e.g. people with mobility problems, older people, children or single parents who cannot get out of the house. Many of the counselling and helping skills are the same, but there are some important differences and for readers wishing to work in, or simply want to know more about telephone agencies, there are some resources available through the Telephone Helplines Association.

Basic helping and counselling skills by email and on the Internet

In recent years there has been significant growth in the provision of counselling and helping services by email (e.g. Samaritans) and on the Internet. Email counselling is often used in educational establishments as a supplement to face-to-face services. Internet counselling and Internet therapy is a specialist service and was pioneered by American companies and groups of practitioners and is now offered in the UK by some therapists in private practice. Practising in this medium brings its own 'rules' for best practice and negotiating the particular ethical dilemmas present in email/Internet/computer-mediated helping. BACP has published documents and guidelines for anyone wanting to get involved with email and Internet counselling.

Support and self-help for women, lesbians, gays, bisexuals, disabled people, ethnic minorities, young people and minoritised groups

Groups of people band together as self-help groups with political leanings, because they experience society's attitudes towards them as oppressive. They may have a view that the particular problems experienced by individuals in the groups are better explained and solved by looking at the issues of oppression first or alongside the problems of the individual.

There is sometimes a culture clash between counselling approaches and political approaches, since some people believe that it is the oppressive system that should change, not the individuals within it. Counselling skills are nearly always used by people in such groups but may not be explicitly acknowledged.

The confusingly complicated array of professionals offering services in the general field of psychological therapies is more confusing and complicated than ever, and it's growing by the day.

The situation has not been helped by an entirely new layer of government-induced complication. The government introduced an important new mental health policy, based partly on the work of Lord Layard in his book *Happiness: Lessons from a New Science*, published by Penguin in 2005, called 'Improving Access to Psychological Therapies'. Two pilot sites, in Doncaster and Newham, were set up in 2006 to trial and evaluate the approach which has since been rolled out across the UK in various manifestations. Just to keep everyone on their toes, the IAPT programme has introduced two new job specifications to the range of helping professions, these are 'High Intensity Workers' and 'Low Intensity Workers'. I will look in a little more detail at these titles later in this short chapter, but for now it is worth mentioning that these titles relate more to the type of work done than the *professional* qualifications of the practitioner.

It is important to understand that in many situations in the helping professions exactly the same work is being done by different people with different job titles. This happens because there is genuine overlap between roles, but also because, as helping has evolved over the decades, only a few job actions have become legally tied to specific job titles, e.g. the prescribing of medication can only be done by a psychiatrist because they are medically qualified. Similarly the law states clearly who (in terms of job title) must be present when someone is detained under Section 3 of the Mental Health Act (more of this later). The different professional groups in the helping sector have been just as concerned with protecting titles, i.e. what you are allowed to call yourself ('psychiatrist', 'psychologist') and how much each are paid. But other than acknowledged *medical* treatments, there are few helping activities practices restricted to a particular job title. Inevitably this has led to both positive and less positive features of how help is delivered in the UK. This idiosyncratic process of development has, over many decades, established one of the most comprehensive networks for delivering help to psychologically distressed people in the world – and there is still room for improvement.

Improving Access to Psychological Therapies (IAPT)

The IAPT programme was developed to implement the National Institute for Health and Clinical Excellence (NICE) guidelines for people suffering from depression and anxiety disorders in England. [Equivalent are: Increasing the Availability of Evidence-Based Psychological Therapies in Scotland and IAPT (Wales)]

Since randomised controlled trials (RCT) research consistently shows that psychological treatment is in many cases as effective as medication, IAPT is designed to provide access to effective front-line treatment, combined where appropriate with medication which traditionally had been the only treatment available.

Full details are available on the IAPT website <http://www. iapt. nhs.uk/> which explains:

From 2011, [IAPT's] focus has broadened, following publication of *Talking Therapies: a four-year plan of action*, one of a suite of documents supporting *No health without mental health*, the cross-Government mental health strategy for people of all ages.

At the time of writing IAPT is dominated by Cognitive Behavioural Therapies, but more evidence from RCTs and other sources demonstrates that other approaches are equally effective (see Chapter 12, pp. 182-3).

Note

Although I haven't mentioned them in the text, the following two professions are key to the web of helping services in the UK.

Psychiatric Nurse

This is a different qualification from *General Nurse* and the different training prepares the psychiatric nurse to specialise in the treatment of psychiatric conditions. They will work in psychiatric hospitals, day units and in the community where they will be called Community Psychiatric Nurses or CPNs. CPNs make home visits, make assessments and carry out treatment plans (usually checking that medication has been taken). Sometimes they will give counselling-type support and therapy, but are not often trained specifically to do this. Some may have limited training in cognitive behavioural therapy.

Some nurses will be trained to deliver 'talking therapies' as low or high intensity workers in the Improving Access to Psychological Therapies programme. See pages 169, 173-4 and 175-6.

Social Worker

Social workers (requiring graduate-level qualification) provide support for socially excluded people and people experiencing crisis by helping service users to help themselves. Their clientele might include: young offenders, people with mental health conditions, school non-attenders, drug and alcohol users, people with learning and physical disabilities, and the elderly.

They work in a variety of settings supporting individuals, families and groups in the community by visiting service users' homes, schools, hospitals, etc. The job is split between face-to-face contact with service users and helping professionals in multidisciplinary teams, and research and report-writing. The face-to-face work requires good listening and relationship skills.

So, the current options in helping careers include:
- Coach
- Low Intensity Worker
- Counsellor
- Psychotherapist
- High Intensity Worker
- Educational Psychologist
- Clinical Psychologist
- Counselling Psychologist
- Psychiatrist

What do they all do, and how are the services they offer different? If we feel distressed or overwhelmed, have a problem at work, have suffered trauma or want to get more out of life, who should we go to see? If we are working as a helper and have reached our limits of expertise, who should we refer our clients to, and what service can they expect to receive?

Starting at the bottom of the list I will give a brief summary of the training and qualifications necessary, the type of clients seen and the type of treatment used for each of the professional groups above. One word of caution: there are differences within each professional group and differences in provision in each geographical area of the UK, so all that I can attempt is a general set of guidelines for understanding who's who in the helping professions. There will be exceptions to these general rules, and I hope the information stays current long enough to be useful.

Psychiatrist

It might have been sufficient a few years ago to say that a psychiatrist is a doctor who specialises in the treatment of mental illness and leave it at that. In recent years the medical profession has become more specialised and has had to become more accountable and we want to know more about the qualifications and responsibilities of medical practitioners. Also, mental health workers have to have an increasingly detailed understanding of the law since legislation has codified the caring of certain groups of vulnerable people, e.g. the Children Act 1989.

After qualifying as a doctor and gaining experience (three years is usual) in general medicine and surgery, specialisation is the next step for medical students. Psychiatry is one of a variety of specialisms such as general practice, gynaecology, paediatrics, etc. It involves some years spent in full-time specialised psychiatry placements supported by training. Look out for the following letters signifying higher qualifications in psychiatry:

DPM (Diploma in Psychiatric Medicine)

MRCPsych (Member of the Royal College of Psychiatrists)

FRCPsych (Fellow of the Royal College of Psychiatrists)
DM or MD (doctoral thesis) in a psychiatric subject

Psychiatry itself is divided into specialisms including:

General adult psychiatry – This involves looking after working age adults with a wide variety of mental health needs.

Old age psychiatry – This involves working with adults over the age of 65. As well as dealing with the mental health problems encountered in general adult psychiatry, a major part of this work involves the diagnosis and management of dementia.

Child and adolescent psychiatry – The management of emotional and behavioural problems of children and adolescents up to school leaving age. This is particularly likely to involve a team of professionals such as social workers, psychologists and education specialists.

Forensic psychiatry – This speciality covers the interaction between psychiatry and the law, particularly the treatment of people who have committed crimes whilst mentally ill, people who develop a need for psychiatric care in prison, and the writing of court reports and giving evidence in court.

The vast majority of psychiatrists work in NHS settings and will have patients referred to them by GPs or other healthcare professionals. Some psychiatrists will see fee-paying patients privately, though there will be little difference in the treatment. Psychiatrists are also usually on call at Accident and Emergency (A&E) departments, so reporting to A&E is a method of self-referral.

The typical caseload of a psychiatrist will include many people experiencing serious mental disturbances of either a temporary or more enduring type. Such serious disturbances often mean that the patient is thought to be a danger to themselves or others (although this can be a contentious issue) or is incapable of looking after themselves. There is an increasing tendency to call for the support of a psychiatrist when all other options are exhausted.

The role of the psychiatrist is changing in the UK from someone who delivers treatment, to someone who manages a treatment plan. Their role is also invested with statutory powers such as prescribing drugs and authorising admission to or discharge from hospital.

Treatments used by psychiatrists reflect the medical history and tradition of psychiatry. They are more likely to use 'physical' treatments, e.g. medication and ELECTROCONVULSIVE THERAPY (ECT). Only medically qualified persons can prescribe such treatments. Psychiatrists are less likely to use 'talking therapies' themselves (possibly due to lack of time), although they may prescribe psychological treatment via a clinical psychologist , psychotherapist,

Note

'Treatment' by any type of psychiatrist mainly involves using medication but when the system is working well, 'psychiatric care' (again, regardless of specialism, but obviously including a psychiatrist) also means a package of care which may try to influence psychological and social factors such as family circumstances, benefits and housing.

Note

When you are sectioned, three people must agree that you need to be detained in hospital, although exceptions can be made in urgent situations, e.g. if you pose an immediate risk to yourself or other people. You can be detained for assessment and/or treatment, and sometimes treatment is compulsory.

The three people involved in the sectioning process are likely to be:

- an approved mental health professional (e.g. a social worker, mental health nurse, occupational therapist or psychologist who has received special training and is approved by a local authority social services department to carry out duties under the Mental Health Act) *or* your nearest relative as specified by the Act
- a doctor who has received special training (a psychiatrist)
- a registered medical practitioner (usually your GP)

ELECTROCONVULSIVE THERAPY (ECT) A physical treatment used by psychiatrists for serious and enduring mental health problems. The treatment involves passing an electric current through the head, or sometimes only on one side of the head causing a generalised convulsion similar to an epileptic fit. Patients are anaesthetised and given a muscle relaxant before the shock is administered. Patients' reactions vary, but some report a relief of depression following treatment.

Note

Psychologist

When used on its own, the title 'psychologist' has little meaning. In order to become a psychologist all that is really needed is a psychology degree (BA or BSc). Psychology is the study of the normal mental life and behaviour, mainly of human beings, but also of some animals where their behaviour can throw light on human behaviour.

Being a psychologist in no way qualifies or prepares a person to offer help to those with any form of mental distress or disturbance. Furthermore, the simple title 'psychologist' (rather than one of the terms in the text, e.g. clinical psychologist), can be used by anyone, whether qualified or not. If you are considering seeking help from, or referring someone to, a psychologist, it is wise to check the nature of their professional status.

In order to check that the person offering psychological services as a clinical, educational or counselling psychologist is properly qualified and registered for practice (backed up further with more codes of ethics and complaints procedures), you should check on the Health Professions Council (HPC) website <http://hpc-portal.co.uk/online-register//>.

Note

Up-to-date information on Counselling Psychology can be found at the Division of Counselling Psychology's website: <http://dcop.bps.org.uk/> or by contacting the British Psychological Society:
St Andrews House
48 Princess Road East
Leicester
LE1 7DR
Tel: 0116 254 9568

Note

Up-to-date information on Clinical Psychology can be found at the Division of Clinical Psychology's website: <http://dcp.bps.org.uk/> or by contacting the British Psychological Society (above).

or specialist nurse or occasionally a counsellor. Psychiatrists are also responsible for admitting people to psychiatric hospitals and specialist units, sometimes compulsorily.

The Mental Health Act is divided into sections and compulsory detainment under Section 3 of the Mental Health Act is often called 'sectioning' or 'being sectioned'.

Counselling Psychologist

Counselling psychologists are psychologists specialising in counselling psychology and members of the Division of Counselling Psychology. They will have a MSc or PhD in Counselling Psychology, gained by full or part-time study and supervised practice. They are expected to have a first degree in psychology or a degree in another subject with a 'conversion' qualification to give them some psychology background.

Counselling psychologists can work in a variety of settings including the NHS (in your local psychological services unit) and private practice and will, according to the British Psychological Society (BPS), work with adults, groups, students and young people, families and couples, the elderly, in health and medical settings, in work settings and in community settings. Counselling psychologists will work using a range of counselling skills, techniques and approaches that are informed by psychological knowledge and research.

Counselling Psychology is the most recent addition to the list of specialisms offered by BPS Chartered Psychologists and the number of Counselling Psychology courses, and practising counselling psychologists, is increasing at the time of writing. As mentioned, a number are in private practice, and full details can be obtained from the BPS or from the Directory of Chartered Psychologists if you want to find one. Because of their relatively small numbers, you are less likely to be referred to one (rather than a clinical psychologist – see below) by your GP or anyone else. You would probably have to specifically ask or look for one yourself.

Clinical Psychologist

Clinical psychologists traditionally work in medical or mental health settings. They will have a MSc or PhD in Clinical Psychology, gained by full or part-time study and supervised practice. They are expected to have a first degree in psychology or a degree in another subject with a 'conversion' qualification to give them some psychology background and they may have a further specialisation, e.g. in child clinical psychology.

They provide a number of psychological assessments and treatment techniques such as psychological testing, behavioural therapies and helping people rehabilitate after brain injury or disease. Many use counselling-type relationship skills alongside the psychological therapies, but not all do. Their clients or patients are likely to be suffering from an acute or enduring mental illness, such as panic attacks, phobias, obsessive disorders, schizophrenia-like conditions, depression, etc.

Clinical psychologists have their own health service structure through which their services are delivered, usually managed by a District Clinical Psychologist. Referral to the clinical psychologist will be from your GP, psychiatrist or other health service specialist. You may ask for a referral if you think a clinical psychologist would help, or you could find one that takes private clients in your locality.

Educational Psychologist

Psychologists working in educational settings or specialising in psychology related to education and children are called educational psychologists. Nowadays they will have a PhD in Educational Psychology, gained by full-time study and supervised practice and are expected to have a first degree in psychology or degree in another subject with a 'conversion' qualification to give them some psychology background.

They work mainly with children and adolescents up to the age of 19 and receive most referrals via the education system or parents. Their clients will be wanting help with a range of social and emotional problems which may manifest themselves through school, or academic and intellectual problems such as dyslexia and special learning needs.

Educational psychologists offer a range of assessments and treatments including counselling approaches, but also behavioural therapies, e.g. for bed-wetting, and learning programmes or resource management for children with special learning needs. If a child is having problems at school, then the educational psychologist will probably use psychological testing to help diagnose the problem before applying specific treatments. They will also work with children in emotional difficulties, including court work if the child needs to be put in a place of safety.

Educational psychologists are usually employed by Local Education Authorities (LEA) and can be accessed through schools or directly by looking up the LEA or School Psychological Service in the phone book. You can also have private consultations if you wish by finding a local educational psychologist in private practice.

High Intensity Worker (HIW)

As I noted on p. 169 of this chapter, the terms high and low intensity worker relate more to the type of work done than the *professional* qualifications of the practitioner. They are umbrella terms describing the type of person delivering certain helping tasks. From the IAPT

Note

Up-to-date information can be found at the Division of Educational and Child Psychology's website:

<http://decp.bps.org.uk/> or by contacting the British Psychological Society:
St Andrews House
48 Princess Road East
Leicester
LE1 7DR
Tel: 0116 254 9568

Note

Chartered Psychologist

Chartered Psychologists are 'gold standard' psychologists and members of the British Psychological Society (BPS) who abide by their own Code of Conduct with its attendant complaints procedure. Chartered Psychologists can use the letters *CPsychol* after their name and a description of the services they offer is described in the Register of Chartered Psychologists, which can be found in your local public library or online: <http://www.bps.org.uk/bpslegacy/dcp>.

A Chartered Psychologist has a first degree in psychology (BA or BSc), a further postgraduate qualification (MA, MSc or PhD) and a period of supervised training in a specialist area of psychology and been judged fit to practise. The specialist area of psychology does not need to be one in the 'helping' sector – it could, for example, be in teaching.

website archive, HIWs are described as follows:

> Clinical psychologists, Counselling psychologists, Nurse therapists, Primary Care counsellors and other qualified Mental Health professionals are eligible to train in delivering High Intensity therapy … To become a High Intensity trainee, you will need to have had considerable experience and training in providing psychological therapies. Some of the staff who would be considered might currently be working as nurses, occupational therapists & social workers, counsellors, experienced graduate workers, psychotherapists or newly qualified clinical psychologists.
>
> Qualified High Intensity Psychological Therapists provide a course of cognitive behavioural therapy (CBT) … These roles are likely to be delivered by a mix of professions including CBT therapists, clinical psychologists, counsellors, nurses, occupational therapists, and psychotherapists.
> (<http://www.iapt.nhs.uk/about-iapt/website-archive/high-intensity-therapy-workers/> retrieved 10/05/11)

It is unlikely that a member of the general public will come across the terms IAPT or high intensity worker, but as a beginning counsellor on the first rung of the helping professions ladder you should be aware of these initiatives. They increasingly determine job opportunities and will figure in training decisions you make in the future.

Psychotherapist

To some extent the difference between psychotherapists and counsellors is as artificial as the difference between psychotherapy and counselling (see Chapter 1, p. 16). It is not uncommon to find two people with identical qualifications and client caseloads, one of whom calls themselves a counsellor, whilst the other calls themselves a psychotherapist. By a similar token you may find the same person calling themselves both a counsellor and a psychotherapist (and sometimes a counselling psychologist too).

Laying aside any such problems of definition, the United Kingdom Council for Psychotherapy (UKCP) is a professional body looking after the interests of psychotherapists and psychotherapy. It monitors standards of training, has a code of conduct and a register of practitioners. The UKCP works alongside other organisations such as BACP in the development of standards in therapeutic helping.

Since the BAC changed its name to BACP (for *psychotherapy*), the public would be forgiven for being even more confused. I'm afraid that I can offer no words of comfort here, except to say that I give a little more time to this issue in Chapter 12.

Psychotherapists work in a range of healthcare settings and in

Note

Things change, so visit the appropriate websites occasionally:

- IAPT <http://www.iapt.nhs.uk/>
- For updates on the policy initiative, Increasing the Availability of Evidence-Based Psychological Therapies in Scotland <http://www.scotland.gov.uk/Topics/Health/health/mental-health/servicespolicy/DFMH>
- IAPT Wales progress can be checked in the NHS Wales Mental Health news section <http://www.wales.nhs.uk/sites3/newslist.cfm?orgid=438>

Note

A United Kingdom Council for Psychotherapy registered therapist

Anyone successfully completing a UKCP registered course can be on the UKCP register. To find a therapist on the register, you must visit the UKCP 'Find a Therapist' website: <http://members.psychotherapy.org.uk/find-a-therapist/> or contact UKCP
2nd Floor, Edward House
2 Wakley Street
London EC1V 7LT
Main switchboard: 020 7014 9955

private practice. They employ a range of therapeutic techniques for helping clients. There are many different 'schools' or approaches in psychotherapy, but any competent therapist will explain the basis of the techniques that they use should you wish to know. There are specialisms within psychotherapy including child therapists, family therapists, art therapists and drama therapists.

If you feel that a psychotherapist can help, you should contact the UKCP for access to the register, or contact BACP for information or ask your GP to refer you.

Counsellor

It might seem flippant to start with the statement: 'Counsellors are people who do counselling', but I fear it's going to be the closest I can get to defining a counsellor in a single statement, see p. 3, Chapter 1.

There is no single route to being a counsellor, and there are many specialisms within counselling: bereavement counsellor, drugs counsellor, student counsellor, HIV/AIDS counsellor, etc. One distinguishing feature which may be helpful is that many counsellors are professional, that is they earn their living as a counsellor. This will usually indicate a degree of training and experience above that usually associated with being a volunteer or someone using counselling skills, *but not always*.

Minimum qualifications would be a Diploma in Counselling or equivalent. The BACP accredits Diploma courses which come up to agreed minimum criteria. Such courses will say 'BACP Accredited Course'.

Many counsellors will be members of BACP (therefore subject to the BACP Code of Ethics and Practice) and some will be BACP Accredited Counsellors (see below and Chapter 13).

If you want to choose a counsellor working in private practice, there are helpful guidelines on the BACP website and you should follow the links to the 'seeking a therapist' page – qualifications and accreditation status are listed along with specialisms. Word-of-mouth recommendation is often the best guide. A job well done is often the best way of choosing someone, alongside checking out their qualifications and membership of a professional body. Do not apologise for being choosy.

You can also check with the UK Register of Counsellors/ Psychotherapists (UKRCP) to see if a particular counsellor is on the Register. Counsellors can become registered if they are Accredited (see above). For a little more on the UKRCP there is a very short section on page 190, Chapter 12 or visit their website.

Low Intensity Worker (LIW)

LIWs can also be known as psychological wellbeing practitioners, graduate mental health workers, or primary care mental health

Note

United Kingdom Register of Counsellors/ Psychotherapists (UKRCP)

This is a voluntary register for counsellors and psychotherapists in the UK. It allows someone to advertise themselves as an 'Independent Registered Counsellor or Psychotherapist'. Entry to the Register is via accreditation with BACP, Counselling & Psychotherapy in Scotland (COSCA), UK Association for Humanistic Psychology Practitioners (UKAHPP) or Federation of Drug and Alcohol Professionals (FDAP). An accredited counsellor or psychotherapist has a certain level of validated training and experience. Website: <http://ukrconline.org.uk>.

If a registered practitioner is not conveniently located near you, the next-best solution is a counsellor who is a member of BACP or a similar professional body so that their practice is governed by a code of ethics and practice.

British Association for Counselling and Psychotherapy

BACP House, 15 St John's Business Park, Lutterworth, Leicestershire LE17 4HB
Tel: 01455 883300
Email: bacp@bacp.co.uk
Website: www.bacp.co.uk

BACP Seeking a Therapist
<http://www.itsgoodtotalk.co.uk/ therapists>/

United Kingdom Council for Psychotherapy
See opposite margin.

Note
UKRCP website <http://www.ukrcon line.org.uk>.

workers (and this list continues to develop). As with the high intensity workers, the term low intensity worker relates more to the type of work done than the *professional* qualifications of the practitioner. It is an umbrella term describing the type of person delivering certain helping tasks.

LIWs provide lots of low-intensity helping tasks characterised by short sessions – around 30 minutes – possibly involving telephone work as opposed to face-to-face sessions, and one-off contacts or short interventions. They use a stepped guided self-help method based on CBT techniques. Since this will probably not involve face-to-face helping it could be helping clients work through self-help books, supporting them with computerised-CBT. Face-to-face work will be short sessions of simple CBT work.

Mostly, LIWs will see clients with mild to moderate anxiety and depression, although a far more varied client group will be seen. They are supervised by high intensity workers (see p. 173).

To quote my last paragraph of the HIW section on p. 174:

> It is unlikely that a member of the general public will come across the terms IAPT or high intensity worker, but as a beginning counsellor on the first rung of the helping professions ladder you should be aware of these initiatives. They increasingly determine job opportunities and will figure in training decisions you make in the future.

Coach

The terms 'coach' and 'coaching' have been used informally in many settings for years. Only recently, however, has the idea of coaching been introduced to the helping professions. The BACP launched its coaching division 'BACP Coaching' in 2010 although the website does not offer a description or definition of the activity of coaching. Many organisations claim to represent coaches and coaching in the UK and internationally, yet still definitions are scarce. In Chapter 10, p. 161, I refer the reader to the International Coach Federation (ICF). Established 10 for years, their website offers a code of ethics and practice plus core coaching competencies. Different accounts and definitions can be found on the Coaching and Mentoring Network website, which is also comprehensive.

I am sure this emerging field in the helping professions will generate coherent definitions as it becomes established. In the meantime, the only certain thing is that whatever I write here will be out of date by the time you read it. As I write there really is no clear consensus on the role, remit, training, pay, or almost any other aspect of coaching. The BACP Coaching website will continue to be the best starting place for your questions.

IF YOU WANT TO KNOW MORE ABOUT COACHING

For more information on coaching, try:
BACP Coaching <http://www.bacpcoaching.co.uk/index.php>
UK International Coach Federation <http://www.coachfederation.org.uk/>
Coaching and Mentoring Network <http://www.coachingnetwork.org.uk/Default.htm>

Counselling as we know it today arrived from the USA in the mid-1960s and was taken up by people working in educational settings and the voluntary sector, notably in the National Marriage Guidance Council (now Relate). The last 30 years have seen great developments in counselling in the UK and now in the early 21st century we have the United Kingdom Register of Counsellors/Psychotherapists and a national professional body (BACP) with over 35,000 members. For most of you reading this, just beginning your exploration of counselling, it may seem that the counselling 'industry' is well established in the spectrum of helping professions.

As I explained in Chapter 2, the ideas behind counselling and psychotherapy are at best 100 years old and many are more recent than that. I also noted that the ideas themselves are probably re-inventions of much older ones. In Chapter 9 I looked at the relatively safe and incident-free history of counselling, compared with, for example, psychiatry. Now I suggest we pause, both to take stock, and to answer some of the questions put forward by the critics of counselling, and to consider some of the important debates within the 'profession'.

For many readers, this introductory course, or this book, will be your only contact with a counselling way of helping. You will go back to your families, communities or jobs with a set of ideas about counselling and I am determined that you should take with you as accurate a view of contemporary counselling as possible. You will be better able to help your friends, family, colleagues and clients locate and gain access to the best counselling-style help only if you think that it is based on honesty and integrity, for self- and community enhancement; not motivated by greed, self-aggrandisement or the need to meet the helper's needs above those of the client.

The counselling community is in a constant state of self-questioning and self-development. The activity of counselling requires that individual counsellors constantly monitor their practice through supervision to ensure that they do not place their own needs over the needs of their clients. This monitoring also happens quite naturally in the wider community of counsellors. There is always someone ready to do the supervisor's job and challenge accepted norms within the counselling 'industry' in case we get

Note

I've put some words in inverted commas to indicate that the word is contentious and debatable. You will find that some experienced helpers are not in favour of counselling becoming a profession, and the use of the term 'industry' in the caring field is pejorative, a thinly veiled insult to many.

Welcome to counselling in the 21st century.

'If it was right to be believing,
and write his name in blood
and then I met him when I died,
well I'd have it out with god.
But if it means degrading scenes
and sanctioning crusades,
I'd know we couldn't stand man to man
without feeling afraid.

If it was wrong for not believing
in fairytale facade
and then I met him when I died,
well I'd apologise to god.
But if it meant I went down on my knees
well where's the spirit gone
where's the love you're all talking of
when you can't stand man to man?
Man to man
When you can't stand man to man.

I find it hard to believe
in these 'gospels' that I've heard
the forked tongue of the bible belt
the ayatollah's word.
I don't believe most anything
spoken by anyone
as hell's fanatic paranoids
fire heaven's loaded gun.

If it was right to be believing,
then it must be in this
that difference is beautiful
and living it is bliss
there are no teams
there is no side
that life on earth is done
by living the love you're only talking of
by standing man to man.'

'If' by Roy Harper, from the album *Once*.
Awareness Records

Halmos, P (1969) *The Faith of the Counsellors*. London: Constable.

driven by self-interest. This is done at large gatherings and conferences, through the pages of journals, etc. Issues such as the effectiveness of counselling, the cost of counselling and the availability of counselling are of central concern to counsellors.

With so many people involved in counselling it is easy for any representative organisation to become distanced and out of touch with the needs of the community of counsellors and helpers. Everyone involved in counselling needs to be vigilant, responsive and vocal regarding important issues in the helping professions. There are critical voices within the profession and I hope I have represented some of these in this chapter.

Is counselling a new religion?

This is a fascinating question, since it reveals how much our culture has, to some people, lost its soul – some say to consumerism, some to global capitalism, others to technology and science. The question is often asked nowadays as if to imply that 'religions' are a bad thing. One, I believe intentional, implication behind the question is that anything non-scientific is untested, unproven and therefore not to be trusted. A further implication is that anything even inadvertently filling the niche of a 'religion' in our society should be treated with at least suspicion, since it might appear to be seeking to replace traditional or 'true' religion (e.g. Islam, Christianity) in our hearts, minds and souls. So, I would argue that what is a fascinating question is sometimes asked with the dishonourable intention to discredit counselling and to do so with a hidden anti-spiritual, 'technology is trustworthy' subtext.

On the other hand, there is a fascinating sociological debate to be had regarding the place of religion and counselling in our increasingly secular society. Paul Halmos elegantly and learnedly explores this notion in his book *The Faith of the Counsellors* (1969).

In the next few paragraphs I will review some of the possible ways in which counselling and religion or spiritual traditions appear to be similar. I am not suggesting that counselling either is or is not supplanting traditional religions, but the similarities and differences are worth looking at and the issue worth debating.

Some people argue that counselling is, amongst other things, filling a void that has developed in contemporary life. The evidence is that thousands of people turn to counsellors every day and are satisfied enough to return each week. It has been suggested that people only seek and return to counsellors because they are so desperate and they have nowhere else to go. And there, I suggest, is the void. In a civilisation which puts men on the moon, we seem unable to provide a place for people when they are desperate.

Every spiritual tradition has something to say about helping others, extending love to others, whether they are your neighbour or not. If there is a void, partly created by the turning away from religious beliefs, then counselling seems ready-made to step into it.

We can debate whether the media causes or reflects trends in society, but if we want our suspicions confirmed, we do not have far to look for confirmation of the parlous state we are in. Many find turning on the television a thoroughly disheartening experience – assaulted by a vision of the world where we reject the weakest link, wish for instant success and quick makeovers, and where democracy is reduced to the telephone vote for a dance competition. The values of counselling and helping as described in this book could not be more diametrically opposed to these sentiments.

A further feature of helping in a counselling way is that all approaches involve some element of self-evaluation or contemplation. Counselling provides a time and space in which the centre of attention is you, a time for reflection on life and your part in it and the world. This contemplation and self-awareness development has many resonances with meditation and similar spiritual practices. One strong theme in spiritual traditions is the idea of self-improvement; this is, of course, the *main* theme in counselling. Perhaps counsellors do fulfil the role of secular spiritual guides for those disconnected from, or without any sense of, their spiritual selves, whether that disconnection is by choice or not.

Again, counselling finds itself at odds with contemporary culture which denigrates the internal world, requiring us to get on-message, live fast, aspire to nothing greater than wearing designer labels and to buy before we think. We live in a world 'Where straight teeth in your mouth are more important than the words that come out of it' (Disposable Heroes of Hiphoprisy, 1992).

Many people have noted that there is, without doubt, a flavour of the confessional in some counselling situations. People come to counselling to unburden themselves. This unburdening is not *necessarily* because they believe they have sinned in a religious sense, or done something wrong in a legal sense, but it can often be

Note

There is more on this on p. 186 under the heading 'Counselling and wellbeing: Solution or part of the problem?'

> 'Television, the drug of the nation
> Breeding ignorance and feeding radiation …
>
> … TV is the reason why less than ten percent of our Nation reads books daily
> Why most people think Central America means Kansas
> Socialism means unamerican and Apartheid is a new headache remedy …
>
> … TV is it the reflector or the director?
> Does it imitate us or do we imitate it?
> Because a child watches 1500 murders before he's twelve years old
> and we wonder how we've created a Jason generation that learns to laugh rather than abhor the horror …'
>
> Disposable Heroes of Hiphoprisy, *Television, the drug of the nation.* Lyrics by M. Franti

Note

Brian Thorne has written extensively and persuasively on this topic from a Christian position (Thorne, 1991, 1998), and such views are not restricted to one spiritual, religious, or even secular viewpoint.

Thorne, B (1991) *Person-Centred Counselling: Therapeutic and spiritual dimensions.* London: Wiley.

Thorne, B (1998) *Person-Centred Counselling and Christian Spirituality.* London: Wiley.

Disposable Heroes of Hiphoprisy (1992) *Television, the Drug of the Nation.* Lyrics by Michael Franti. Island Records.

because they feel the weight of assumed guilt or having failed to meet either their own or others' high expectations. In an increasingly secular world it could be that counsellors are seen as offering a safe place for people to confess and heal themselves.

It appears that some people are turning towards the spiritual in our culture at the same time as turning away from organised religion. If it is a common feature of human life that we seek a spiritual connection, it does not seem so surprising that people will use whatever is handy to make the connection they desire. Whilst counselling would appear to fit the bill in a number of ways, we must not lose sight of the fact that counselling is not offered primarily as a spiritual activity. It is a helping activity which can be carried to professional levels and may, for some people, have a wider or deeper spiritual meaning, just as people have 'peak' or spiritual experiences when climbing mountains, running marathons or listening to music.

Does counselling work?

Berk, RA & Rossi, PH (1990) *Thinking about Program Evaluation.* Newbury Park CA: Sage.

This is an important and difficult question. It is rather like an iceberg – only one-tenth of it is visible and all of the danger lurks, hidden from view. On the face of it it's a reasonable question; a question we should surely all ask, so what's the problem? In 1990, Berk and Rossi suggested that the initial question *Does counselling work?* has to be immediately followed up with *Compared with what?* In real life, we sometimes offer no help or support to people in distress, so we must compare the effectiveness of counselling with how frequently people feel better without any special, deliberate treatment. Sometimes, in the case of specific forms of disturbance and distress, we can compare counselling with another more established form of treatment such as drugs.

Most of the time when this question is asked, the questioner makes the assumption that the 'scientific method' will yield the answer. It has proved to be extremely difficult to conduct credible 'scientific' experiments on the outcome of counselling.

The scientific method used in testing the effectiveness of, say, medical treatments is, in principle, quite simple. The researchers arrange for one group of people to receive treatment whilst another group receives none. If the first group get better more quickly or more of them get better than the second group then the treatment 'works'. This approach is fine for physical treatments like drugs, laser beams and surgery. However, when we try to use it on counselling, a number of problems arise.

- Firstly, most science concerns itself with measurable things, and helping, based as it is upon *relationships* and *subjective feelings,* is notoriously difficult to measure.

- Secondly, the whole of a person's life impinges upon their mental state, so even if we treated a series of counselling sessions as though they were pills (i.e. we give the sessions to one group but not another) there is no telling what the people in either group have been doing in-between times to make them better or worse.
- Thirdly, the 'treatment' itself, i.e. counselling, is rather variable to say the least. With pills, the dosage can be measured accurately, but how can the 'dosage' in counselling be measured? Are four sessions always twice as good as two, or can some sessions be more powerful than others? Also, it is difficult to allow for the variation in the treatment that comes with different counsellors.

As you can see, 'testing' what works and what doesn't is fraught with complications. I will summarise some of the remaining complications:

- Whenever we ask whether something works, we need to define what we mean by 'works'. You might think that, in counselling or helping terms, we might simply be interested in whether someone feels better. But then we need to ask how long they need to feel better for before we would feel assured that they *really are* better. On the other hand, an employer asking the question might want to know whether their employee will be able to get back to work next week. Or a teacher will want to know if their star pupil will pass their exams as expected. Or the anxious parent will want to know how much weight their teenager has put on. Unless we work hard to define this term we are never sure that we are talking about the same thing.
- Those counselling approaches which lend themselves to measurement have the appearance of being more scientifically credible, such as cognitive and behavioural approaches. This doesn't mean that they *are* more effective – just that the concepts are simple, instrumental and countable.
- Not all science is good science. We need to be very careful about how the results of scientific experiments are interpreted. Some grave mistakes have been made in recent times where people's lives have been ruined by the too hasty application of what was (often in good faith) thought to be sound science. However, it must be remembered that often, another motive (profit, or a quick fix) can become tangled up with the honourable desire to help others. Such hellish mixtures have historically led to, e.g. the deadly combination of BARBITURATES used to relieve the stress of everyday life coupled with AMPHETAMINES used as stimulants or slimming pills, and the overprescription of BENZODIAZEPINES and resulting addictions.

BARBITURATES Highly addictive drugs used as anaesthetics and (in the 60s) as sleeping pills. Easy to take lethal overdose.

AMPHETAMINES Stimulant drugs (street name 'speed') unscrupulously prescribed as 'slimming' drugs. In the 60s they were prescribed, mainly to women, as 'uppers' to overcome the debilitating effects of the prescription of BARBITURATES (sleeping pills). Highly addictive.

BENZODIAZEPINES Addictive minor TRANQUILLISERS, e.g. Valium.

TRANQUILLISERS A type of drug which has a mood-flattening effect, often popularly referred to as 'downers' or sedatives. Sometimes referred to in medical literature as either 'major' tranquillisers such as Largactil (*chlorpromazine*) or 'minor' tranquillisers such as Librium and Valium (*diazepam*). Many of these drugs cause serious dependency and all have 'side' effects, some serious and permanently debilitating.

Research on the effectiveness of counselling

In the past 10 years, counselling and psychotherapy in the UK have woken up to the fact that we now live in an evidence-driven world. There are still debates about what constitutes evidence and what constitutes a good outcome at the end of counselling, but these are academic and philosophical debates. They are important, but not much use when funding for the service you are working for requires number-crunching 'gold-standard' evidence of randomised controlled trials (RCTs – see below). It is neither possible nor appropriate to go into much detail on these issues here, but there are suggestions for further reading below, and this is essential if you are to pursue a career in counselling, psychotherapy or psychology.

Systematic research into counselling and psychotherapy started in the 1950s and much of it was concerned with looking at theoretical concepts, rather than effectiveness. Academic psychologist Hans Eysenck threw the cat amongst the pigeons somewhat in 1952 by conducting one of the first reviews of research into the effectiveness of psychological therapies (he only used 19 studies) and concluding that psychotherapy was no better than no treatment. Since then psychotherapy research has become increasingly oriented towards scientific methods and number crunching. I'll briefly look at two ways of collecting effectiveness data to give you an idea of the dynamics of the 'effectiveness' debate.

Randomised controlled trials
Briefly, in a medical setting (where the method originated) patients are allocated to one of two groups by chance (the toss of a coin). One group is give an active treatment (e.g. a pill), the other group is given a sugar-coated pill (the control group). The groups don't know which pill they've been given and neither do the people giving the pills. A second group of scientists knows which group is which and they have no contact with the patients. So everything is kept the same across both groups except one thing (what's in the pills), meaning that any improvement in the health of the group given the active treatment must be due to the make-up of the pill – the active ingredient. This sounds fine until you imagine how you might do this with psychotherapy:

- What would the control group be given that would 'look' like the active treatment, yet you could be sure would not have any therapeutic effect?
- How do you measure improvement, since, unlike treatments for, say, diabetes, there are no blood tests to confirm improvement? The more symptom-specific (i.e. take a single symptom like anxiety) the easier it is.
- How do you make sure each 'dose' of treatment is the same (not as easy as formulating pill doses)?
- People have a tendency to drop out of therapy experiments before the study is finished for complicated reasons – including feeling better – but then cannot be included in the results.

RCTs can be done on talking therapies (counselling 'treatments') as long as the treatments are very simple and can be arranged in easily deliverable standard units ('doses' like pills). That's why CBT techniques have been used in RCTs – they are easily 'chunkable', arranged in doses – and tend to be used more where simple diagnoses and single symptoms are involved.

Auditing – collecting practice-based evidence
Another method of studying the effectiveness of talking cures is to collect a huge amount of medium-grade data. (RCTs rely on a small amount of high-grade data.) This approach is strengthened by standardising as many aspects of the measurement and collection of the data as possible and in the UK, the advent of Clinical Outcomes in Routine Evaluation (CORE) system. CORE is a set of measures (questionnaires that have been tested to make sure they reliably measure what they claim to measure) – the idea behind which is to get counsellors to use them *routinely* with all clients. This way of doing things is called auditing practice – routinely collecting evidence from practice. The idea is that data is collected for every single client and some shorter versions can be used after every single session, if the counsellor wants and the client agrees. It is not very intrusive if explained to the client as a way of improving standards and effectiveness.

An advantage of CORE is that it can be used as an overall measure of outcome for complicated relational therapies that are not restricted to manualised methods which mimic drug doses. So whether you are person-centred, psychodynamic or integrative, you can audit your practice with CORE and if you join their computerised data collection system, your data goes into a huge data bank which can be used for effectiveness research where two or more therapies are compared.

Which is best, RCT or practice-based evidence?
It depends who you ask – CBT therapists tend to refer to RCTs, person-centred therapists prefer CORE data studies. The reason is simple, CBT can be 'proved' to work with simple diagnoses and single symptoms. In large scale analysis of CORE data, all therapies come out more-or-less equally effective (sometimes, CBT is slightly better, sometimes person-centred therapy).

The more important thing to be aware of, though, is that the National Institute for Health and Clinical Excellence (NICE, the government body that says which treatments are effective and can be recommended and therefore funded by the NHS) have RCTs as the highest quality evidence and prefer to take notice of a few RCT studies at the expense of the several thousands of measures supporting a variety of treatments. It may be that NICE is correct to use RCTs as the gold standard. Since it is a health service organisation, it has applied medical research tools and criteria to psychological distress. As I pointed out above, this debate rages amongst practitioners, but any debates are academic unless and until NICE reviews its policies.

Resources to follow up on the effectiveness of counselling
• The best place to start if you do not have a social sciences background is: Cooper, M (2008) *Essential Research Findings in Counselling and Psychotherapy.* London: Sage.

• Jewel (1992) published a report of evaluative study of counselling in general practice in 1992. Counselling led to a reduction or cessation of prescribed drugs (such as tranquillisers and antidepressants) in between 20 and 50% of patients taking such drugs.
[Jewel, T (1992) *Report of an Evaluative Study of Counselling in General Practice.* Cambridge: Cambridgeshire FHSA.]

• In 2000, Professor Michael King conducted a large study directly comparing three treatments in primary care: person-centred therapy (PCT), CBT and routine general practitioner care with patients suffering from depression and mixed anxiety and depression. The study found:
  • Both PCT and CBT obtained significantly better results than 'usual general practitioner care' at the four-month follow-up.
  • There was no difference in therapeutic effectiveness between person-centred and cognitive-behavioural therapies.
  • Higher patient satisfaction scores were recorded for the psychological therapies than the usual GP care.
[King, M, Sibbald, B, Ward, E, Bower, P, Lloyd, M, Gabbay, M & Byford, S (2000) Randomised controlled trial of non-directive counselling, cognitive behaviour therapy and usual general practitioner care in the management of depression as well as mixed anxiety and depression in primary care. *British Medical Journal, 321*, 383-8.]

• Two large studies (totalling almost 7000 patients) using CORE data found no differences in outcome between the major therapeutic approaches, CBT, person-centred and experiential therapies, psychodynamic, and integrative.
[Stiles, WB, Barkham, M, Twigg, E, Mellor-Clark, J & Cooper, M (2006) Effectiveness of cognitive-behavioural, person-centred and psychodynamic therapies as practised in UK National Health Service settings. *Psychological Medicine, 36*, 555-66.
Stiles, WB, Barkham, M, Mellor-Clark, J & Connell, J (2007) Effectiveness of cognitive-behavioural, person-centred and psychodynamic therapies in UK primary-care routine practice: Replication in a larger sample. *Psychological Medicine, 37*, 1-12.]

For more research evidence, visit the BACP website research pages <http://www.bacp.co.uk/research/>

ELECTROCONVULSIVE THERAPY (ECT) A physical treatment used by psychiatrists for serious and enduring mental health problems. The treatment involves passing an electric current through the head, or sometimes only on one side of the head causing a generalised convulsion similar to an epileptic fit. Patients are anaesthetised and given a muscle relaxant before the shock is administered. Patients' reactions vary, but some report a relief of depression following treatment.

Activity
• *How would you set about finding out if counselling works?*
• *Would you be satisfied by your own experience, i.e. if you went for counselling yourself and it seemed to make you feel better?*
• *Discuss this issue with others in your training group.*

QUANTITATIVE research is concerned with measuring the countable quantities of human experience.

QUALITATIVE research is concerned with the qualities of human experience, those which are very difficult or impossible to measure without destroying or altering the experience.

| IF YOU WANT TO KNOW MORE ABOUT |
| DOING COUNSELLING RESEARCH |

Read:
Sanders, P & Wilkins, P (2010) *First Steps in Practitioner Research: A guide to understanding and doing research in counselling and health and social care.* Ross-on-Wye: PCCS Books.

We often assume that medical treatments are subjected to scientific analysis before they are used, so it is reasonable to assume that counselling 'treatments' are subjected to the same sort of testing. The truth is that some medical treatments or techniques were never subjected to scientific testing before they were used (e.g. X-rays and ELECTROCONVULSIVE THERAPY), so it is not safe to assume that science is always the benchmark. But we should not dismiss science, either. Just remember that expediency, political gain or profit are also likely to be the guiding rules when decisions are made.

Furthermore, sociologists and psychologists have been developing a different sort of 'science', based not on the measurement of things in terms of numbers, but on an appreciation of the qualities of things. This new way is just as difficult, rigorous and demanding a research method as the more traditional measuring with numbers or 'QUANTITATIVE' method. The method is able to use the more natural experiences of people (including clients) to tease out how people *experience* counselling rather than trying to condense these complicated human moments into a set of numbers. This turns out to be much more in keeping with the whole ethos of counselling, but medical research does not yet accept the validity of this 'QUALITATIVE' approach to science.

These questions and those in the margin undoubtedly have a relevance much wider than counselling. What kind of evidence do *you* require before you believe something? Most people rely heavily upon personal experience, and once they have had an experience, they tend to hold on to it come hell or high water! Do you require 'personal experience' as evidence that counselling works?

I will leave you with what I call the 'Loch Ness Monster Effect'. In the Polygram film *Loch Ness* the following dialogue takes place between the sceptical American scientist John Dempsey, played by Ted Danson, and a young Scots girl Isabel, played by Kirsty Graham, who has seen and made friends with the monster. Isabel shows John Dempsey a drawing she made of the monster:

Dempsey: *'So this is your Kelpie.'*
Isabel: *'It's my friend.'*
D: *'Are you telling me you actually saw ...'*
I: *'Aye!'*
D: *'... Aye ...' (Dempsey laughs.)*
I: *'You're laughing at me. You don't believe me. No one does. I shouldn't have drawn it.'*
D: *'No, no, no, I'm not laughing at you, it's just that ... (Dempsey sighs)... I have to see it before I can believe it.'*
I: *'No, Mr Dempsey, you've got to believe it before you can see it.'*

Does counselling do more harm than good?

This question raises similar issues to the 'Does Counselling Work?' question, since firstly, it depends upon how you define the words *harm* and *good,* and secondly, it depends upon whose viewpoint you are taking. I remember reading a tabloid headline many years ago which shouted '*He only wanted to give up smoking, but ended up walking out on his family*'. The story concerned a man who went to see a hypnotherapist with the aim of giving up smoking, but the treatment so changed his personality that he fell in love with his next-door neighbour and left his wife. This headline represents one of a number of commonly held fears that certain experiences (counselling being one) will change us beyond recognition. Is there really anything to be afraid of? Again, without the space to cover the ground fully on these issues (and whole books are devoted to these subjects), I will give you some discussion starters so that you can debate the issues in your training group, with your friends or just in your head.

Common fears about counselling and change and some answers

- I will change in a way that I cannot control and that people around me, my family and friends, will not be able to keep up with.
- I will uncover things about me that I don't like, things that are better kept under wraps.
  - *There's no getting away from it – counselling is a form of helping that involves change. At the very least the person being helped is expected to change from feeling generally bad about things to feeling better about things. Such changes don't come in nice neat units because the causes of unhappiness rarely come in nice neat units. There is a chance that there will be more change than you initially bargained for in counselling, but two things should limit the notion of 'runaway' change:*
    - *There is the skill and professionalism of the helper. (Although you will not be practising counselling at this stage in your training, you will still be expected to behave ethically and properly. The safeguards are there to protect your client.)*
    - *Implicit in the workings of the majority of counselling approaches is the notion that the client or person being helped is in control of the rate of change.*
- The counsellor might plant ideas and even false memories in my head when I am in a suggestible state.
- When people are desperate and vulnerable they may say things, do things and make decisions that they will regret later.
- Vulnerable people could be exploited by counsellors by getting

IF YOU WANT TO KNOW MORE ABOUT
CRITIQUES OF COUNSELLING

Now out of print, originally published in 1988, but reissued and available 'used' online:

> Masson, J (1992) *Against Therapy.* New York: Flamingo.

From the client's perspective:

> Sands, A (2000) *Falling for Therapy: Psychotherapy from a client's point of view.* Basingstoke: Palgrave Macmillan.

For the more advanced student:

> Howard, A (1996) *Challenges to Counselling and Psychotherapy.* Basingstoke: Macmillan.

them to continue to attend for counselling when there really is no need.

• *Codes of Ethics and Practice are there to ensure that counsellors don't exploit their clients when the clients are vulnerable or desperate. Add to this the central notion of all counselling approaches, that the aim is to empower clients to take full control of their lives, and it is difficult to see how a vulnerable person can be harmed, unless the person being helped is a victim of bad practice.*

   Most counsellors are trained specifically to not actively give advice or make suggestions to clients, vulnerable or not.

• Counselling encourages people to look on the dark side of things and *forces* people to look at unpleasant experiences which can easily make people feel worse if they are already depressed.

• *Helping in a counselling way does not encourage people to talk about anything they don't want to, or to look at anything they don't want to. However, given the opportunity to talk freely without being judged, some people have a tendency to gravitate towards the things that are troubling them. They may have sought help with a particular problem in mind. This may mean that for a while, as they dwell on the unpleasant feelings associated with their problem, they may feel worse than when they started. This can be distressing and any responsible counsellor would explain this. It should pass in a short time, but it is possible that the person being helped will revisit these negative feelings from time to time during counselling.*

Counselling and wellbeing: Solution or part of the problem?

In the margin I look very briefly at IATROGENESIS, the harm done by measures intended to help or heal. Could the therapy industry itself be iatrogenic?

Concern has been growing in many circles over the increasing tendency to say that what used to be thought of as everyday troubles in life are 'mental illnesses'. Would you rather be shy or have 'social anxiety disorder', rather be a naughty boy or have 'conduct disorder', rather be throwing a temper tantrum or have 'temper dysregulation disorder with dysphoria'? This tendency to medicalise everyday life has led to a huge increase in the number of diagnostic categories in the past 100 years, and of course, a concomitant increase in the number of treatments for them. The questions we have to answer are:

1. Has there really been an increase in distress to this extent?
2. Are 'illnesses' being manufactured from everyday troubles?
3. If so, why? Who would stand to benefit?

Activity
• *What have you learned about a counselling way of helping that prevents vulnerable clients from being exploited?*
• *Make a list and share it with others in your training group.*

'The victims of this world, are advertised on posters
A beach and a pretty girl, if you just drink their potion …'

The Levellers, 'Fifteen Years' from the album *Levelling the Land*, China Records

---

IATROGENESIS Inadvertent harm caused by medical treatment e.g. the side effects of some drugs require further drugs to relieve the patient's symptoms caused by the first prescription of drugs.

IF YOU WANT TO KNOW MORE ABOUT
IATROGENIC MEDICALISATION

An accessible, but powerful and challenging book:
Kutchins, H & Kirk, SA (1977) *Making us Crazy: DSM – the psychiatric bible and the creation of mental disorders.* London: Constable.

One uncomfortable conclusion is that it is the legion of helping professionals that stand most to gain from the proliferation of new mental illnesses, whether or not there is any scientific basis for them.

You may wonder what I mean when I say 'whether or not there is any scientific basis for them'. What we consider to be a mental illness is determined by social forces rather than medical science. This is mentioned briefly in Chapter 9 pp. 146 & 148). There I relate how 'homosexuality' was classified as a mental illness up until 1973, when after years of protest and social action by the lesbian and gay communities in many countries, it was no longer deemed to be an illness. This medicalisation of what is, essentially a natural function or difference between human beings has been applied, over the years to some aspects of being a woman, e.g. menstruation and pregnancy (both natural, but medicalised and the subject of campaigns by the women's movement), and disability (again a natural difference between people, which after campaigns by disabled people has been, to some extent, demedicalised). The key question is whether you consider differences between people to be illnesses, or simple – indeed wonderful – human diversity, to be celebrated, not medicalised.

Who protects clients from bad practice?

Again, much as I would like to report that there is a simple answer to this question, encouragingly, there is a vigorous debate within counselling and psychotherapy regarding the best way to protect clients. Some argue for a strong 'profession' of counselling with a comprehensive system of regulation backed up with complaints procedures, whilst others argue against this. I will not be able to summarise all of the arguments, but I will try to present the main ones. Then I will explain the role of organisations such as the British Association for Counselling and Psychotherapy (BACP), and the United Kingdom Register of Counsellors/Psychotherapists (UKRCP).

Regulation – statutory and otherwise
The past five or so years have seen much activity in professions which provide psychological services. I am not going to go into great detail here – again, several books have been written on the subject, not to mention journal articles, entire websites, government committees and working groups in the professional bodies. The issues, however, are of great importance to everyone wanting to become a counsellor or offer help in a counselling way.

For a variety of reasons the government instituted a process that was intended to bring the provision of psychological services (psychology, psychotherapy, counselling, occupational therapy, etc.)

Note
In 1976, Ivan Illich described the over-activity and over-confidence of the medical establishment, resulting in three levels of harm caused by structures and activities intended to cure:
• Clinical IATROGENESIS – the harm done to patients by medical treatments
• Social IATROGENESIS – the damage done by the unnecessary medicalisation of life
• Cultural IATROGENESIS – the destruction of culturally traditional ways of dealing with pain, illness and death.

When my grandmother was a young woman, there were family/community/cultural ways of dealing with events in life (positive and negative), from childbirth through growing up and relationships to death and grief. Now all of these natural events have been medicalised. That is the product of social and cultural IATROGENESIS.

Illich, I (1976/1995) *Limits to Medicine. Medical Nemesis: The expropriation of health.* London: Marion Boyars.

IATROGENESIS See margin opposite.

IF YOU WANT TO KNOW MORE ABOUT REGULATION

Although not progressing in the foreseeable future, visit the appropriate BACP webpage for history and any developments <http://www.bacp.co.uk/regulation/>

For a comprehensive critical viewpoint read:
Postle, D (2007) *Regulating the Psychological Therapies: From taxonomy to taxidermy.* Ross-on-Wye: PCCS Books.

under one umbrella and *regulate* the practitioners and services they provided. At this point there was an opportunity for the various professional groups to get together to cooperate on the formation of a unitary body specially for providers of psychological services, rather like the General Medical Council, but for psychologists, counsellors, psychotherapists and the like. However, the professional bodies representing these groups could not agree and the opportunity was lost.

Determined to have regulation, the government stepped in and decreed that the body which would do the regulating would be the Health Professions Council (HPC). This was not received with unanimous support. Some psychotherapists and many counsellors did not think that the helping relationships they provided were best organised under the HPC – the organisation which regulates, amongst others, biomedical scientists, hearing aid dispensers, operating theatre practitioners, paramedics, and radiographers. A consultative process sparked a vigorous debate, but it looked as though those in charge were set on regulation. Then the government changed in May 2010 and the new coalition government opted for voluntary rather than statutory regulation, in keeping with their views – anti big government, and pro saving public money (establishing and maintaining the regulation process would have cost millions).

For: Regulation will bar bad practitioners from harming the public.
Against: *A regulated register (like the one run by the HPC) will have just as many bad practitioners on it as not on it. There is no real way to stop all bad practice.*

Note
You will have seen many news items devoted to members of the public having bad experiences of regulatory systems operated by professional bodies for the police, lawyers and the medical profession. Critics claim that professionals just close ranks and that these systems also favour those with enough money to fund their complaint.

For: Regulation processes will be able to operate complaints procedures whereby those successfully complained against would be sanctioned or struck off.
Against: *Complaints procedures in the professions cannot be relied upon to protect the public from bad practice, or satisfy the person that makes the complaint.*

For: People (including counsellors) should not be trusted to not exploit the people they serve or work for. We need to have government regulation to keep these basic human tendencies in check.
Against: *Since counselling is a helping method based on the best human qualities, to have monitoring systems based on lack of trust is against the ethos of counselling. We have to have procedures in harmony with this ethos, even if it makes us look (to some) hopelessly optimistic and trusting.*

For: Our modern world demands that customers are placed first and that counsellors, as service providers, are forced to provide the best service by close regulation and penalties for poor practice.

Against: It is precisely because of the breakdown in trust between persons in our society (as evidenced by our increasingly litigious modern world and the tendency to seek financial compensation) that counselling should not become part of the system which eschews resolving conflicts in personal relationships in favour of the courtroom.

Whatever we think on this topic, the activity of counselling *is* being subjected to increasing voluntary regulation from professional bodies, and the non-statutory voluntary registration of counsellors has already happened in the form of the United Kingdom Register of Counsellors/Psychotherapists.

The British Association for Counselling and Psychotherapy

The British Association for Counselling and Psychotherapy (BACP) was born in 2000 out of the British Association for Counselling, which in turn was founded in 1977, itself growing from the Standing Conference for the Advancement of Counselling (SCAC). Since then the membership has steadily grown to its present level of over 35,000. BACP has had to deal with rapid change in the nature of counselling in the UK and the field of helping is still evolving. As well as providing a discussion forum for counsellors, the BACP has provided a regulatory structure by continually developing a framework for ethical practice and managing complaints.

In order to join BACP, applicants have to fill in a comprehensive application form and sign a declaration agreeing to abide by the *Ethical Framework for Good Practice in Counselling and Psychotherapy* and be subject to the disciplinary procedures. These application procedures are now more comprehensive and stringent, preventing casual applications or applications from those using membership simply to attempt to gain status.

If members have a complaint upheld against them, they will be subject to sanctions decided by the panel that hears the complaint. The ultimate sanction is expulsion from the Association and having any special status removed (e.g. Accredited Practitioner). This would then affect the individual counsellor's inclusion on the UK Register of Counsellors/Psychotherapists.

It is worth noting that the BACP is a professional association, not a trade union (unlike the British Medical Association, which is both, see margin overleaf). If counsellors and psychotherapists want the kind of protection and solidarity provided by a trade union, they should join one related to their sector of work, such as the health or education sections of UNITE or UNISON.

Activity
- *What arguments can you assemble for or against the regulation of counselling and the registration of counsellors?*
- *Where do you stand on the subject? [Don't worry if you think you haven't enough experience of counselling or helping yet. Use your experience as a customer or potential client of counselling.]*
- *Imagine you are going to a see a counsellor – would you want to be protected? If so, what safeguards would you like to see in place?*
- *Debate the issue in your training group and amongst your friends. They might be past, present or future consumers of counselling or helping services too.*

Activity
- *What views do you have about how professions should be regulated?*
  - *Who should pay for this?*
  - *How should it be organised?*
- *Remember: hard cases make bad law.*

Note
After much consultation, in 2002 a new *Ethical Framework for Good Practice in Counselling and Psychotherapy* was adopted by BACP in place of the older codes. You will find in Chapter 7 more details of the *Ethical Framework* and how it might inform your basic helping. You can read the document in full on:

<http://www.bacp.co.uk/ethical_framework/>

or purchase a printed copy from:

BACP
BACP House, 15 St John's Business Park,
Lutterworth LE17 4HB
Tel: 01455 883300

Activity
- *As a beginning helper in terms of counselling skills, do you think you have a place in BACP?*
- *What would you want from the organisation?*

Note: UKRCP contacts
Website: <http://www.ukrconline.org.uk/>
Tel: 01455 883335

Activity
- *Looking back at your answers to the question of how you would wish to be protected if you were a client, having read the above section do you think the BACP and UKRCP do enough?*
- *If not, what else needs to be done?*

Note
General Medical Council
Is the regulatory body set up to protect, promote and maintain the health and safety of the public by ensuring proper standards in the practice of medicine.
British Medical Association
Is the professional association and trade union for doctors in the UK.

Note: IPN contact
Website: <http://i-p-n.org/home.htm>
Tel: 03333 213 004

The United Kingdom Register of Counsellors/ Psychotherapists

BACP, along with other interested organisations, developed a Register of Counsellors (UKRC). Officially 'launched' in September 1997, it is now called the United Kingdom Register of Counsellors/ Psychotherapists (UKRCP). Only those with certain qualifications and experience are allowed on to the Register – they are called *Registered Independent Counsellors*.

The UKRCP is a *held* register, not a *published* register. This means that you cannot see a copy in a library or buy a copy in a bookshop. The register is held by the Registrar and if a member of the public wishes to check whether a counsellor is on the register or not, it takes just one phone call to UKRCP or a visit to the website.

Who pays for the regulation of counselling?

The BACP and UKRCP are funded entirely by membership fees and donations. The BACP is a registered charity and receives no funding from the government to assist in its activities. Each area of activity within the BACP, such as publications, accreditation, complaints, etc. has a paid manager.

Membership of a committee is done on a voluntary basis and involves several days' attendance at meetings per year, plus several days' work at home. Would your employer give you leave to attend BACP meetings? Would they let you have time off in lieu or would you have to take unpaid leave? If you are self-employed, could you afford to lose several days' pay per year?

The average salary of a BACP member will probably be at or below the national average because many BACP members are voluntary counsellors or working part time or in private practice, which is relatively poorly paid. This directly affects the fees that the Association can set, which then affects the number of employees, the services to members and the general public, and the publicity that the Association can afford. So, the BACP is not able to ask for high fees whereas doctors, for example (who earn more, on average, than counsellors), can afford to have a much better-funded professional regulatory body in the form of the General Medical Council.

The Independent Practitioners Network (IPN)

As I explained earlier in this chapter, not everyone supports the idea of increasing regulation and professionalisation in counselling and psychotherapy. Some eminent academics and practitioners believe it runs counter to the fundamental principles and values of counselling.

The Independent Practitioners' Network (IPN) was formed to

organise the voices calling for an alternative to the headlong rush towards what some disparagingly refer to as the 'MacDonaldisation' of therapy. There is an excellent web resource giving details of the IPN and other alternatives if you want to explore the other side of the argument on registration and professionalism. To give you an idea of the IPN position, below are a couple of extracts from their information – both can be found on the website.

It is noteworthy that the IPN method of dealing with complaints is based on conflict resolution, rather than an adversarial, courtroom-style evidence-weighing judgement. The BACP and the British Psychological Society (BPS) both have adversarial complaints procedures. In the case of the BPS, the Society employs a barrister to prosecute the case against its own member. Whilst without doubt, rigorous, some may think this legalistic procedure is incongruent with the ethos of a helping profession. The IPN method is explained fully on the website and a flavour can be gained in the extracts below and overleaf.

From the IPN Homepage <http://i-p-n.org/home.htm>

What is IPN?
The Independent Practitioners Network offers an authentic model of best practice accountability through open, committed relationships with peers. We are a nationwide, network of practitioners of equal status rather than a hierarchical organisation. We work together in linked groups to offer each other mutual support and challenge. We believe that high quality ethical practice is grounded in honesty, integrity and transparency. We welcome counsellors, psychotherapists, educators, growth workers and allied practitioners.

IPN structure
Non-hierarchical, low bureaucracy. IPN is inclusive of more or less qualified or registered members, since we recognise that there are many routes to being an effective practitioner. The structure is horizontal and multi-centred rather than vertical and pyramidal. There is no central, standardised code of practice, each peer group creates and circulates its own.

Freedom of practice
We are committed to defending freedom of practice, and to creating a culture of openness and challenge. The Network grows out of the belief that no centralised organisation has the right or the ability to decide who should practise therapy, facilitation or equivalent skills.

Open definitions
Has a commitment to encouraging diverse forms of practice, training or therapeutic relationship, since we value a richly pluralistic and multi-skilled ecology.

The structure provides for:
- A powerfully effective means of supporting the interests of both client and practitioner.
- Self and peer assessment and accreditation through a continuing process of accountability.
- An exciting, stimulating and creative context for ongoing practitioner development.
- Willingness to own mistakes and take responsibility for constructive approaches to improving situations that may result from them.

continued /…

.../ continued

Peer validation
The unit of membership is a group of at least five practitioners who know and stand by each other's work; who take responsibility for supporting each other's good practice and the good practice of other groups in the Network; and who address any problems or conflicts in their work. The group seeks to establish the quality of its members' work through personal ongoing interaction – consistent with our belief that this most effectively facilitates authentic practice. A full member group is required to have formed cross-links with other groups, through which the process of peer support and challenge is widened and deepened.

From the *IPN Users' Guide* <http://i-p-n.org/IPNDocuments.htm>

'Standing by'
A key element in all this is the concept of 'standing by'. What creates an IPN group is the willingness of its members to stand by each other's work (P&P [Principles & Procedures] 3-4). This does not (of course!) constitute a guarantee of that work – everyone makes mistakes. But it means that, in the event of a conflict arising, the group members promise to commit themselves to sorting out whatever has gone wrong. In order to make this commitment, group members must clearly have achieved some degree of understanding about what each other does, and positive feelings about it.

There is no set procedure for reaching a position of 'standing by'. Every group does this in their own way. For example, some use fairly formal methods, whereby each person writes an account of their work, and other people 'rattle and shake' this account until they feel satisfied. At the opposite pole, other groups simply develop an informal sense of each other as people and practitioners, through interacting and perhaps group supervision.

My aim in this chapter has been to attempt to answer some of the common questions asked about counselling. You have discovered that behind each question is a debate – debates that I hope you can now take part in. These questions and debates concern everyone with an interest in helping and counselling; perhaps you will continue these and other debates about the place of counselling in our society, whether you choose to go further in your training or not.

ALL PURPOSE LATE TWENTIETH CENTURY CREED   Simon Rae

I believe in my beliefs.
It's my belief that my beliefs
Are truer far than your beliefs,
And I believe that your beliefs
Are threatening to my beliefs,
So I'm defending my beliefs
And all who hold the same beliefs
Against your dangerous beliefs
And all who share your false beliefs
Or what I think are your beliefs.
And I will die for my beliefs;
And you will die for my beliefs.

And what, in fact, are my beliefs
Beyond the complicating reefs
Of tedious theology
And arid ideology?
The usual: a divine Creator,
Whose love rings earth like the equator;
Justice and the Rule of Law
(And giving hand-outs to the poor);
Respect, of course, for Mother Nature,
Care for every living creature;
And that in the pursuit of Peace
All wars (excepting mine) should cease.

As you come to the end of this book and your introductory course there are several options open to you. You may have already decided what your next step is going to be. Or perhaps you are not so sure, nor even sure what the next step *could* be.

In Chapter 10, I wrote that some people seek counselling for self-development rather than to resolve a problem or in response to a crisis. So it is with counselling training at an introductory level. You may have started such a course with a view to increasing your self-awareness and general knowledge of helping processes. Initially you may not have considered any career as a helper either paid or voluntary. On the other hand, you may have started the course certain that you wanted to progress to more advanced training.

Regardless of why you started the course, the process of the course will have helped some of you to make the decision that counselling or helping in a counselling way is not for you. If that is the case, I hope that you can be an advocate or ambassador for counselling after your experience on the course. By this I mean that you may be able to explain to friends, relatives and colleagues what a counselling way of helping is, that through your own experience you have found it to be helpful, principled, led by a body of knowledge. You may be able to point those around you in the right direction for good quality help should they wonder whether they need it, and help them realise that getting help at the right time improves the quality of our lives.

In my view, it is perfectly acceptable to pursue training in counselling to the next stage with the sole intention of developing self-awareness and self-improvement. I say this because I firmly believe that counselling skills are no more than good relationship skills and that I would support anyone seeking to improve their relationship skills. These more highly developed skills could be used in a community sense amongst one's family, friends or colleagues, and such 'communities' will be all the better for it.

The starting point – an Introduction to Counselling

The structure of counselling training varies slightly between the organisations offering training. The most basic introductory courses

Important note

Counsellor education in the UK

After a decade or more of a stable framework for counsellor training in the UK, the advent of IAPT (see Chapter 11), the 'unresolved' move towards the regulation of helping professionals and the perceived need to create a career path for counsellors, we are in a period of great change in counsellor training.

Whilst I will try to give an up-to-date picture, readers must understand that choosing the next step in training requires research. Do not make a snap decision, and unless forced to, do not simply go to the nearest provider. Take a good look around and ask lots of questions.

Check with BACP for any updates on the levels of training required for admission to the UK Register of Counsellors/ Psychotherapists, and check with IAPT for the latest requirements for low and high intensity workers on the following websites:

UKRCP <http://www.ukrconline.org.uk/>
IAPT <http://www.iapt.nhs.uk/>

The one certainty is that there will be many further changes in the next few years.

The higher education progression of qualifications

Counsellor training has been moving towards the model of progression that exists in higher education in the UK, as follows:

• Higher Ed Diploma – one year full time or part-time equivalent
• Higher Ed Certificate – two years full time or part-time equivalent
• Degree – three years full time or part-time equivalent

Postgraduate courses – Masters (MA and MSc) and Doctorate level (PhD) are then available to people who achieve a good degree. These courses are sometimes taught and sometimes achieved by independent study and research, supervised by an experienced academic.

are between 10 and 30 hours spread over a weekend or several weeks of two to three hours per week. There will be little or no formal assessment on such a course. Some are organised as 'taster' courses where you will get the briefest of introductions to different approaches. Some dedicate themselves as an introduction to a single approach. Make sure you ask before you start so that you are choosing the right course for you.

Certificate and Higher Education Certificate courses

The aim of these courses is to continue development of theory, self-awareness and counselling skills and attitudes for those wishing to train as counsellors, whilst providing a genuine stopping-off point for those wishing to train only in the use of counselling skills, but no further. So a certificate course would be of use to:

• Teachers, nurses, social workers, youth workers, police officers, managers, indeed, anyone who is aiming to use counselling skills alongside their already established professional skills.
• Those wanting to proceed to professional training in order to be a counsellor.
• Volunteers for advice and counselling agencies who want to continue development of their counselling skills beyond that offered by their basic agency training.
• Anyone wanting to continue a 'counselling training' route to personal improvement and to use their counselling skills in the community, without any firm intention to become a paid or 'professional' counsellor.

Completion of a certificate course does not qualify someone to practise as a counsellor nor apply for a job as a counsellor under most circumstances. Certificates only qualify someone to use counselling skills.

Professional level courses

A *Diploma in Counselling* at a college of further education or university used to be the professional practitioner level course. A few diploma courses are still available of around 300 to 500 hours duration spread over one or two years part time. Diploma level courses also require students to practise with bona fide clients (up to the BACP Accredited Course requirement of 450 hours) and have this work assessed in some way (e.g. via audio-taped sessions). This practice is also supervised, usually by external supervisors.

Degrees in counselling (BA or BSc) are now commonplace. They are most likely to be called a degree in counselling studies because whilst they give a good grounding in the subject of counselling, they are unlikely to have a sufficient (if any) component of clinical practice.

Completion of a diploma course is unlikely to qualify someone to practise as a counsellor nor apply for a job as a counsellor under most circumstances. Degrees in counselling studies give a broad academic understanding of counselling theories.

A *Masters in Counselling/Psychotherapy* is the first level of postgraduate course and is usually completed over two or three years of part-time study. The emphasis is predominantly academic, will require the completion of a lengthy dissertation and will almost certainly include completion of a modest research project. These courses are post-practitioner level and usually require a degree or equivalent as an entry qualification. Some courses also require some years' experience as a practitioner.

Completion of a masters' course is very likely to qualify someone to practise as a counsellor and apply for a job as a counsellor under most circumstances. However, you must check with the training provider to be sure.

A *PhD in Counselling/Psychotherapy* is the highest level of qualification. On successful completion of such a course you can call yourself 'Doctor …'. Study at this level is extremely demanding. Some courses are taught (i.e. comprise lectures and seminars) and will have very lengthy dissertations as the major assessment. Others are research based and again require very lengthy writing. Both types take several years (five or six years) to complete and they require a huge investment of time and effort. Almost all of the 'course' is self-directed study, so be ready to work almost entirely on your own. Admissions criteria are high and a significant number of those accepted do not complete the qualification. These courses are expensive and require a huge commitment of time and energy – they are not for the faint-hearted.

A doctorate is a postgraduate qualification and it will be a requirement of admission that you are already an experienced practitioner.

Attention – reality check

Some people enter counsellor training with unrealistic expectations. They may completely misconstrue the nature of the training process, in which case, although disappointed, they will probably drop out during the intermediate level course or decide not to continue to

Note
Part time or full time?
The vast majority of counsellor training is provided on a part-time basis, either over a series of weekends or one session (a half or full day) per week for one or more years, depending on the level of the course. A very few institutions offer full-time counsellor training and will take applicants who have completed an introductory course or have equivalent experience. Full-time courses are usually of one year's duration and are eligible for BACP Accreditation.

Note
IAPT training
In Chapter 11, pp. 169 and 173–6, I looked briefly at the Improving Access to Psychological Therapies initiative. This government-funded project has implications for counsellors who wish to practise in primary care (GP practices). Those primary care service providers wishing to deliver IAPT must have a sufficient number of staff trained to deliver the high and low intensity work. Your counselling training may or may not include modules that would qualify you for IAPT work and you should check on application.

Note
Primary care service provision
This is the part of the NHS that deals with GP practices, prescriptions, etc. Readers will be aware that the government is planning to change the way this provision is funded by giving more control to groups of GP practices that get together to form a local consortium. It is not at all clear at the time of writing how this will affect IAPT or counselling in GP surgeries, but readers wanting to work in that setting should monitor developments carefully.

Note

BACP Accredited Counsellors

The BACP has a grade of membership called Registered Practitioner (Accredited Counsellor) which means that the qualifications and experience of the counsellor meet certain criteria, importantly including 450 hours of training and 450 hours of supervised practice.

BACP Senior Accredited Practitioner

BACP are in the process of revising the requirements for Accredited Members to become Senior Accredited Members. Suffice to say that it requires evidence of continued supervised experience and professional development.

Both of these qualifications can be considered 'quality marks' for counsellors and can be used when choosing counsellors or supervisors – you may want to assure yourself that they have an appropriate amount of training and experience. You can check the details of the criteria yourself by visiting the BACP accreditation page: <http://www.bacp.co.uk/accreditation/>

BACP Accredited Courses

Courses as well as individual practitioners can seek a seal of approval from BACP if they meet certain rigorous criteria, including a minimum of 450 hours of tuition, 150 hours of supervised practice, 50 hours of further placement activity, fully qualified staff, approved assessment procedures and course policies. For a full list of criteria, visit: <http://www.bacp.co.uk/admin/structure/files/repos/416_course_accreditation_scheme_.pdf>

diploma. This would be considered a success. It would be a failure if such a person continued to a professional level only to become disillusioned then. Professional training is financially expensive, personally demanding and very time-consuming. Once you have started a course, it is frustrating and extremely disappointing to withdraw during the course at that level and it can mean that you feel a failure.

Others enter training with unrealistic expectations of the life and work of a counsellor. Some people leave well-paid jobs to train as a counsellor only to find that counselling jobs are few and far between and most pay only modest salaries. No one should enter the world of counselling in the belief that it is a well-paid job. At the time of writing, only a few counselling posts pay on a level with, for example, teaching or nursing. The majority do not come up to these levels. Take a look at Chapter 11 for a little more on employment possibilities.

- Some counsellors are able to obtain part-time (or rarely, full-time) employment in a GP practice.
- When reaching the status of Accredited Counsellor, some are able to get sufficient work with Employee Assistance Programmes (EAPs) to make up a week's work.
- Some generate sufficient work in private practice as a counsellor.
- Some work part time as a counsellor (for example, one or two days a week or in the evenings) to supplement or complement another part-time job.

Some people train as a counsellor in order to enhance the job they are already doing, e.g. as a nurse or social worker. For example, a nurse in a renal unit may start to offer informal support to patients and relatives. After training as a counsellor this may develop into a formal counselling post for a part of the week if the need for counselling can be demonstrated.

A teacher may choose to specialise in tutorial support work upon completion of a counselling skills course or certificate and may be able to make the move to school counsellor after qualifying as a counsellor at a higher level.

The voluntary sector benefits from the over-provision of qualified counsellors because recently qualified counsellors will want to continue seeing clients in order to gain BACP Accreditation. One of the best ways of doing this is to work for a voluntary agency. Occasionally, a paid post as a co-ordinator of a voluntary service becomes available and might require a counselling qualification, but these jobs are not completely satisfactory as the bulk of the work is desk-bound administration, not face-to-face counselling. Such jobs are few and far between.

Readers of this book should be aware that they will find precious few jobs advertised in the local (or even national) newspaper that read 'Counsellor Wanted …'. Many posts are individually tailored to the person. Once you have gained a diploma in counselling, only a fortunate few make counselling a career without a considerable wait, or lots of effort, or both.

Increasingly, people are opting for what is euphemistically called a 'portfolio career', that is one that is made up of a number (at most a small handful) of possibly related part-time jobs. For example, some people continue their old employment as a teacher or insurance salesperson part time whilst working for an afternoon in a voluntary agency, another half day paid at a GP practice and at the same time building up a private practice in counselling. After a number of years, they may add supervision or involvement in training to their portfolio.

If you are dedicated in your pursuit of a career in counselling and you succeed, the rewards can be great, but probably not in terms of your bank balance.

endings

For some of us, endings of things just come and go along with the rest of everyday life – we are not very sensitive to them. For others, the end of something is an emotional time, a time to celebrate, mourn or otherwise mark in some way. In helping, endings have special meaning since the end of a helping relationship can be symbolic of many moments of moving on in our lives.

The end of the course may also be a special time for course participants, perhaps marked by some exercises, at least to help you reflect on the experience of the course and review your learning on it. What do endings mean to you? What words and pictures come up for you?

The flip chart in the margin is the last from our imaginary group. How do their responses fit in with your own? The end of the course is the end of the life of the group, the end of the relationships in the group as you knew them. Of course, some relationships may continue beyond the end of the course – you may have made new friends whom you will continue to see after the course. Perhaps some of you have decided to continue your training and will meet up with new people on the next course. It is easy to see endings either as closure, as new beginnings or as transitions from one state to another offering new and different opportunities.

How we handle endings on the course may reflect the way we feel about endings in our lives. Some may dread endings and put off thinking about them, others may eagerly look forward to them – impatient to move on to the next thing. You might also have a sense of the timing of endings; do they feel right and natural – has the course come to its natural end? Or does it feel too soon, and that you are unprepared for the end? Are any of these familiar to you? What other endings can you remember, and how did you feel about them? Here are some to get started:

- last day at school
- separation from spouse or ending a long-term relationship
- someone close to you dying
- moving house

These endings may seem to have something in common with the changes we looked at in Chapter 3. Endings *are* change in the

> What we call the beginning is often the end. And to make an end is to make a beginning. The end is where we start from.
>
> TS Eliot: *Four Quartets*

MAKE A SKETCH OF ANY IMAGES OR A NOTE OF ANY WORDS.

ENDINGS

PARTING   NO REGRETS   SORROW

DEATH FINISHED GONE FOREVER

'YOU CAN NEVER GO BACK
TO THE PAST'

LOSS   PAIN   GRIEF   SADNESS

'AS EACH DOOR CLOSES ANOTHER
ONE OPENS'

MOVING ON TO BETTER THINGS

GOODBYE

....

Activity
*Make a note of important endings
in your life.*
• How did you feel about them?

sense that they signal a point of change that is inescapable. Some changes are gradual, but an ending or transition has a fixed moment. Sometimes we try to extend the ending by having a false ending before the 'real' one, or by putting the ending off, or by trying to recreate the way things were before the ending. For example, when someone close to us dies, we might want things to be the way they were – to bring that person back, or if we have a relative who is terminally ill, we begin the grieving process before they die (called anticipatory grieving).

If endings are such strong symbolic events for us, we must be ready to pay them special attention in any helping relationships we have. The people we are helping may have strong feelings about the end of the helping relationship:

- They may feel relief and want to get away from the 'old them' that the helping relationship reminds them of.
- They may want to hang on to the security of the helping relationship because they think they can't cope on their own.

The way we conduct ourselves as helpers in the final stages of a helping relationship will have an effect upon those we are trying to help. We must have an awareness of the meanings that endings have for us and not let our own meanings get in the way of our helping. The end of the course provides us with an opportunity to experience some feelings about endings, past and present, enabling us to look at our patterns of behaviour.

Reviewing our learning

I've deliberately written 'our learning', because, as you may remember, I started this book by saying that it would be better if I could form a relationship through the pages with you, the reader. Now the end of the book is here, I am aware that it is an ending for me. An end to sitting in front of my computer, a sense of relief and some anxiety because I'm not sure how the book will be received. What have I learned? I like to ask the following simple questions to help review my learning at the end of courses. You could try it too.

- What have I learned about counselling?
- What have I learned about myself?
- What would I add to improve the experience and my learning?
- What would I remove to improve the experience and my learning?
- What will I do differently from now on?

Activity
- *How will you end the relationships with the people on your course?*
- *Does your answer to this question have any resonance with other endings in your life, good or bad?*

YOU MIGHT LIKE TO MAKE THIS THE FINAL ENTRY IN YOUR JOURNAL. 🖎

'This is not the end. It is not even the beginning. But it is, perhaps, the end of the beginning.'

Winston Churchill
November 1942

index

THE TRIBES OF THE PERSON-CENTRED NATION, 2ND EDITION
AN INTRODUCTION TO THE SCHOOLS OF THERAPY RELATED TO THE PERSON-CENTRED APPROACH

edited by Pete Sanders   ISBN 978 1 906254 55 1, 2012

This book has a mission to gather the tribes of the person-centred nation for dialogue; to discover common ground and debate differences; to celebrate the fact that it is, as Margaret Warner declared, 'one nation, many tribes'. The first edition has become a widely used set-text and this new edition has been revised and considerably extended for both students and practitioners.

New to this edition are:

- revised contributions from Nick Baker, Mick Cooper, Campbell Purton and Richard Worsley;
- a chapter on Emotion Focused Therapy by Prof Robert Elliott;
- an entire section on 'new developments' comprising:
  - Person-Centred Expressive Therapies (Dinah Brown)
  - Pre-Therapy (Pete Sanders)
  - Relational Depth (Rosanne Knox)
  - Counselling for Depression (Andy Hill)

PERSON-CENTERED AND EXPERIENTIAL THERAPIES WORK
A REVIEW OF THE RESEARCH ON COUNSELING, PSYCHOTHERAPY AND RELATED PRACTICES

edited by Mick Cooper, Jeanne C Watson & Dagmar Hölldampf
ISBN 978 1 906254 25 4, pp. 272+vi, 2010

Person-Centered and Experiential Therapies Work provides a comprehensive, systematic and accessible review of the evidence base for the approach and the methods and measures by which it can be evaluated. It gives clear evidence for the effectiveness of person-centered and experiential therapies, and is an essential resource for students and practitioners who want to know more about the empirical support for their work, and to promote it with confidence.

THE THERAPEUTIC RELATIONSHIP
PERSPECTIVES AND THEMES

edited by Sheila Haugh & Stephen Paul   ISBN 978 1 906254 04 9, pp. 278, 2008

This book explores the therapeutic relationship in the psychological therapies, reviewing the importance of the therapeutic relationship within the key modalities of person-centred, psychodynamic, existential, gestalt, transactional analysis, cognitive behavioural therapy, relational and transpersonal approaches. The place of power and oppression and the social context of the relationship in therapy are further reviewed.

Authors examine what the research really tells us about outcomes in therapy and explore the place of research for the psychological therapies.

In a series of commissioned chapters significant themes are presented which enable the reader to consider their impact on therapeutic practice. These include: touch, a Japanese perspective, spirituality, I–Thou relatedness and the contribution of Buber, the creative therapies and working with groups.

permanent discounts, free UK p+p   www.pccs-books.co.uk

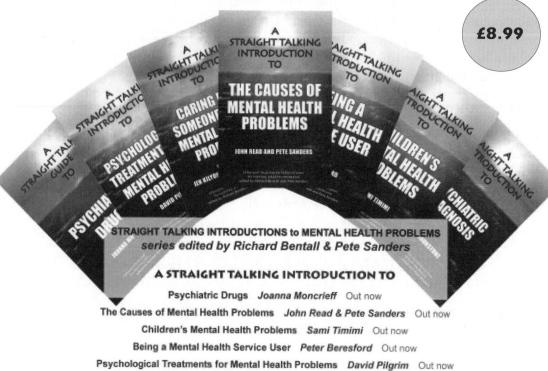